To Retain Command of the Mississippi

To Retain Command of the Mississippi

The Civil War Naval Campaign for Memphis

Edward B. McCaul Jr.

University of Tennessee / Knoxville

First Edition.

The paper in this book meets the requirements of American National Standards Institute / National Information Standards Organization specification Z39.48-1992 (Permanence of Paper). It contains 30 percent post-consumer waste and is certified by the Forest Stewardship Council.

Library of Congress Cataloging-in-Publication Data

McCaul, Edward B., 1951-
To retain command of the Mississippi : the Civil War naval campaign for Memphis / Edward B. McCaul Jr. — First edition.
pages cm
Includes bibliographical references and index.
ISBN 978-1-62190-088-7 (hardcover)
1. Memphis, Battle of, Memphis, Tenn., 1862
2. Mississippi River Valley—History—Civil War, 1861-1865—Naval operations.
I. Title.
II. Title: Civil War naval campaign for Memphis.

E473.5.M33 2014
973.7'32—dc23
2014023334

To my father, Edward B. McCaul,
who served in the United States Navy
during World War II.

Contents

Illustrations

Figures

Maps

Preface

> Take the battle [Battle of Memphis], together with its results, it was one of the handsomest achievements of the war, but it did not receive that general notice which it deserved.
>
> —Admiral David D. Porter[1]

A number of battles were fought for control of the Mississippi River, and much has been written about them. The Battle of Memphis was one such battle; however, this battle was pivotal, as the results determined the course of the Civil War on the Mississippi. Unfortunately, as Admiral David Dixon Porter acknowledged, the Battle of Memphis has never received the notice it deserves—a belief that remains true today. Although most authors writing about naval warfare on the Mississippi do in fact discuss the battle, no one—in my opinion—has given it adequate attention. Two reasons account for this lack of critical consideration: the battle was decided very quickly and was very one sided. Had it been a longer, bloodier fight with substantial losses on both sides, the battle would have received more attention; but it was not. Because the battle was so one sided, the results appear to have been foreordained and, thus, are considered by many to be insignificant. However, the battle could have easily been a Confederate victory—or, if the battle had never occurred, the Confederate River Defense Fleet could have survived as a "fleet in being." In either case, future Union operations in the Mississippi River valley would have been severely hindered. But, the battle was a decisive Union victory that allowed the Union to continue its march down the Mississippi.

As with many historic events, the Battle of Memphis and its immediate predecessor, the Battle of Plum Point, have been subjected to many misconceptions over the years. Unfortunately, many of these inaccuracies endure as fact. Information about the battles is available in the *Official Records of the Union and Confederate Navies in the War of the Rebellion*, *The War of the Rebellion: A Compilation of the Official Records of the Union and Confederate Armies*, autobiographies, biographies, letters, newspaper reports, as well as books written about the history of the war on the Mississippi. Despite all of this information, some major issues arise when researching these battles. First, the Navy's

Official Records has described the volume of information from the Confederates as "very scant."[2] Also, the precise time at which certain actions occurred can be very confusing, as different individuals reported varying times for the same event, although the general time of day is not in question. In addition, conflicting reports and statements present a challenge that all historians confront. For my part, when facing different times or conflicting information, I chose the source I believed to be correct and articulate my rationale in a footnote.

Three fleets were involved in the Battle of Memphis, all of which were under United States Army or Confederate States Army control.[3] Consequently, some—but not all—of the pertinent reports and messages can be found in the Army's *Official Records.* Duplicates, as well as messages and reports not found in the Army's *Official Records*, can be found in the Navy's *Official Records.* This distribution may cause confusion, as researchers may assume that all pertinent reports and information are in the records (Army's or Navy's) they are reviewing. One result of this archival arrangement has been that many researchers have not read Confederate Commodore Joseph E. Montgomery's report on the Battle of Memphis. As such, some books that address this battle assert that his report cannot be found, and that he disappears from history; however, his report on the Battle of Memphis can be found in the Army's *Official Records* in Series I, Volume LII, Part I. Beyond information on the battle are details regarding the construction of the boats in the Confederate River Defense Fleet. In addition, Montgomery's obituary and photograph can be found in Volume 10 of the *Confederate Veteran*, although the obituary greatly exaggerates his wartime achievements. Backing up Montgomery's official report on the Battle of Memphis is an overlooked article in the Houston, Texas *Tri-Weekly Telegraph* newspaper. The article was written from information provided by First Assistant Engineer William H. Reeder, who was on the Confederate flagship *Little Rebel*, and who, unfortunately, disappears from history.[4] From these two overlooked sources—along with the better-known sources—one may closely determine the disposition of the Confederate fleet before the Battle of Memphis. Not surprisingly, the disposition is very different from what official Union reports, newspapers, and reminiscences described.

Two issues with Montgomery's name that have likely confused many researchers are its commonplaceness and that both the Navy's and Army's *Official Records* refer to him as James Montgomery in their indexes. However, James was not Commodore Montgomery's first name; it was Joseph. There was a Union pilot on board the *Queen of the West* by the name of James Montgomery, which may have led people to use of the wrong first name.[5] Compounding this issue is that Montgomery's first name does not appear on any of his reports, as they are signed J. E. Montgomery; and reports written by other individuals refer to him as Montgomery—again, with no first name. In addition, Commodore Montgomery's obituary in the *Confederate Veteran* only refers to him as Commodore J. E. Montgomery, whereas the Army's *Official Records* confuses Commodore James E. Montgomery with Captain James E. Montgomery, United States Army.[6] Compilers of the Navy's *Official Records* missed one source of Montgomery's first name in a series of messages, dated July 1865, between Joseph E. Montgomery's lawyer, John Colerick, and the departments of the Treasury and Navy. These messages concern clarification of Montgomery's claim that he was authorized to raise twenty-seven civilian steamboats that had been sunk by the Confederate government in the Yazoo River.[7] Confirmation that the Montgomery involved in the dispute is Commodore Montgomery comes from *A Genealogical History of the Montgomery's and Their Descendants*, published in 1908, six years after Commodore Montgomery's death, and written by immediate members of his family. In addition, this family history gives Montgomery's name as Joseph Edward Montgomery.[8] The messages concerning Montgomery's dispute with the Treasury and Navy Departments, along with the information in the Montgomery genealogical history, led me to conclude that Commodore Montgomery's first name is Joseph, not James.

Montgomery is not the only name compromised by confusion. The commander of the *General Beauregard*, Captain James H. Hurt, has various spellings in the Navy's *Official Records*. Cities also suffer in this regard, as Pittsburgh, Pennsylvania, is spelled Pittsburgh and Pittsburg in both the Army's and Navy's *Official Records*, with Pittsburg being the most common spelling. Because the Union ironclad involved in the Battle of Memphis was named *Pittsburg*, I decided to use that spelling when referring to the city. Adding to the confusion, some individuals—specifically Charles Ellet Jr. and David G. Farragut—mention Fort Wright in some of their messages when, in fact, they are referring to Fort Pillow. In those cases, I changed their references to Fort Pillow. All of this conflicting information inevitably makes researching the battles that much more challenging.

The Union gunboat fleet had a similar issue, as its name kept changing. At various times, it was called Naval Forces, Western Rivers; Gunboat Flotilla, Western Waters; Cairo Flotilla; and Western Flotilla; until its final designation as Mississippi Squadron in October 1862. I

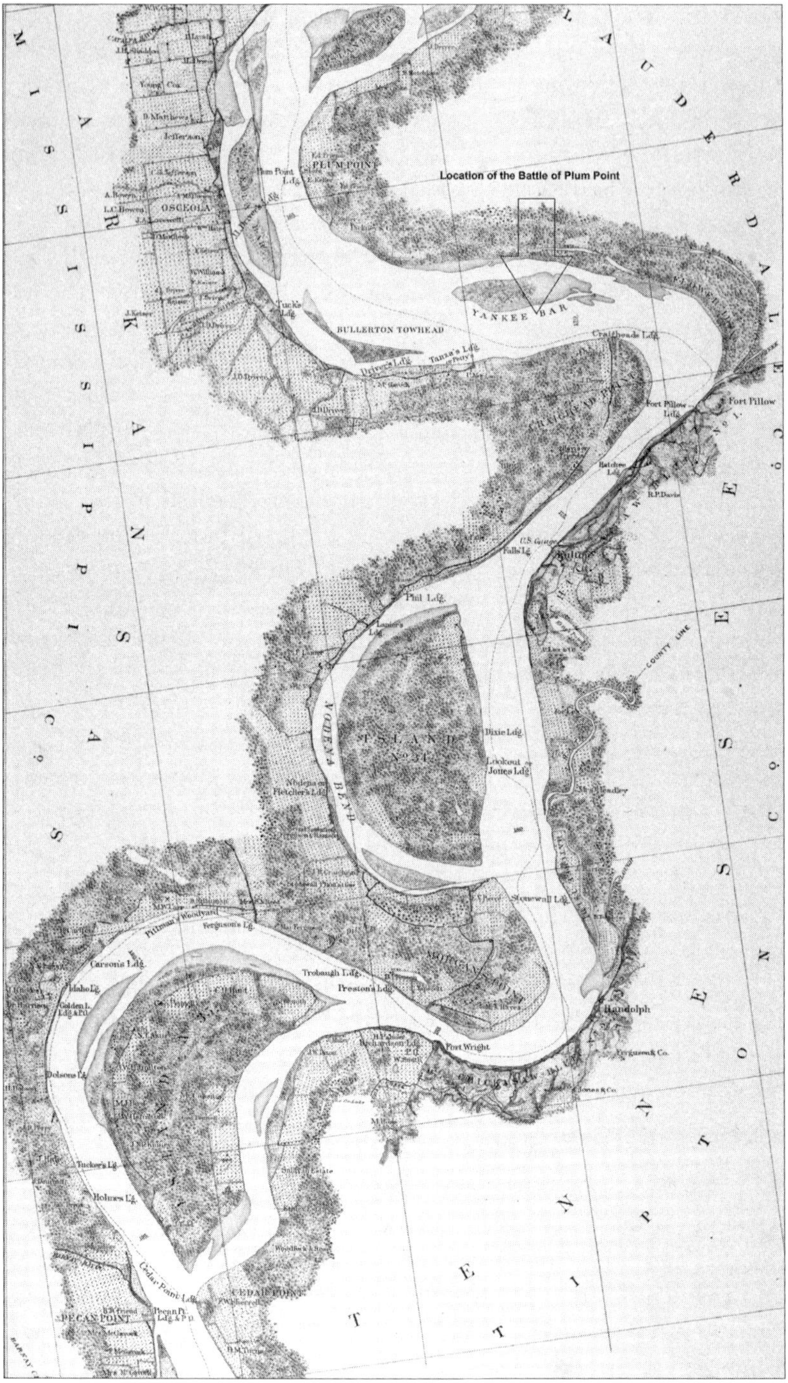

Plum Point and Fort Pillow, 1891, Mississippi River Commission, 1891, Map Sheet #6. Courtesy of the Orton Memorial Library of Geology, The Ohio State University.

decided to call the Union gunboat fleet the Western Flotilla—the title its commander, Flag-Officer Charles H. Davis, used at the time of the Battle of Memphis. In addition to the various designations for the Western Flotilla, the term used to describe all of the vessels in these battles varies depending on the source; however, most official reports and news articles from the time refer to the vessels as boats, although

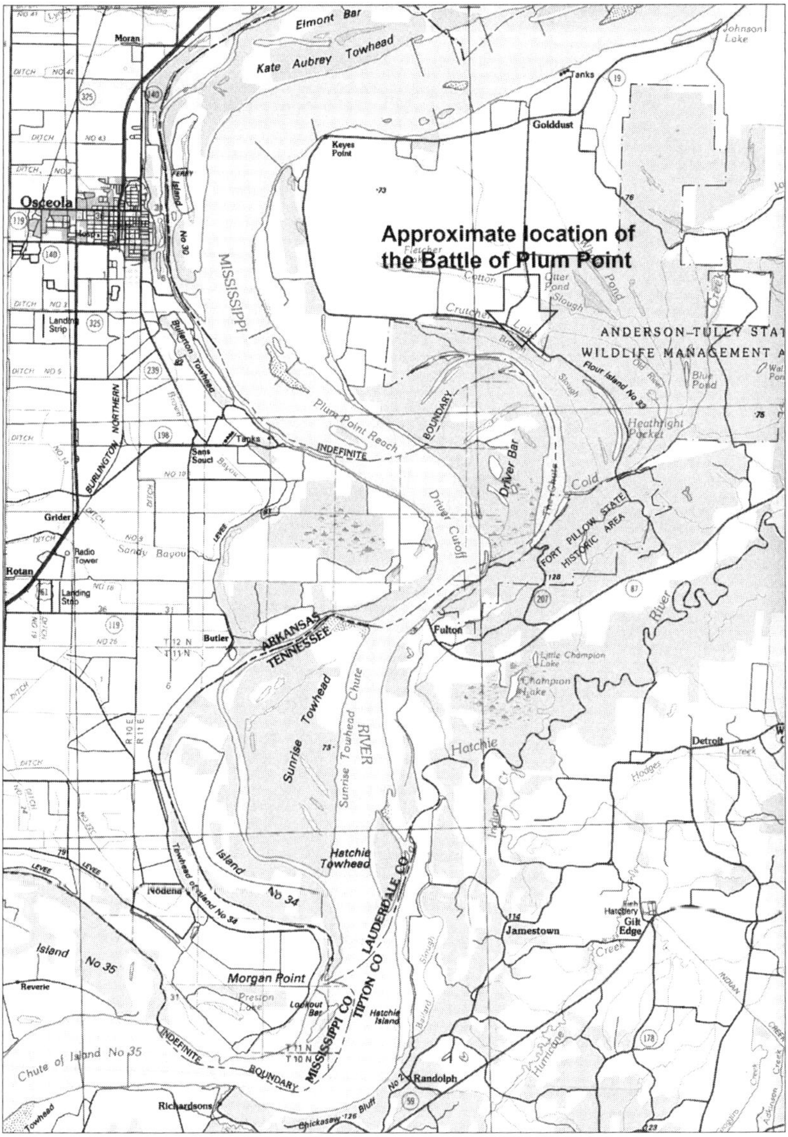

Plum Point and Fort Pillow, 1986, Tennessee Valley Authority in cooperation with the United States Geological Survey, Blytheville, 1986. Courtesy of the Orton Memorial Library of Geology, The Ohio State University.

two of the Confederate vessels were ocean-going ships. To avoid confusion, I use the term boat, in keeping with the perspective of most of the participants.

I also decided to capitalize the words Army, Navy, Soldier, and Sailor, as I use them as proper nouns. Numerous other definitions are

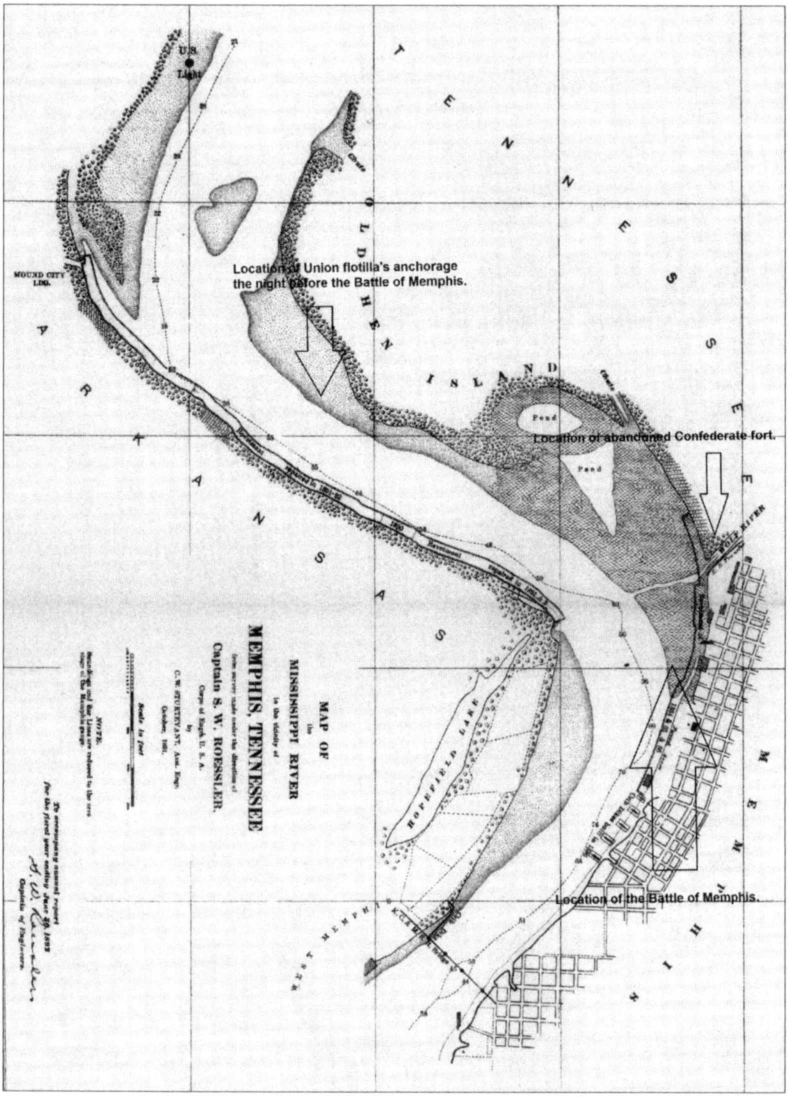

Memphis, Tennessee, 1891, Corps of Engineers, 1891. Courtesy of the Orton Memorial Library of Geology, The Ohio State University.

attributed to each of these words, but I only employ them in a military context. Where any confusion could have arisen, I added either US or CS in front of these nouns.

Unlike many land battles, these engagements left no permanent mark on the land, and the course of the Mississippi River has changed

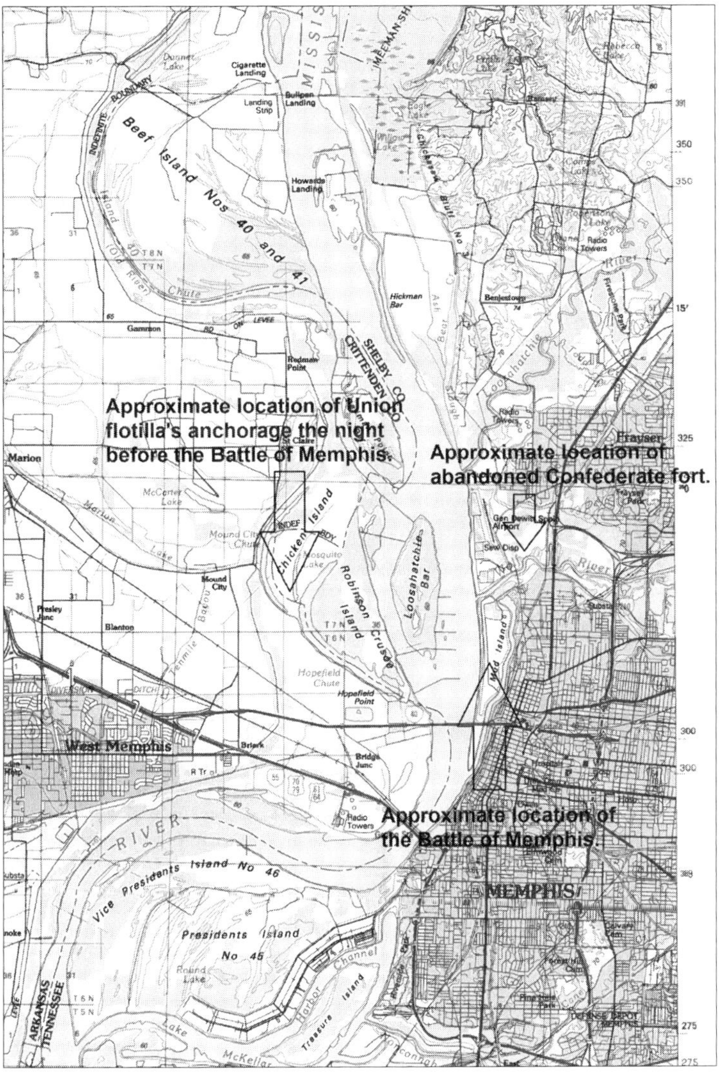

Memphis, Tennessee, 1986, Tennessee Valley Authority in cooperation with the United States Geological Survey, Memphis West, 1986. Courtesy of the Orton Memorial Library of Geology, The Ohio State University

since the Civil War. No maps showing the channel and other details of the Mississippi River in the vicinity of Plum Point or Memphis were made during the Civil War. Detailed maps were not produced until 1891, and show a different river channel than the battle maps in Chapters 5 and 7, as the river channel shown on the battle maps is based on maps from Henry Walke's *Naval Scenes and Reminiscences.* I based my battle maps on Walke's, as he was the captain of the *Carondelet* in both battles, and, as a knowledgeable observer, he likely produced maps that accurately reflect the major geographical features during the battles. The Mississippi River has changed even more since 1891, as shown on the maps created by the Tennessee Valley Authority in 1986. These maps indicate that the location of the Battle of Plum Point is no longer part of the river, and that the Mississippi flowing past Memphis has undergone tremendous changes to its channel since the war. Visitors to either battlefield—if they know what to look for—will see evidence of where the Mississippi used to flow; but the uninformed will assume that the Mississippi has not changed course, and will not correctly locate the site of either battle.

Unfortunately, each of the battle sites has only one historic marker to indicate where these battles took place, and it is the rare individual who can show the actual location of each of the battles. Part of this forgetfulness is that during the postwar period, the Confederate River Defense Fleet did not get the credit it deserved due to the bias of former regular Confederate Naval officers toward these "amateurs." Such bias can be seen in John Thomas Sharf's *History of the Confederate States Navy,* in which he, a former regular Confederate Navy officer, gives them little credit and much criticism. Sharf's introductory paragraph on the Battle of Memphis indicates his bias, as he states: "To that disparity [the disparity in the number of guns in the Union fleet versus the number of guns in the Confederate fleet] must also be added the *morale* and experience of educated naval and army officers, and the *esprit de corps* of both United States services as against the total want of both in Montgomery and the other Mississippi pilots who had been improvised into officers afloat, without any of the essential characteristics, except that of personal courage."[9]

The U.S. Navy was not exempt from this bias. In 1864 Commander Robert Townsend asked Lieutenant-Commander James A. Greer to take his boat, the *Benton,* to Vicksburg for the purpose of being in charge and control of naval operations on the Mississippi from the mouth of the White River down to Natchez.[10] Townsend informed

Grier that the reason for the request was "the logic of events shows that the volunteer commanders hereabouts have been unequal to the responsibility of their position."[11] Greer reinforced this attitude when he informed his commander about the request by telling him that Townsend "deems the presence of a regular naval officer there [Vicksburg] essential on account of the rascality that is going on."[12] Their bias is all the more interesting given that, by 1864, volunteers commanded the majority of boats on the Mississippi. Obviously, neither Confederate nor Union regular Navy officers thought highly of their volunteer officers and, subsequently, when writing their reminiscences, many of them either ignored or belittled the contributions of the volunteers.

One technological development, the steam engine, must be included and understood in any discussion of naval warfare on the inland rivers. In the decades before the war, the development of efficient steam engines allowed boats and ships to easily go upstream against the current, an ability that oar- or sail-powered vessels found difficult However, Civil War–era steam engines were not very powerful, and heavy ironclad boats had difficulty overcoming the current when they went upriver. Although Union ironclads struggled going upriver, Confederate ironclads on the Mississippi—specifically the CSS *Arkansas*—with their poor quality engines had even more trouble. Moreover, steam engines, of that time period, required a tremendous amount of fuel, with quality coal being preferred.[13] Consequently, having an adequate amount of coal available was an issue that commanders on both sides had to manage as it directly impacted their operations. Even with these issues, however, steam power made naval warfare on the country's inland waterways possible.

* * *

The struggle for control of the Mississippi River was long and bloody, but the Union gained naval control of the upper Mississippi with its victory at Memphis in June 1862, gaining complete naval control of the Mississippi when the CSS *Arkansas* was destroyed in August 1862. However, not until Port Hudson surrendered on the 9th of July 1863 did the Union gain sufficient control of the entire river such that unarmed and unprotected civilian steamers could travel up and down the Mississippi.[14] Still, due to attacks by the Confederate Army on shipping and the threat of Confederate boats coming from tributaries of the Mississippi to make raids, the Union did not gain absolute control of the Mississippi River until the end of war. This struggle was complex and only won by the joint effort of the US Army and Navy, an objective neither could have accomplished alone. Many armies and naval squadrons were involved in this effort—too many to discuss in any one book. Thus, this book does not attempt to describe all of them or to enumerate all of actions in which they were involved. Its purpose is to highlight the Battle of Memphis, one of the forgotten pivotal battles of the war, and the naval units involved in it. I hope I have achieved my purpose by adding to our knowledge of the struggle for the Mississippi River during the American Civil War.

Acknowledgments

As with any book, there are a number of people I need to thank. I would first like to thank John Montgomery, who introduced me to the Battle of Memphis, provided information about the battle, and read a number of versions of the manuscript. My wife, Sherri, also needs to be thanked for proofing the manuscript and for her patience while I worked on this project. Mary Scott and Jan Wagner at The Ohio State University library need to be thanked for providing maps and continually looking for additional maps. David Slay and Jake Kock at the Vicksburg National Military Park were very courteous during my visit there and provided much appreciated information. Bill Roberts was also supportive in providing crucial information on the construction of the monitor being built at Cincinnati and for critiquing part of the manuscript . Bill Reynolds, who belongs to The Sons and Daughters of Pioneer Rivermen, provided information on Acting Volunteer Lieutenant Commander William R. Hoel, as well as a photograph of a Navy jacket that Hoel wore during the Civil War. Elaine McConnell at the United States Military Academy kindly provided information on Edward D. Mansfield, while Dot Abbott at the United States Naval Academy supplied information on Colonel William S. Lovell. Yeosany Yoon, a graduate student in Geomatics Engineering at The Ohio State University, also needs to be thanked for his work on the maps of the Battle of Plum Point and Memphis. Other individuals who provided information required to complete this book include Corey Black at the Naval Historical Foundation, Harry Miller at the Wisconsin Historical Society, Elizabeth Gaines at the Cotton Belt Rail Historical Society, and Joan Albert at the Virginia Historical Society.

Finally, I would also like to thank Gary Joiner and Douglas Cupples, along with an anonymous reader who helped make this a better book. In addition, Scot Danforth and Thomas Wells at the University of Tennessee Press need to be thanked for allowing this book to be published along with Annalisa Weaver for her excellent editing. In the end, responsibility for the book is mine.

Chapter 1

The Importance of the Mississippi River

> Among the successful operations of the late war, none were more gallant, none resulted in greater public benefit, than those executed by the gunboats of the Mississippi squadron.
>
> —Rear-Admiral Henry Walke, USN, 1887[1]

> It is no exaggeration of the services rendered in the late war by the navy of the United States, to say that without its aid the armies of the Union would not have been successful.
>
> —J. Thomas Sharf, *History of the Confederate States Navy*[2]

The importance of the Mississippi River and its tributaries during the American Civil War cannot be overemphasized. Whichever side controlled them gained a tremendous advantage. The Union needed to control the rivers to divide the Confederacy; keep Confederate ships from attacking Northern cities and shipping on the rivers; allow produce and manufactured goods from the midwestern states easy access to the ocean; and provide a safer supply route to their armies than the railroad.[3] Indeed, the Union considered control of the Mississippi so important that Assistant Secretary of the Navy Gustavus V. Fox informed Admiral David D. Porter in October 1862, "The opening of the river as early as possible is the imperative act to be considered above even the capture of Charleston."[4] For its part, the Confederacy had to maintain control of the Mississippi and its tributaries to keep from being separated into disjointed parts; have access to the Gulf of Mexico for import and export; and retain the option of using the river system as a means of attacking Northern states bordering the river. Consequently, Confederate commanders were as aware of the importance of controlling the Mississippi as their Union counterparts. Major-General Leonidas Polk wrote President Jefferson Davis in December 1861 that "with the enemy in possession of the river [Mississippi] the injury we shall sustain is incalculable."[5] As a result, both sides expended considerable resources to control these rivers.

However, control of the rivers did not make them easily navigable. Travel on the Mississippi River and its tributaries was a difficult and dangerous undertaking in this era before flood control, dredging, and the ability to maintain an adequate level of water. Accordingly, it took years for a river pilot to become proficient because the channels constantly changed, the level of the water in the rivers varied tremendously from season to season, and obstacles—such as snags—abounded. When the war started, these navigational challenges forced both sides to modify their actions based on what the rivers were doing. One specific problem both fleets had to deal with was low water during the summer—the main campaigning season for the armies. During those months, many boats suffered frequent groundings on sandbars, and the larger boats could not go up the tributaries. This problem affected resupply efforts of both sides as well as the US Navy's ability to provide protective gunfire to the US Army from its large guns.

Before they could start down the Mississippi, the Union forces had to secure Cairo, Illinois. As shown on the Mississippi River and Tributaries map, Cairo is located at the junction of the Mississippi and Ohio Rivers. If it successfully blocked this junction, the Confederacy would stop the vast majority of the river traffic and keep the Union Navy from moving down river. This potential menace explains why the Union made such a tremendous effort to gain control of the terrain opposite Cairo in Kentucky and Missouri. Even with Cairo secured, another threat had to be neutralized. This threat came from the Tennessee and Cumberland Rivers, which enter the Ohio River upriver from Cairo. Union control of these rivers would prevent Confederate boats from suddenly appearing on the Ohio River and disrupting shipping. Indeed, the danger from Confederate gunboats was considered so severe that, in October 1861, Captain Andrew Foote ordered the *Lexington* to blockade the Tennessee River to prevent Confederate gunboats on the Tennessee from gaining access to the Ohio River. The *Lexington* was ordered to remain on blockade duty until relieved by the more heavily armed and protected *New Era*.[6] These threats explain why the initial Union efforts in the Mississippi River Valley were concentrated on securing Cairo and these two rivers rather than on immediately forcing a passage down the Mississippi. Only after Cairo and the Tennessee and Cumberland Rivers were secured could Union forces safely move down the Mississippi.

Due to its topography, the Mississippi River only had a few major ports during the Civil War, Memphis being one of them. Memphis was the largest city on the Mississippi between New Orleans and

Mississippi River and Tributaries, ORN, series I, vol. 22, p. 276. (Notes added by the author.)

Saint Louis, the fifth largest city in the Confederacy, and the largest city in Tennessee. It was important enough that the 1860 census listed it as one of the forty-four principal cities and towns in the country.[7] Memphis's importance was based on its location on the Mississippi, its geographical advantage as the site at which all three eastern rail lines converged, and the western rail line's position across the river from it.[8] When war appeared inevitable, citizens of Memphis wrote letters to various newspaper editors, emphasizing their city's importance and how its loss would have a devastating effect on the Confederacy. However, such letters were written by the citizens of all major Southern cities, as they all considered their city essential to the survival of the Confederacy.

Memphis's strategic location had already been recognized by the Federal government, which had established the United States Navy Yard there in 1844. Memphis was selected because it had a good port and was far enough inland to be protected from potential naval raids, such as ones the United States had experienced in the War of 1812. However, the Navy neither wanted nor supported the yard, and Congress eventually donated the yard to the city in 1853.[9]

When the war began, only two ports controlled by the Confederacy on the Mississippi could support shipbuilding or repair: New Orleans and Memphis.[10] However, as with New Orleans, the Confederacy neglected to properly fortify Memphis, in part because high command felt that the upriver forts—to include Island No. 10 and Fort Pillow—would protect it from any naval threat, and the Army would protect it from any attacks by land. General Pierre G. T. Beauregard informed President Jefferson Davis, when asked about the dispositions to defend Memphis during an inquiry after the retreat from Corinth and the capture of Memphis, that "The best way to defend Memphis, having no forces or guns to send there, was to hold Fort Pillow and Corinth."[11] Beyond the lack of resources, Beauregard's reasoning was probably based on the fact that Memphis was 251 winding, torturous river miles from Cairo, almost a fourth of the way to New Orleans from Cairo.[12] This distance was considered to be so substantial that a Union fleet would not be able reach the city without suffering tremendous loses from the upriver forts. Moreover, the city was about 150 miles by land from Cairo, making any threat from the land side unlikely without control of the river.[13] Thus, when the city was threatened by Federal forces, the Confederacy had not constructed an extensive defensive system there, and it was too late to build one, even if the troops and heavy artillery had been available.[14]

For the Union, securing Memphis meant that its fleet would had a more convenient location for resupply and repair; and, fortifying Memphis with heavy guns or stationing a warship there would help prevent any Confederate raider from going upriver. Edward Mansfield, an 1819 graduate of the United States Military Academy who lived just north of Cincinnati, was asked by General Joseph Totten, Chief of the Corps of Engineers, to provide information on the number and type of boats available on the Mississippi as well as information on navigating the river.[15] As part of his report Mansfield stated that he considered "Memphis the most valuable military point on the Mississippi between New Orleans and Cairo-as a defensible and as an aggressive point more valuable than either of them. It is not only one of the very few high and comparatively healthy places on the river, but in its relationship to Arkansas, Mississippi, and Tennessee it has peculiar advantages. The recent construction of railroad [*sic*] centering there has quadrupled its advantages."[16] The railroads to which Mansfield was referring were the four previously mentioned railroad lines that came into Memphis. One line ran north and joined the Baltimore and Ohio system; one line ran east to Corinth; and the third line ran south to Jackson, Mississippi, then on to New Orleans. The fourth line linked Memphis to central Arkansas, although all goods traveling on that line had to be ferried across the Mississippi. These four railroads made Memphis a vital hub for goods being shipped from the Confederacy's western states to the central and eastern armies. Of these four railroads, the one running east from Memphis was considered by Secretary of War Judah P. Benjamin to be vital to the defense of the Confederacy.[17] Consequently, when Confederate disasters in Tennessee threatened the safety of this railroad, Benjamin reported the following to General Robert E. Lee in Savannah, Georgia: "The railroad line from Memphis to Richmond must be defended at all hazards. We can only do this by withdrawing troops from the seaboard. You are therefore requested to withdraw all such forces as are now employed in the defense of the seaboard of Florida, taking proper steps to secure the guns and munitions of war, and to send forward the troops to Tennessee, to report to General A. S. Johnston, by the most expeditious route."[18] However, these reinforcements were not able to stop the Union advance, and the loss of Corinth and other positions along this railroad cut this vital means of transportation. Then, Union control of Memphis cut all four rail lines, and the Confederacy lost another center of communications, manufacturing, and population.

An important factor affecting Union naval strategy is that no major rivers flow into the Mississippi between Cairo and Memphis. This geographic reality meant that Confederate warships could not go up a side river on the upper Mississippi and slip out behind the Union fleet to create havoc upriver. Down river from Memphis, a number of major rivers enter the Mississippi, and these rivers were capable of hiding Confederate warships. Thus, once it went below Memphis, the Union Navy was forced to leave warships behind to continually patrol and blockade these rivers. This strategy was a response to the Union naval commanders' enduring fear that a fast Confederate warship would get upriver of the Union fleet. Controlling Memphis and placing heavy guns there partially alleviated this fear.

As previously mentioned, numerous battles were fought over who was to control the Mississippi and its tributaries. Two of these battles were fleet engagements that have been all but forgotten, having been overshadowed by bloodier land battles as well as the siege of Vicksburg. Many histories of the war do not mention them, even though the Union victory in the pivotal Battle of Memphis opened the Mississippi down to Vicksburg for the Union. If both battles had been decisive Confederate victories, Union control of the Mississippi River would have been delayed by at least six months, which would have had a ripple effect on the rest of the war. These two battles also demonstrated that ramming was an effective tactic in a relatively confined maneuver area during the age of muzzle-loading guns.

The first of these two battles, the Battle of Plum Point, occurred on May 10, 1862. The Battle of Plum Point was an empty Confederate victory because it taught the Union flotilla important lessons it applied during the Battle of Memphis. In addition, the damage inflicted on the Union flotilla was not decisive, and the damaged boats were quickly repaired. The Battle of Memphis was a decisive, one-sided Union victory that gave the Union control of the upper Mississippi. There were two Union fleets at the Battle of Memphis, one under Commodore Charles H. Davis and one under Colonel Charles Ellet. Interestingly, both fleets were under the command of the US Army. Davis was under the command of Major General Henry W. Halleck.[19] Ellet was more independent and reported directly to Secretary of War Edwin Stanton.[20] The Confederate fleet involved in both battles was commanded by Commodore Joseph E. Montgomery.[21] In turn, Montgomery, reported to General Beauregard.[22] These were three very different fleets, all under Army command—one commanded by a professional naval officer with no experience in river warfare, one by a former bridge engineer with neither riverboat nor military experience, and the third by a former Mississippi River pilot with no military experience. This combination is hard for us to believe today; yet, the actions of these three men had a tremendous influence on the outcome of the war.

While the loss of Memphis was a long-term blow to the viability of the Confederacy, the loss of the River Defense Fleet was, at least in the short term, a greater loss. As long as it existed, the River Defense Fleet severely limited the Union river fleet's ability to operate freely, as stationary shore-based batteries could be bypassed, but an enemy fleet could not. Thus, the destruction of the Confederate River Defense Fleet allowed the Union fleet greater flexibility, as it now had control of the Upper Mississippi River. However, before these battles could occur and the struggle for control of the Mississippi River could begin, the boats had to be built or purchased and converted, armed, and crewed, and logistical bases had to be established.

Chapter 2

The Confederate River Defense Fleet

> Their views [Riverboat Captains Joseph E. Montgomery and James H. Townsend[1]] in regard to an independent organization and action, in order to give greater efficiency to the undertaking, has [*sic*] impressed me very strongly, and I can but urge the reasonableness of their demand and the adoption of their views in this respect.
>
> —Major-General Leonidas Polk, 27 December 1861, letter to President Jefferson Davis[2]

> In short, unless some competent person of education, system, and brains is put over each division of this fleet [the River Defense Fleet] it will, in my judgment, prove an utter failure. No code of laws or penalties has been established, and it is difficult to decide how deserters from the fleet are to be tried and punished. There is little or no discipline or subordination—too much "steamboat" and too little of the "man-of-war" to be very effective.
>
> —Major-General Mansfield Lovell, 15 April 1862, letter to Confederate Secretary of War George Randolph[3]

These two quotations demonstrate the range of opinion about the Confederate River Defense Fleet. While some authorities were very receptive to the idea, others did not think very highly of it. Part of the problem was the regular officers' perception of non-regular officers and units. Volunteers on both sides encountered this problem, even though many of their ideas were more inventive than those of the professional officers. The difficulty faced by the volunteers was putting their ideas into action and proving their effectiveness without the full support of the regulars. As J. Thomas Sharf, a former regular Confederate naval officer, stated in his book *History of the Confederate States Navy,* "This anomalous, inefficient, useless and expensive expedition was planned and gotten up by the pilots, Montgomery and Townsend, and urged upon Congress by the whole Mississippi delegation [The Navy's *Official Records* state that it was the Missouri delegation] and Gen. Polk."[4] While Sharf's opinion summarized that of most of the regular Navy toward the River Defense Fleet, some of its officers—especially those who dealt directly with Montgomery's fleet—developed a good opinion of it. In his reminiscences, Charles Read, another former regular Confederate naval officer who had direct knowledge of Montgomery's fleet, stated that the Montgomery rams were "the most serviceable and formidable war vessels of [*sic*] the river on either side."[5]

Contempt was not one sided, as the Mississippi River boat men, along with many residents along the river, expressed equal disdain for the regular Confederate Navy officers. Their scorn only increased when the regular Navy failed to prevent the Union fleet from advancing down the river. Even some of the regular naval officers were ashamed of the regular Confederate fleet on the upper Mississippi. Charles Read wrote in his reminiscences that, when he was traveling on a river steamer from Memphis to Fort Pillow to rejoin the regular Confederate fleet after the fall of New Orleans, "the ridicule of '[George] Hollin's [*sic*] fleet' was so great and general, that I was really ashamed to own that I was on my way to join it."[6] In the end, Montgomery's fleet became the Confederacy's last hope for stopping the advancing Union flotilla, a state of affairs recognized by the Confederate high command. At the beginning of May 1862—before the Battle of Plum Point—General Braxton Bragg sent a message to General M. Jeff Thompson,[7] whose men were serving as gunners on the boats, "Hope ere long you will be able to test with success the efficiency of your boats, which are now the last hope of closing the river to the enemy's gunboats."[8] Unfortunately for the Confederacy, even with the best wishes of General Bragg, the contempt both groups felt toward each other hindered cooperation and, thus, effectiveness.

Due to the rivalries, creating the River Defense Fleet and other Confederate fleets on the river was a major effort, because there were no warships on the Mississippi River or any of its tributaries at the start of the war. Realizing the need to control the river, both sides quickly converted available boats by adding guns and strengthening them where necessary. The Confederacy was the first to produce results, even though the initial work in New Orleans focused on high seas cruisers. In June 1861, a converted tug, the CSS *Jackson*, entered Confederate service at New Orleans.[9] However, the Confederacy quickly fell behind, because it possessed very limited ship building facilities on the Mississippi. The Confederacy's best shipyards on the Mississippi were located in New Orleans, while Memphis was the only Confederate city on the upper Mississippi capable of building or repairing a ship.[10] This capacity was in part due to the previously mentioned former United States Navy shipyard.

The lack of quality shipyards was not the only reason the Confederacy was unable to compete with the construction efforts of the Union. There was also a shortage of the necessary related industries and trained shipyard workers, and a lack of interservice cooperation. In December 1861, Confederate Secretary of the Navy Stephen R. Mallory wrote to General Leonidas Polk asking to use mechanics in Polk's command to assist with the construction of an ironclad gunboat at Memphis. With their assistance, Mallory wrote, the boat could be completed in sixty days.[11] General Polk sent about seven men—although Mallory had requested one hundred.[12] One reason Polk may not have fully cooperated was that he had earlier purchased a boat that he was having converted into a gunboat. Although the boat was to be used on the Tennessee River, due to the inadequate facilities in Nashville, his boat had to be taken to New Orleans for the conversion to be completed.[13] Lack of cooperation extended beyond not lending skilled workers. Parts were in such short supply that Confederate officers in Nashville seized bolts and spikes intended for the CSS *Arkansas* for use on the boat that was being converted in Nashville.[14] The dearth of critical manufacturing facilities also delayed the construction of Confederate ironclads on the Mississippi. One such facility was sawmills with the capacity to cut large pieces of lumber. To keep up with his schedule, the contractor responsible for constructing the *Arkansas* and *Tennessee* was forced to rebuild two saw mills so they could cut the necessary long pine boards.[15]

The appropriation of the bolts and spikes designated for the *Arkansas* and *Tennessee* was not the only example interservice rivalry. In March 1862, the Confederate Army detained, for its own use, eight cannon intended for the Confederate Navy in New Orleans, although the cannon were later returned to the Confederate Navy when Secretary of War ordered their return.[16] The Confederate Army also commandeered a train carrying ammunition for Navy cannon.[17] Because of the interservice competition and the lack of an adequate industrial base, the construction of the ironclads *Arkansas* and *Tennessee* at Memphis was delayed. This delay was fatal, for when Union forces threatened

Memphis in April 1862, the *Tennessee* was burnt, and the *Arkansas* was towed to the Yazoo River for completion.[18] Had both ironclads been available for the defense of the upper Mississippi, the results of the naval battles there might have been very different. In the end, the combination of an insufficient industrial base, the absence of cooperation, and the lack of skilled workmen doomed Confederate fleets attempting to control the Mississippi River to a perpetual material disadvantage.

Beyond inadequate resources, the Confederacy was plagued by multiple naval commands that included the regular Confederate Navy and a number of independent commands. These independent commands comprised state navies, the River Defense Fleet, and—at the beginning of the war—privateers. Even these multiple commands did not include the gunboat being converted for General Polk. However, the regular Confederate Navy had a much more orderly chain of command. Captain George N. Hollins,[19] Confederate States Navy and former US Navy officer, was commander of all Confederate vessels afloat on the Mississippi and of the naval station at New Orleans.[20] Hollins was an experienced naval officer; having become a midshipman in 1814 and promoted to the rank of captain in 1855, he appeared to be an excellent choice.[21] However, Hollins had responsibility for a geographical area that was too large for any one individual. Consequently, when Hollins went up river in early 1862, taking all of the Confederate Navy's boats with him, Commander William C. Whittle, CSN, assumed command of the naval station at New Orleans but not the vessels afloat.[22] Later, Commander John K. Mitchell, CSN, another former US Navy officer, became the commander of the few remaining regular Confederate warships at New Orleans on April 10, 1862.[23] Even though the regular Confederate Navy had an efficient chain of command, the overall Confederate naval command structure was, at best, a confusing, multilayered command organization with each command competing for the same resources. A truly unified command could have resolved many of these issues, but each command wanted to remain independent, and the regular Confederate Navy wanted to remain separate from the Confederate Army.

The idea for the River Defense Fleet originated with Riverboat Captains Joseph E. Montgomery and James H. Townsend. In December 1861, they were able to convince Major-General Polk of the feasibility of using a fleet of riverboats to contest the Union fleet's advance down the Mississippi. Consequently, Polk wrote a letter to President Jefferson Davis endorsing the idea. Polk's letter stressed that the Confederacy, to resist the advance of the Union fleet, "should resort to any and every scheme that is at all feasible to thwart their purposes and defeat their designs."[24] Montgomery and Townsend, with the backing of Polk's letter and the support of the entire Missouri delegation, eventually convinced Davis and enough congressmen and senators to support their idea.[25] Consequently, the Confederate Congress passed two acts in January 1861 that were used to create the River Defense Fleet. The first act, Act Number XXXIV, appropriated $1,000,00 for floating defenses for the western rivers and was to be expended "at the discretion of the President, by the Secretary of War, or Secretary of the Navy, as he shall direct."[26] Approved on January 9, 1862, the second act, Act Number XXXIX, was supplementary to an act making appropriations for certain floating defenses, and, authorized the president "to raise a corps for the temporary and special service on the Western waters, to cause to be enlisted a number of men not exceeding six thousand, and of such commissioned and non-commissioned officers, and of such rank, either naval or military, as the President may deem necessary, who shall severally receive such pay and allowances as he may determine."[27] Although both acts had their limits, the Confederate legislature had given Davis a very broad mandate.

Davis acted quickly: On January 14, shortly after the passage of the acts, Secretary of War Judah P. Benjamin directed Major General Mansfield Lovell in New Orleans to seize fourteen steamships.[28] The message was considered important enough that Benjamin made the unusual request of having Lovell's telegraph operator let him know when the message had been delivered to Lovell. A few days later, Benjamin sent a more detailed message outlining the mission of the River Defense Fleet and how it was to be organized. In another confusing command structure decision, Benjamin informed Lovell that the fleet was not to be under the command of the Confederate Navy, but was to be "subject to the general command of the military chief of the department where it may be ordered to operate."[29] The boats were to be commanded by steamboat captains and fitted out based on their judgment. President Davis selected Captains Joseph E. Montgomery and James H. Townsend to command two of the boats; they were, in turn, to select twelve other captains and recommend them to President Davis for appointment as boat commanders.[30]

Montgomery and Townsend selected twelve individuals, but approval of the appointments had a political nature to them. In a message to General Lovell in early March 1862, Secretary Benjamin noted that the citizens of New Orleans considered three of the twelve individuals unreliable. Benjamin asked Lovell to replace them with captains who were acceptable to the government, as well as to Montgomery and Townsend, as "public opinion ought to be satisfied, if possible."[31] Replacements were found, as three of the captains who accompanied Montgomery north were not on the original list.

Beyond the question of who the captains were to be, no one had yet been selected as commander of the fleet. The lack of a designated commander had become an issue for multiple reasons, and Secretary Benjamin had already received several communications about command of the fleet that embarrassed both him and the president. To solve the command issue, Benjamin, in a message from March 1862, requested that General Lovell ask Captain Thomas P. Leathers, a steam boat captain who was not on the list of boat commanders, to take command of the fleet, with Montgomery as second in command, Townsend third, and the seniority of the other boat commanders determined by Montgomery. If Leathers turned the command down, then Montgomery was to be appointed the commander,[32] which is apparently what happened.[33] Montgomery was offered command of the fleet because he was a well-known and respected Mississippi River pilot. He had trained a number of pilots, including Mark Twain (Samuel Clemens).[34] His obituary in the *Confederate Veteran* states that he was a personal friend of Jefferson Davis and that Judah P. Benjamin had been his attorney.[35] These connections probably helped him get authorization from the Confederate government for his ram fleet. So, at the age of forty-four, Joseph Edward Montgomery, an individual with no experience in naval warfare, became commander of the River Defense Fleet, the largest Confederate naval force on the Mississippi and, indeed, in the entire Confederacy.[36]

Secretary Benjamin's message of January 19 to General Lovell included an outline of why the fleet was created, how it was to operate, and what was expected of it. The fourteen boats in the Mississippi River Defense Fleet were created with the intention of ramming and sinking Union gunboats and mortar rafts while traveling at a high speed. Confederate officials believed that ramming the Union boats would be more successful than opposing them with artillery due to iron plates that protected the boats—especially because the extra weight of the iron plates made Union ironclads slow and unwieldy and a much easier target to ram than a faster, more maneuverable boat. The Confederate boats were to have their bows reinforced to increase the force of the impact and to protect them from cannon fire as they steamed toward the

Union boats. The rams were not to rely on cannon or firearms because the riverboat men who manned the boats were not considered skilled in using them; rather, the crews were to be armed with cutlasses. However, each boat would be armed with one stern-mounted heavy gun that would be used to defend the unprotected stern of the boat when it was withdrawing. Benjamin's message also specifically stated that the fleet "is not to be part of the Navy, for it is intended for service on the rivers, and will be composed of the steamboat men of the Western waters." However, the fleet was to "be subject to the general command of the military chief of the department where it may be ordered to operate."[37] Because the fleet operated in General Pierre G. T. Beauregard's[38] department, he would have command over both land and naval forces, making him one of the first joint commanders in American military history.[39]

The idea of a boat or ship being sunk by ramming was a principle well understood in 1860. All of the Confederate riverboat captains had probably seen or experienced two boats colliding, as many riverboats had been sunk by accidently ramming or hitting a submerged snag. Consequently, to survive a ramming while inflicting maximum damage on their target, the Confederate boats were designed to absorb the impact. Montgomery's boats were transformed into rams when their bows were made solid by reinforcing their interior with 12-inch square timbers bolted together. In addition, the outside of the bows was sheathed with 4-inch oak planks for twenty feet on each side. Lastly, 1 by 2½-inch iron was bent around the bow to cover the planks.

However, the boats had to survive the cannon fire they would face before they could ram their opponent. This protection could not reduce the speed that was crucial to creating the necessary impact momentum. Accordingly, protection was only provided to the bows, as previously noted, and the engines. The engines were protected by an inner and outer bulkhead filled with compressed cotton and then covered by railroad iron. The inner bulkhead consisted of 12-inch square timbers that were bolted together every 18 inches. The outer bulkhead consisted of 6 by 12–inch timbers, again bolted together every 18 inches. The 22-inch space between the bulkheads was filled with compressed cotton bales, with the bulkheads joined by two iron bolts over the top of each bale. Finally, the outer bulkheads were plated with inch-thick railroad iron that was 2½ inches wide.[40] The offensive power of the reinforced bows and the defensive protection provided to the engines would prove their effectiveness at Plum Point.

General M. Lovell seized the fourteen named boats as ordered on January 15, and informed Secretary Benjamin that he had done so.[41] However, problems began immediately. First, at least one of the boats was not considered adequate, and Lovell asked for permission to replace it with a more suitable boat.[42] In addition, some of the boats were appraised at a high value, and local naval experts advised Lovell to replace them with less expensive boats that would be equally adequate for their intended purpose. However, the cost for the fourteen boats was still substantial at $620,000 even though Lovell had been able to reduce the cost by $280,000. Lovell apprised Secretary Benjamin that the appropriated $1,000,000 would not be enough to both purchase the boats and convert them.[43] Benjamin acted quickly and, on March 22, sent $350,000 to Lovell to help with the costs. Benjamin also wrote that he had applied to the Congress for a $500,000 appropriation to finish paying for the boats.[44] A more critical issue for constructing the boats was the scarcity of materials and mechanics. Consequently, it took several weeks longer than Montgomery—who became responsible for converting the boats—had anticipated to prepare the boats.[45] This delay had an impact on the deployment of the boats, as the Confederates had evacuated Columbus, Kentucky, before the boats were ready.

The first six boats (*Stonewall Jackson*, *Warrior*, *Defiance*, *Resolute*, *General Breckinridge*, and *General Lovell*) were completed by April 22, 1862, but were retained by General Lovell for the defense of New Orleans.[46] Lovell kept the six boats for two reasons. First, as mentioned, the Confederates had evacuated Columbus, Kentucky, which was located twenty river miles down the Mississippi from Cairo.[47] Then, all of the boats in the regular Confederate Navy had been ordered up river and Rear Admiral David Farragut's fleet had begun assembling near the mouth of the Mississippi. Consequently, Lovell wanted Montgomery's boats available to assist in repelling any naval attack.[48] The next three boats (*General Bragg*, *General Price*, and *General Van Dorn*) left New Orleans on March 25. The remaining five boats (*Colonel Lovell*, *General Beauregard*, *General M. Jeff. Thompson*, *Little Rebel*, and *General Sumter*) left New Orleans as each boat was completed. The last one, the *General Sumter*, left on April 17 with Commodore Montgomery onboard.[49]

All of Montgomery's commanders were experienced riverboat pilots and captains. James H. Townsend, Montgomery's second in command, captained the *General Price*. William H. H. Leonard was in command of the *General Bragg*, William W. Lamb commanded the *General Sumter*, Issac D. Fulkerson commanded the *General Van Dorn*, James H.

Hurt commanded the *General Beauregard*, James C. Delancy commanded the *Colonel Lovell*, and John H. Burke commanded the *General M. Jeff Thompson*. Montgomery, in addition to being the overall commander, captained the *Little Rebel*. Townsend never commanded the *General Price* in combat, as, for some unknown reason, he was unable to perform his duties, and Thomas E. Henthorne, his first officer, took command prior to the Battle of Plum Point. Other than that change, these men would be Montgomery's commanders at Plum Point and Memphis.[50]

The shortage of iron in the Confederacy caused some of the boats—at least the *General Price* and *General Van Dorn*—to leave New Orleans without having their ironwork completed.[51] On their way to Memphis, the boats stopped at various ports looking for iron to complete their rams and protect their engines. On March 31, the *Price* reached Eunice, Arkansas, and its captain, James H. Townsend, asked the railroad agent there if he had any iron. He replied that he did not, at which time Townsend informed him that he would have his crew tear up the track and take what they needed. True to his word, Townsend ordered his crew to take up about three miles of track from the Mississippi, Ouachita and Red River Railroad—enough to finish the needed ironwork on both the *Price* and the *Van Dorn*.[52] On April 3, the *Price* and *Van Dorn* arrived in Memphis and, by April 10, all of the necessary ironwork had been completed. [53] Captain Townsend's resolve in getting the needed iron for the two boats demonstrated the determination of these riverboat captains not to be stopped by bureaucracy. Luckily, Captain Townsend's actions did not have any long-term impact on the Confederate railroad system, as the Mississippi, Ouachita and Red River Railroad was incomplete, and the part that was finished could only handle very light traffic.[54]

Beyond being prepared as rams, the boats were lightly armed. Many authors have mistakenly ascribed to these boats many more cannon than they actually had while in Confederate service. This error comes from assuming that the armament on the boats as fitted out in Federal service was the same as it had been when they were in Confederate service. When Montgomery's eight boats left New Orleans, they had between them two guns—a 32- and 24-pounder smooth-bore cannon—all that could be provided. When the boats arrived at Fort Pillow, General John B. Villepigue, the fort's commander, furnished each unarmed boat with a 32-pounder smooth-bore cannon. All of these guns were mounted on the stern of the boats. Later, after the

Battle of Plum Point, and as Fort Pillow was being evacuated, General Villepigue gave the fleet four 8-inch, also known as a 64-pounder, smooth-bore cannon.[55] These guns were mounted on the bows of the *General M. Jeff Thompson*, *General Sumter*, *General Beauregard*, and *Colonel Lovell*.[56] Although more of the boats were capable of mounting the large 8-inch cannon, lack of time and the amount of work involved in moving and mounting the cannon, which weighed well over 8,000 pounds each, precluded this undertaking.[57]

Even with this armament, Montgomery was not interested in engaging in a ship-to-ship gunnery engagement, because his boats would never survive such a battle. He wanted to make a surprise attack and sink enemy ships by ramming. Moreover, most of Montgomery's men and officers did not know how to operate heavy guns. Lieutenant Colonel William S. Lovell, a former US naval officer, was questioned about the effectiveness of the river-defense fleet at General Lovell's Board of Inquiry after the loss of New Orleans. He stated:

> The boats were fitted up generally very well for use as rams. I considered most of them as better for that purpose than the Queen of the West [an Ellet ram captured by the Confederates near Fort de Russy on February 14, 1863], a ram taken from the enemy, which I have well examined since her capture. There was no discipline, no organization, but little or no drill of the crews. I frequently requested the commanding officers [Montgomery and Townsend] to drill their men at a gun I placed on one of the vessels expressly for that purpose. I offered to employ a Navy officer to drill them. I also employed a person who had been a gunner in the U.S. Navy to act as such to the fleet; to mount the guns; to have a general superintendence of everything belonging to the gunner's department; also to teach the officers and men of the fleet how to use and manage the guns. I do not believe one of the officers in command of any of the vessels of the fleet knew how to load or manage heavy guns. Some of the vessels had men employed as gunners. Some of the captains told me they knew nothing about heavy guns and must have gunners.[58]

While the riverboat men eventually developed some proficiency in operating the heavy guns, Montgomery used artillerymen from General

Jeff Thompson's command to man his guns during the Battle of Plum Point. Unfortunately for the Confederacy, these men were not available during the Battle of Memphis, and the riverboat men had to depend on their own skills, with abysmal results.

The eight boats that went upriver with Montgomery varied tremendously, and each warrants separate description. The differences among the boats included tonnage, speed, type of propulsion, and draft, as well as what they had been designed to do as a civilian vessel. These differences made Montgomery's battle plans more difficult to make and the fleet harder to manage. However, Montgomery knew that his boats were faster and more maneuverable than the Union's ironclad gunboats, although they all had a deeper draft by about six feet.[59] This difference was substantial and would become an important factor in both the Battle of Plum Point and the Battle of Memphis.

In most cases, only limited information and few photographs exist of the Confederate boats, especially for the ones destroyed at Memphis. The boats captured at Memphis by the Union had photographs made of them, but these pictures were taken after the boats were re-armed for Union service. One source for illustrations of all of the boats is Alexander Simplot, an artist working for Harper's Weekly magazine. Simplot was at the Battle of Memphis, and his drawings present accurate representations of many of the Confederate boats. Another source of information is General Jeff Thompson, who recorded the relative speeds of the boats in his reminiscences—data collected during the attack at Plum Point, at which time the boats were aligned fastest to slowest.[60]

General Thompson considered *General Bragg* the fastest boat in the fleet, with a speed of 10 knots, and the best overall boat.[61] Originally named the *Mexico,* the three-masted, 700 to 1,043 ton, fourth rate, wooden side-wheel steamer had a draft of twelve feet and was built in Westervelt, New York.[62] Its low-pressure engines powered a solid shaft walking beam making it quieter than any other boat in the fleet.[63] A photograph was taken of the *Bragg* in 1862 or 1863 at Cairo or Mound City, Illinois, when the boat was the USS *General Bragg.*[64]

The second fastest boat in the fleet, the *General Sumter,* was built in Algiers, Louisiana.[65] It was a 400-to-524-ton wooden side-wheel river towboat.[66] Originally named *Junius Beebe,* the boat worked in the New Orleans area prior to the war.[67] Alexander Simplot made two drawings of the *General Sumter,* showing it in action during the Battle of Memphis and after capture. Both drawings were published on June 28, 1862, in *Harper's Weekly.*

USS *General Bragg*. Courtesy of the Naval Historical Foundation, NH 46642.

The *General Sterling Price* was considered the third fastest boat.[68] Built in Cincinnati, Ohio, it was a 633-ton, fourth rate, wooden side-wheel steamer with a draft of thirteen feet.[69] Originally named *Laurent*[70] *Milledon*, it worked as a commercial towboat in the New Orleans area before the war. A. D. Lytle took a photograph of the *Price* in Baton Rouge, Louisiana, when it was the USS *General Price*.[71] Alexander Simplot made a drawing of the *Price*, showing it damaged and the crew abandoning it during the Battle of Memphis. The drawing was published in *Harper's Weekly* on June 28, 1862.

Next came the *General Van Dorn*, a wooden side-wheel steamer, known as the *General Earl Van Dorn*.[72] As the fourth fastest boat in the fleet, it was fast enough—with a head start—to outrace the Union rams that pursued the *Van Dorn* after the Battle of Memphis. Alexander Simplot made a drawing of the *Van Dorn* showing it after the Battle of Memphis, but the drawing is distant and in all probability was based on Simplot's imagination. The drawing was published in *Harper's Weekly* on June 28, 1862.

The *General Beauregard*, the fifth fastest boat in the fleet, was a 454-ton wooden side-wheel steamer built at Algiers, Louisiana.[73] Originally named *Ocean*, it was used as a towboat in the New Orleans area before becoming a Confederate warship.[74] The *Beauregard* was Alexander Simplot's favorite subject as he made three drawings of it. One shows *Beauregard* being rammed by the *Monarch* during the

The *Queen of the West*, *General Price*, *Little Rebel*, and *General Sumter*, with the *Monarch* ramming the *General Beauregard* during the Battle of Memphis. From a drawing done by Alexander Simplot, an eyewitness to the aftermath of the battle. The *Queen of the West* can be seen in the far left distance, disabled. The *Price* is shown on the front left with her crew jumping overboard. The *Little Rebel* is just to the right of the *Price*. The *Monarch* can be identified by the capital M between her smoke stacks. The *Beauregard*, in the center of the drawing, shows her crew jumping overboard as she is being rammed by the *Monarch*. The *General Sumter* can be seen sinking on the far right. Although Simplot's drawings of the battle are considered historically questionable, his drawings of the individual boats are considered to be fairly accurate. Courtesy of the Naval Historical Foundation, NH 902707.

Battle of Memphis, the next its appearance immediately after the battle, and the third as it appeared sunk after the battle. All of the drawings were published in *Harper's Weekly* on June 28, 1862.

The *Colonel Lovell* was the next to slowest boat in the fleet, a 521-ton wooden side-wheel steamer originally named *Hercules.*[75] The *Colonel Lovell* is the only boat in the fleet whose name warrants some explanation. The *Colonel Lovell* was named after the previously mentioned Lieutenant Colonel William S. Lovell, an officer on General Mansfield Lovell's staff and appointed the ordnance and disbursing officer of the River Defense Fleet.[76] As ordnance officer, Colonel Lovell superintended the necessary work on the vessels of the fleet to include receiving and placing their limited armament. He also furnished their ammunition and small arms, and established a system of signals.[77] This work earned him the honor of having a boat named after him. Colonel Lovell was different from most Confederate Army officers because he graduated from the United States Naval Academy in 1853.[78] After being commissioned, he served in the Navy until 1859, spending his last three years in command of steamers.[79] The *Colonel Lovell* thus has the honor of being the first warship named after a Naval Academy graduate.[80]

The largest and slowest boat in the fleet, the *General M. Jeff Thompson*, was a wooden side-wheel steamer.[81] In his reminiscences, General Thompson said that it was the best boat in the fleet, even though he wrote to General Beauregard during the war that the *Bragg* was.[82] Thompson's opinion was likely biased given the boat was named

USS *General Price.* Courtesy of the Naval Historical Foundation, NH 53870

The *General Beauregard* (left), sunk down to its upper deck, and the *General Jeff Thompson* (right), shown in a cloud of smoke, after the Battle of Memphis. From a drawing by Alexander Simplot. The boat in the middle is probably a Union tug. Courtesy of the Naval Historical Foundation, NH 59054.

after him, and he had forgotten his wartime statement. Alexander Simplot made two drawings of the *Jeff Thompson,* showing it after the Battle of Memphis—but all that can be seen are flames and smoke as the *Jeff Thompson* caught fire and blew up. The drawings were published in *Harper's Weekly* on June 28, 1862.

The *Little Rebel* was the flagship of the fleet, a 125- to 161-ton wooden screw steamer with a draft of twelve feet when deeply laden. The boat was originally named *R. E. & A. N. Watson* or *R. & J. Watson.* Its speed relative to the other boats cannot be determined as it did not have a specific location in the battle line at Plum Point, but the US Navy gave *Little Rebel* a maximum speed of 10 knots and ranked it a fourth-rate boat.[83] One advantage the *Little Rebel* had over the other boats was that, as a screw steamer, its means of propulsion were not as vulnerable to enemy fire as the side-wheelers were; however, its engines were just as vulnerable, and screw propulsion was more vulnerable to damage from grounding. Why the *Little Rebel* was selected to be the flagship of the fleet is unknown, but it must have been a very good boat because Flag-Officer Charles H. Davis and Colonel Charles Ellet argued over who would get *Little Rebel* after it was captured at Memphis. Alexander Simplot made a drawing of the *Little Rebel* showing it in action during the Battle of Memphis. The drawing was published in *Harper's Weekly* on June 28, 1862.

The six River Defense Fleet rams that General Lovell kept at New Orleans to defend the city confirmed his poor opinion of them. Lack of unity hurt their efforts as Captain John A. Stephenson, their commander, refused to take orders from Commander John K. Mitchell,

The *General Van Dorn*, *General Sumter*, *General Beauregard*, and the *General Jeff Thompson* after the Battle of Memphis. From a drawing by Alexander Simplot. The *Van Dorn* is seen in the distance on the far left as she is escaping. The *Sumter* is seen in the front center after being captured. The *Beauregard* is to the right of the *Sumter* and in the process of sinking. The *Thompson* is exploding in the distance on the far right. Courtesy of the Naval Historical Foundation, NH 59053.

commander of the Confederate Navy's ships, and insisted that they not be placed under Navy command.[84] The results were predictable when the Union Navy attacked the city. General Mansfield Lovell's Court of Inquiry, conducted after the loss of New Orleans, concluded that the "river-defense fleet was wholly useless as a means of resistance to the enemy."[85] Only one boat, the *Stonewall Jackson*, appeared to have been any aid in the effort to defend New Orleans as it was credited with helping to sink the USS *Varuna*.[86]

The loss of New Orleans made the need to keep control of the upper Mississippi even more important, and its defense after the loss of New Orleans was left to Montgomery's River Defense Fleet. Montgomery's fleet was the only Confederate naval force left on the upper Mississippi, as the "fleets" organized by various Confederate commanders and states along the river played little or no role in the war. In addition, the regular Confederate Navy fleet that was responsible for defending the upper Mississippi prior to the arrival of the River Defense Fleet either went to the defense of New Orleans or dispersed without helping Montgomery. As a result, the final major Confederate naval effort to control the upper Mississippi was in the hands of a fleet officered and commanded by former river boat captains, using converted steam-powered river boats and ocean-going ships. Still, this group of men, whom the regular Confederate Navy looked down on, performed much better and outshone them on the upper Mississippi.

Chapter 3

The Union Fleets

> That the party of the first part [James B. Eads], for and in consideration of the matter hereinafter referred to and set out, covenants and agrees with the party of the second part [Brigadier General Montgomery C. Meigs, Quartermaster-General, acting for the United States] to build, on the Mississippi River, and deliver to the party of the second part at the wharf in the city of Cairo, State of Illinois, seven gun-boats, as described and referred to in the printed specifications, a copy of which is annexed to, and is to be deemed and taken as part of, this contract, and to do the same in conformity to said specifications and to the directions he may from time to time receive from the superintendent in charge.
>
> —From the first section of the contract for gun-boats on the Western rivers, 7 August 1861[1]

> The boats which approach nearest my wants are the *Switzerland*, now at Portland [Ohio], price $13,000, and *Queen of the West*, at Cincinnati, price $16,000. Please authorize Mr. Butler, of Cincinnati, to purchase both.
>
> —Message from Charles Ellet Jr. to Secretary of War Edwin Stanton, 10 April 1862[2]

These two quotations illustrate the very different approaches the Union used to create the two river fleets involved in the Battle of Memphis. The majority of one fleet, the Western Flotilla, was created based on a traditional contractual approach (the exceptions being the first three timberclads and the ironclads *Benton* and *New Era*, later named the *Essex*), whereas the other, the Ram Fleet, was created by a direct line from the fleet commander to Secretary of War Edwin Stanton.[3] How the fleets were created was not the only difference between them. Regular Navy officers commanded the Western Flotilla, while Army officers who had recently been given commissions commanded the Ram Fleet. Both fleets were under Army command but reported to different individuals: The Western Flotilla reported to local Army generals, while the Ram Fleet reported directly to Stanton. The situation was, at best, confusing and would lead to misunderstandings that would not be resolved until a few months after the Battle of Memphis when the fleets were combined.

In addition to a confusing command structure and the inevitable problems with construction, other issues challenged commanders of the Western Flotillas. First was their rivalry with the US Army as well as internal Navy rivalries and misunderstandings. The US Navy was a "blue water" navy to which sailing skills were considered more important than steam engine skills and, thus, had no understanding of the culture on the western rivers. Consequently, commanders on the western waters had to continually explain their policies to their superiors in Washington. All too often, river—"brown water"—operations were not considered as important as coastal—"blue water"—operations. Secretary of the Navy Gideon Welles reinforced this impression when he informed Captain Andrew Foote in his orders to assume command that "whatever the Army can not furnish the Navy will endeavor to supply, having due regard to the operations on the coast." Welles contradicted himself later in that message when he stated that "the Western movement is of the greatest importance."[4] In reality, for a variety of reasons, the US Navy never considered the Western Flotilla as important as its ocean-going squadrons.

Beyond these complications, the Western Flotilla faced a persistent manpower shortage, especially for pilots. Although both the US Army and US Navy were continually short of men, such shortages impacted the US Navy differently than the US Army. Warships need a minimum number of men to operate and those men must have specific skills. Although there were a few positions on the boats, such as coal heaver, for which a strong back was the only requirement, most positions required training, with some requiring years of training. Among the positions demanding training were pilots, engineers, and gunners. Qualified pilots were needed or the boats would run aground; qualified engineers were needed or the engines would not work properly or, worse, explode; qualified gunners were needed to operate the heavy guns that made the boats so feared by the Confederates. In contrast, an infantry or cavalry regiment could be at 25% strength and still function, although at a much lower level of efficiency, but a gunboat could not. Inevitability, the shortage of men for the crews and the shortage of skilled pilots negatively impacted the flotilla's ability to conduct operations. Even with all of these issues, the Western Flotilla was able to retain control of the Mississippi and was a major contributor to final Union victory, although it has never received as much recognition as its "blue water" navy counterpart.

* * *

The creation of the Western Flotilla began with a study by the Corps of Engineers based on "conversations with intelligent and reliable persons."[5] The study was extensive and included information on the number of passenger steamers and how many men they could carry; freight barges and how many barrels they could carry; coal barges and how much coal they could carry; and the fact that a steam-tug could tow enough barges to supply a great number of steamers.[6] The draft for boats on the rivers, along with the available ship yards needed to construct the boats (Pittsburg, Pennsylvania; Wheeling, Virginia; Cincinnati, Ohio; Madison, Indiana; New Albany, Indiana; and Mound City, Illinois[7]), was also discussed, including a caveat that "every gun-boat and passenger steamer must carry a good river pilot."[8] Additional information was provided regarding the quality of coal, with the statement that Pittsburg coal was the best and Pomeroy coal nearly as good.[9] The report also included a table giving all of the landing places from Cincinnati to Cairo and from Cairo to New Orleans, as well as the distances between them. Along with distances, the table included information on the location of known artillery batteries. In addition to the information collected by the Corps of Engineers, a statement by John Lenthall, Chief of the Navy's Construction Bureau, offered data on specifications for gunboats.[10] In early June 1861, Lieutenant-General Winfield Scott endorsed the report, stating that he approved Lenthall's description of the proposed gunboats and hoped that the gunboats would be immediately constructed. In his endorsement, Lieutenant-General Scott asked Secretary of War Simon Cameron that the Secretary of the Navy be requested to detail an experienced naval officer to contract for the construction and supervision of the building of the gunboats. A Navy officer was also requested to command each gunboat.[11] However, Secretary of the Navy Gideon Welles had already ordered Commander John Rodgers to report to Major-General George McClellan on May 16, 1861, for "the expediency of establishing a naval armament on the

Mississippi and Ohio rivers" based on a letter from James B. Eads, who would later construct the City Class gunboats, and in consultation with Secretary Cameron.[12]

The assignment of Commander Rodgers was controversial. The issues were whether the US Army or US Navy was going to be responsible for building the boats, who was going to officer and crew the boats, and who would control the boats. James K. Moorhead, an influential Republican Representative from Pennsylvania, wrote to Secretary of War Simon Cameron on May 27, 1861, objecting to Rodgers's purchasing and arming steamboats. Moorhead believed that the Navy Department had no jurisdiction on the Ohio and Mississippi Rivers and that "an old sea captain, however well he may understand the sea and seagoing vessels, can, of course, know nothing of rivers and river steamboats." Moorhead also stated that Major-General George McClellan had already "made arrangements to secure the best skill amongst our river men for the purpose of purchasing boats and transporting men and munitions of war."[13] Service rivalry was also a reason behind Moorhead's letter, as he had been the Adjutant General for Pennsylvania and was referred to, at times, as General.[14] as he included the statement, "Besides, it is giving to the Navy a jurisdiction that I think clearly belongs to the Army, and I am proud to be able to add that the public have [*sic*] much the greater confidence in the latter." Another issue—the one that probably pushed Moorhead to write to Cameron, because it came from his constituents—was that McClellan had already consulted with Captain William J. Kountz and informed him that he would be needed to "purchase and prepare boats for transportation."[15] However, the assignment of Rodgers only temporarily ended this informal agreement as the Union Army maintained its own fleet of transports, and Kountz was one of the riverboat captains involved in this effort.[16]

Secretary of the Navy Gideon Welles was very aware of this issue and wrote Rodgers on June 11, 1861, that "The movements on the Mississippi are under the direction and control of the Army. All purchases of boats for army movements must be made by the War Department. You are not authorized to make requisitions except for armament and crew."[17] Welles followed this message up with a much longer one on June 12, 1861, in which he informed Rodgers that he had been

> directed to proceed West and report to General McClellan, commanding the forces on the upper Mississippi, and it

> was distinctly stated in your instructions that that officer would make the necessary requisitions. The movement in that quarter pertains to the Army and not the Navy. Nor must the two branches of service become complicated and embarrassed by separate action or any attempt at a combined movement on the rivers of the interior. You are, then, subordinate to the general in command, to aid, advise, and cooperate with him in crossing or navigating the rivers or in arming and equipping the boats required for the army on the Western waters. Should naval armaments be wanted for any of the boats, or crews to manage them, you are specifically authorized to make requisition for either or both, but nothing further. The Department can not recognize or sanction any contract for boats. They are not wanted for naval purposes. If they are required for the Army, those whose business and duty it is to procure them will make requisitions on the War Department. There has been and is great sensitiveness among the boatmen and others on the Western rivers in relation to the water craft that might be required for the Army, and it was an especial object of the Department in framing your instructions to so restrict them as to avoid jealousy. Repeated applications have been made to the Department in regard to your movements and powers by Members of Congress and others, to all of whom unequivocal answers have been given that you were not authorized by this Department to purchase or build boats or make contracts.[18]

Welles also wrote to Cameron on May 12, informing him that the Navy would not be able to furnish officers "to superintend the building of boats and engines on the Western waters." Welles also stated that it would be better if the boats that would be used on the Western waters were "built by Western men, who are educated to the peculiar boat required for navigating rivers." However, Welles did volunteer that he would provide "one of our naval constructors to advise and assist in so building as to adapt them [the boats] to war purposes should you desire it."[19] Samuel M. Pook, a Navy constructor, was selected for this job, and on May 20 was ordered to report to Rodgers in Cairo, Illinois.[20]

The flotilla was a mix of the Army and Navy at its beginning. The Army's Quartermaster's Department paid for the construction of most of the boats, but the Navy supervised it. Command of the boats was also mixed, as the initial commanding officers of the gunboats were regular Navy officers, but the commanders and officers of the transports and some of the other vessels were employed by the Army's Quartermaster's Department. The crews were a combination of Sailors from the Navy and Soldiers detailed from the Army. Arming the boats was also a joint effort, as some of the armament and ordnance was supplied by the Army's Ordnance Department while some was provided by the Navy. It was an expensive operation; during the 1861–1862 fiscal year, the Army's Quartermaster's Department spent $2,400,000 on the fleet.[21]

Pay was a similarly hybrid affair with equally confusing results, as the Navy officers were paid by the Navy while all of the other men were paid by the Army.[22] Although the Navy officers did not have problems with their base pay, they did have an issue with sea pay. Sea pay increased an officer's pay by 25%. For example, a commander on shore duty received $2,240 a year, but at sea received $2,800.[23] The problem was that the officers serving with the Western Flotilla were not receiving sea pay. Rodgers was forced to write to Secretary of the Navy Gideon Welles to ask him to override the decision of the Fourth Auditor, who had decided that "the officers attached to the gunboats on the Western rivers are not entitled to sea service." Rodgers appealed on the bases that "officers of steamers passing up and down the Potomac are allowed sea service. Officers of the steamer *Michigan* on the lake, perform technical sea service. Officers in seagoing vessels are allowed sea service, even in port; officers of Coast-Survey vessels on rivers and bays receive sea service."[24] It appears that sea pay was granted, as no future flotilla commander complained about the issue.

Rodgers quickly learned that the skills and pay needed to crew a boat on the Mississippi were very different than those required on the ocean. Less than a month after being given the assignment, he wrote Secretary of the Navy Gideon Welles requesting "permission to engage the necessary pilots, engineers, and firemen here [in Cincinnati]. The management of these engines in the muddy waters of the Mississippi requires a peculiar experience, which it is cheaper to employ than to teach."[25] Rodgers also quickly learned that paying the men the same rate as their equivalent rank in the Navy was not adequate.[26] By the time Foote assumed command, the pay rate had increased and, fortunately, Foote—prior to leaving Washington to assume command—had also been given permission by Quarter Master-General Montgomery Meigs

> to appoint such assistants as I deemed necessary to carry out effectively the objects of the flotilla, and he informed me that masters of Western steamboats often received $200 per month, and that I could not be governed in all cases by salaries or pay given at the East. In the case of masters and pilots, I have been obliged, in order to secure the services of efficient men, to pay first masters $150 per month, second masters $125, third masters $100, and fourth masters $80 per month, while pilots are paid $175 per month.[27]

Because the Army paid these men, the Navy did not have any problems creating ranks that did not exist in the Navy or paying them more than what their naval equivalent earned. However, this arrangement would become an issue when the Navy assumed full control of the flotilla. The Navy only had one master's rank—a rank between ensign and lieutenant, which in today's rank structure would be a lieutenant j.g.; the pay for that rank was $1,200 per year on shore duty and $1,500 per year at sea.[28] In the Western Flotilla, a first master would have received $1,800, a second master $1,500, a third master $1,200, and a fourth master $960 per year—all of whom, except a fourth master, received more than the $1,200 an ensign at sea would have been paid.

Engineers were also considered officers in the Western Flotilla, even though they were not listed as officers on the Navy officers' pay table. In addition, they were well paid.[29] As with masters, there were a number of ranks for engineers, chief engineer, first assistant engineer, second assistant engineer, and third assistant engineer. Chief engineers were paid $1,500, first assistant engineers $1,200, second assistant engineers $960, and third assistant engineers $720 per year. Foote quickly learned, as Rodgers had, that the skills the river men possessed and service on the Western waters were different than those required by the "blue water" navy. In mid September 1861, he informed Secretary of the Navy Gideon Welles, "I earnestly request that the Department [Navy] will not send any engineer here, as the Western engineers, from their experience, can better perform their duty and it will be more gratifying to the Western people:"[30] The river men wanted to be well paid for their defined skillset and knowledge that the Navy's "blue water" officers lacked.

One reason a number of Navy officers did not want to serve on the western rivers was that they viewed the assignment as lacking in glory, providing little opportunity for advancement, and offering limited prize money. Secretary of the Navy Gideon Welles wrote in October 1862 to Captain John Dahlgren, "One captain in the Navy preferred the command of a sloop of war [a relatively minor ship] instead of the chief command of the Western Flotilla."[31] Still, enough regular officers accepted the assignment to provide the necessary initial leadership, but most of the officers were recently commissioned civilians.

Being one of the eight ironclad captains during the Battles of Plum Point and Memphis did not hurt the careers of most of these men. One, Henry Walke, captain of the *Carondelet*, became a rear admiral, two, Roger Stembel, captain of the *Cincinnati*, and Augustus Kilty, captain of the *Mound City*, became rear admirals on the retired list. Two, Egbert Thompson, captain of the *Pittsburg*, and Benjamin Dove, captain of the *Louisville*, obtained the rank of captain, with Thompson receiving it while on active duty, and Dove receiving it on the retired list. Nathaniel Bryant, captain of the *Cairo*, was promoted to commander in 1862, while Wilson McGunnegle, captain of the *St. Louis*, was promoted to lieutenant commander in 1862. McGunnegle probably would have achieved a higher rank, but he died in April 1863. Seth (S) Ledyard Phelps, captain of the *Benton*, was promoted to lieutenant commander in July 1862. However, Phelps was an ambitious man and felt the he was not receiving the recognition and promotions he desired and deserved. Consequently, he resigned his commission in October 1864. As a civilian, Phelps was very successful and became the United States Minister to Peru just prior to his death.[32]

The captains of the ironclads were also very experienced and averaged 28 years of service. The least experienced captain, Wilson McGunnegle, become a midshipman in 1845, while the most experienced captain, Augustus Kilty, became a midshipman in 1821. The advantage these regular naval officers brought with them was a discipline lacking in many of the boats captained by former civilian river boat captains. But, these "blue water" officers initially lacked the knowledge needed to operate on the inland rivers; also, being a regular naval officer did not guarantee that the officer was aggressive or competent.

Beyond personnel, an issue the first commanders of the Western Flotilla had to face was a question of rank. The problem was that the Army only considered a Navy captain the equivalent of a lieutenant-colonel. Consequently, Captain Andrew Foote found that Army colonels were giving him and his boat commanders' orders, a situation that he brought to the attention of the Gustavus Fox, Assistant Secretary of the Navy, in early November 1861. As he wrote:

> We suffer a good deal for my want of rank. The Army say [*sic*] I rank only with a lieutenant-colonel, and in one instance a colonel ordered a gunboat to go with his regiment for a certain duty. General Frémont never intended this. I want, for the efficiency of the fleet, the appointment of flag-officer. At Cairo a week since, the brigadier-general said he would not give a place assigned by General Frémont to our stores had it not been a positive order from General Frémont. I am considered merely as a captain, and find that I want rank in order to render my command more effective. My own boat will carry 16 heavy guns of 8,000 or 6,300, and of 4,200 weight – nearly the armament of a frigate – and there will be 12 boats, also 38 mortar boats, in addition, if we get them ready, which will constitute a large squadron, and am I not under the law entitled to the rank and to the appointment of a flag-officer? Now, when afloat, there is nothing to distinguish my vessel from the others. Hence I am embarrassed on all sides for want of rank.[33]

The difficulty was due to how the Navy viewed its forces on the western rivers. Captains in command of squadrons were to be addressed as flag-officer and Navy flag-officers ranked as major-generals.[34] The problem was that the Western Flotilla was not initially considered nor called a squadron. The Western Flotilla was referred to by a number of names other than Western Flotilla, including Naval Forces on Western Rivers; Gunboat Flotilla, Western Waters; and the Cairo Flotilla. Not until October 1, 1862—after the Battle of Memphis—did it became known as the Mississippi Squadron.[35] Luckily, even before the organization was considered a squadron, Foote was appointed a flag-officer on November 13, 1861.[36] Unfortunately, his replacement, Commodore Charles H. Davis, had the same command relationship difficulties as Foote. Davis was not immediately promoted, as he was a temporary replacement for Foote until he recovered from a wound he received at Fort Donelson.[37] Davis's assignment did become permanent, but not until June 17, 1862, after the Battle of Memphis, at which time he was appointed commander and a flag-officer.[38] None of the commanders after Davis had this issue as they were automatically appointed as a flag-officer when they assumed command. The reason for the change was that the Navy assumed responsibility for the Western Flotilla on October 1, 1862, and changed its designation to the Mississippi Squadron.[39] In addition, the command relationship with the Army changed from one of subordination to one of cooperation.

However, the transfer of the flotilla to the Navy caused another set of problems. In many cases, when the flotilla was part of the Army, officers had ranks that did not exist in the Navy. This discrepancy caused problems for paymasters, and Fleet Paymaster Elisha W. Dunn was forced to write to Secretary of the Navy Gideon Welles in April 1863 asking for instructions, as he did not know how to settle the men's accounts. He explained:

> Allow me to state that at the time of transfer of this squadron from the Army to the Navy was made the new appointments which were issued from the Navy Department to the officers then on duty here were in many cases a reduction of pay and of rank. For instance, some, both first and second masters, had new appointments given them as ensigns, some first masters had new appointments as masters. The old rate of pay was, first master $1,800 and second master $1,500 per annum; a reduction of first master to ensign was a reduction of his pay $600, a second master to ensign of $300 per annum.
>
> In some instances, when such reductions took place, the officers declined to accept the new appointments, but owing to the fact that they were absent on distant duty, or their services much needed, or perhaps other reasons, they were for a time continued in the service at rates exceeding the amount authorized by law.[40]

This arrangement represented a tremendous reduction in pay and prestige, and many of the men declined to accept the new appointments. Doing so was probably not a tough decision as shipping on the Mississippi was increasing, and men with their skills were in high demand and well paid. The loss of these knowledgeable officers must have hurt the flotilla's efficiency as it would have been difficult to get equally skilled replacements.

The enlisted men had their own set of problems. For example, many of the Soldiers that were transferred to the flotilla stopped being paid by the Army, as their units dropped them from their rolls. Eventually, this issue began to affect morale, and Foote was forced to ask Major-General John Frémont in September 1861 to direct the Quartermaster General to issue monetary drafts to the paymasters so that the crews of the *Tyler*, *Lexington*, and *Conestoga* could be paid.[41] However, this action did not settle the issue. In January 1862, Foote, now a Flag-Officer, was forced to write directly to Quartermaster-General Montgomery Meigs in reference to the mortar and tug boats of which he had been given command that "The question of pay and rations requires to be settled."[42] The problem became serious enough that President Lincoln had to get involved and, in March 1862, he issued instructions to the War Office to pay the men transferred from the Army.[43]

Another pay issue was how much the men were to be paid. Even though the Army paid the men, their pay was based on their rating in the Navy whether they joined directly as a volunteer or indirectly by being transferred from the Army. In the "blue water" Navy recruit seaman, known as "Landsmen", received $12.00 a month; ordinary seamen received $14.00 a month; and able seamen received $18.00 a month.[44] Initially, the Navy tried to imposed these same pay rates, but found that this strategy was not possible. Flag-Officer Andrew Foote learned that he had to pay his enlisted men more than the norm, as had Rodgers, and he informed Gustavus Fox, Assistant Secretary of the Navy, in late December 1861, "Commander Rodgers had paid all his men $18 per month, as he informed me none could be had at a less prices, as river men receive $30 per month usually, and I therefore have been compelled to continue this rate of pay to the men, and rate all over 20 years of age as seamen, at $18 per month."[45] Foote realized less than two weeks later that $18.00 per month may not be enough, as "The river men enlisted in June, or went South, and as our pay is $18 per month and their old pay $30, the remaining men are indisposed to go or ship in the gunboats."[46]

The increased pay led to further complications in that men who had enlisted in the West were being paid less than men who had come from the East or had been transferred from the Army. This incongruity impacted the morale of the Western men, as the ordinary seamen and landsmen on the *Carondelet* were only being paid $14 and $12, respectively. They petitioned Foote to have their pay increased to $18.00, as they thought "that we are equally entitled to this increase in pay, for as far as efficiency is concerned we acknowledge no superior in the flotilla."[47] Foote acknowledged their complaint and increased their pay.

The differential in pay between the flotilla and the "blue water" Navy continued until the flotilla became part of the Navy. However, Commodore Charles Davis, who was still the commander of the flotilla when the transfer took place, tried to convince the Navy that the difference in pay and rank was justified. In September 1862, Davis sent Paymaster Elisha Dunn to Washington to prepare for the financial turn off of the flotilla. Davis instructed Dunn:

> You are acquainted with the pay given to the various rates in the flotilla and can explain to the Department [Navy] how it is that all men under the grade of petty officers uniformly receive the pay of seamen; the custom of the river to give coal-heavers $25 per month; the high wages habitually paid to pilots; how it happens that there are so many classes of engineers, and all other peculiarities that have been unavoidably taken from the usages of the Western waters.[48]

Dunn was unsuccessful and Secretary of the Navy Gideon Welles informed Davis that "The ratings of petty officers, complement of men, and their pay, of the vessels of the flotilla must, after the transfer, correspond with those of other vessels of similar classes in the naval service."[49] However, it took some time to make all of the changes in rank. Assistant Secretary of the Navy Gustavus Fox admonished Acting Rear-Admiral David Porter in October 1862, after the flotilla had been transferred to the Navy, that "I notice the first assistant engineer in tugs where we have seconds. Our highest is first in charge of the largest ships; seconds take all others." In all likelihood, some of the commanders, in the interest of keeping up their men's morale, continued to try and pay their men at the higher Army rate. One reason the Navy did not want to pay the higher Army rate was its desire to show how much more economical the Navy was than the Army. Fox emphasized this rivalry when he told Porter in the same message that "When the day of examination comes, we must show an economical administration over our West Point friends, which, I have no doubt, will be the case."[50]

The crews were a mixed lot. A few of the men were regular Navy with years of experience, some were newly enlisted with experience on Mississippi riverboats or ocean-going ships, and others were newly enlisted with no experience. Recruiting stations were opened in various cities along the Mississippi and Ohio. Because few men signed up at the recruiting station in Cincinnati, it was moved to Cleveland. There, it was hoped that men with experience on the Great Lakes would enlist.[51] However, the Navy Department had issues with the Western Flotilla recruiting men from the Great Lakes because these men were needed in the "blue water" navy. Less than two weeks after Captain Andrew Foote was informed that his recruiting on the Great Lakes was "regarded as antagonistical to the interests of the Navy,"[52] he received a message from Gustavus Fox, Assistant Secretary of the Navy, that "We have sent you off 500 men, but I am inclined to think it is all we can do. You may have Carter's rendezvous [Commander John C. Carter commanded the recruiting station in Erie, Pennsylvania, but was only able to provide 100 in March 1862[53]], as we wrote to you. Every means is being used to recruit, but the large number of vessels put afloat absorbs them."[54]

Because the Navy could not provide the number of men that were needed, the Army was asked to furnish them. As a result of the Navy's request, Major-General George McClellan, now the General-in-Chief, ordered Major-General Henry Halleck to provide 1,100 men for the Western Flotilla in December 1861.[55] Halleck was already aware of the shortage, as Foote had written him on December 7, 1861, that he was short 1,100 men for the gunboats. In addition, men were needed for the mortar boats.[56] The shortage was severe enough that on January 17, 1862, Major-General George McClellan informed Major-General Henry Halleck that "The flotilla, together with the naval officers on duty with it, is completely under your orders, and it is expected that you will devise the means of overcoming the obstacles that have presented themselves. It will be more economical, and it seems quite proper, to use volunteer troops to supply the deficiencies in gunners."[57]

Soldiers either volunteered or were ordered to serve on the boats, with some even coming from the Army of the Potomac on the East Coast.[58] However, the Army was not very willing to give up any of its Soldiers, as it—like everyone else—was shorthanded. Commanders frequently discouraged their men from volunteering, and the ones who were drafted were seldom the best men available, as commanders saw this draft as an opportunity to get rid of their troublemakers. Another hitch was that the Army wanted entire units to volunteer along with their officers, an arrangement that was not acceptable to the Navy, as Flag-Officer Andrew Foote wrote Secretary of the Navy Gideon Welles that "Our flotillas will be seriously affected, as will be seen by the following telegram to General Halleck, if his orders are carried out, who has written to me that officers of the regiment of volunteers must come to the flotilla with their soldiers and all to be regarded as marines and to be under command of no navy officer except the commander of the gunboats." Foote was informed that the issue would be taken up with

McClellan, and it was resolved in the Navy's favor, as no officers joined the flotilla with their men.[59]

As with any unpleasant task, the responsibility for getting enough volunteers was shifted to a lower headquarters; in this case, it fell under the purview of Brigadier-General Ulysses Grant, as Cairo—the Navy's main base—was in his area of responsibility. Because not enough men were volunteering, Grant suggested, in early January 1862, that "There are quite a number of soldiers in the guard house here for desertion, disorderly conduct, &c. I would suggest, in view of the difficulty of getting men for the gunboat service, that these men be transferred to that service; also that authority be given to transfer unruly men hereafter, I have spoken with Commodore Foote on the subject, and I believe it meets with his approval."[60] Foote apparently changed his mind, for in late February he wrote Secretary of the Navy Gideon Welles that the men the Army sent him—with a few exceptions—were "the offscourings of the Army." Foote proceeded to state that "We want no more [men] from the Army. I prefer to go into action only half manned than to go with such men."[61]

When Grant's initial plan did not provide enough men, he had to come up with additional ideas of ways of getting volunteers for duty with the gunboats. In late January 1862, he issued an order stating the following:

> Commanders of regiments will report to these headquarters without delay the names of rivers and seafaring men of their respective commands who are willing to be transferred from the military to the gunboat service. Seeing the importance of fitting out our gunboats as speedily as possible, it is hoped there will be no delay or objections raised by company or regimental commanders in responding to this call. Men thus volunteering will be discharged at the end of one year, or at the end of the war, should it terminate sooner.[62]

The early discharge offered by Grant came back to haunt the Navy when the men who volunteered requested their discharge based on his order. Acting Volunteer Lieutenant William Hoel, commander of the ironclad *Pittsburg*, discovered this complication in February 1863, when 14 of his men, who had volunteered under this order—but had not signed anything with the Navy lengthening their service—requested their discharge.[63]

In the short term, the Army's incentives provided enough volunteers that Soldiers serving on the gunboats made up a significant portion of the crews. When the *Carondelet* ran pass the batteries at Island No. 10, approximately 20% of its crew were Soldiers, in addition to the Army sharpshooters that had volunteered for the mission.[64] These men, once trained, served well and were an important part of the flotilla, as without their services at least half of the gunboats would not have been available for duty. However, even with the Army volunteers, additional men were needed, and the Navy eventually began recruiting contrabands.

At first, even though blacks were already serving in the Navy, Foote did not want any "colored people" with the flotilla. He informed his Chicago recruiting officer in September 1861 that "As there are objections or difficulties in the Southern country about colored people, we do not want any of that class shipped."[65] By May 1862, the attitude of the Navy was changing, and Acting Secretary of the Navy Gustavus Fox issued the following order to Flag-Officer David Farragut: "The difficulty of meeting the demand for seamen renders it important that those now serving on board the storeships should be employed to a better advantage. You will, therefore, on arrival of the *Potomac*, transfer as many of its crew as can be spared without detriment to the service to the seagoing vessels of the squadron and supply their places with enlisted contrabands, as they are termed."[66]

The Western Flotilla was slower to employ contrabands than the rest of the Navy, as it was not until the Navy was preparing to assume command of the flotilla that Davis received orders to employ contrabands. Even then, they were only to "be employed as coal heavers, but are not to be allowed the pay of that grade."[67] Davis's order was based on a message that the Secretary of the Navy Gideon Welles had issued on April 30, 1862. Welles wrote:

> The large number of persons known as contrabands flocking to the protection of the United States flag affords us an opportunity to provide in every department of a ship, especially for boats' crews, acclimated labor. The flag-officers are required to obtain the services of these persons for the country by enlisting them freely in the Navy, with their consent, rating them as boys, at $8, $9, or $10 per month and one ration.[68]

This message was sent to all of the Navy's flag-officers, but was not sent to the Western Flotilla, which was still under Army command. The Western Flotilla had a completely different attitude about contrabands, as seen in July 1862 with Flag-Officer Charles Davis's reprimand of Lieutenant Nathaniel, commander of the *Cairo* that "I again call your particular attention to my instructions in relation to contrabands; they are not to be received promiscuously on board the ships of the squadron."[69] However, Davis's attitude changed as more of his men became incapacitated due to the hot southern climate. By the end of July, he wrote in his diary, "As we approach Helena I am satisfied, from reports received from the transports, towing vessels, etc., that if we had remained a week longer at Vicksburg I should not have had engineers nor firemen enough to bring the vessels up. As it is we have depended very much on the contrabands to do the work in front of the fires."[70]

As attitudes toward the use of contrabands changed, the Navy allowed them to have a higher rating than "boy" in December 1862, when it issued a circular that

> Persons known as "contrabands" will not be shipped or enlisted in the naval services with any higher rating than that of landsman; but if found qualified after being shipped may be advanced by the commanding officer of the vessel in which they serve to the ratings of seaman, ordinary seaman, fireman, or coal heaver, if their services are needed in such ratings, and will be entitled to the corresponding pay. They will not be transferred from one vessel to another with a higher rating than that of landsman, but if discharged on termination of enlistment, or from a vessel going out of commission, will retain their advanced rating in the discharge.[71]

This circular was probably based on the need for men. As Acting-Rear Admiral David Porter informed Secretary of the Navy Gideon Welles in October 1862:

> We will want more men soon to fill up the vacancies caused by 400 sick, who will never be fit for service again. I have commenced substituting contrabands for firemen and coal heavers, reducing the expenses in that way. I have so far only obtained forty, but have sent down river to get enough for

> all vessels here [Cairo], and have ordered all commanders to use them hereafter in place of white men. I have also distributed the mortar men among the different vessels, thus keeping up a partial supply. I have also opened a rendezvous in Louisville, St. Louis, and Cincinnati; but have not, as yet, secured any men. We will want about 1,000 men to fill up the vessels fitting out, and fill vacancies; and I beg leave to recommend that a rendezvous be opened in Chicago for the squadron.[72]

By December 1862, Acting Rear-Admiral David Porter was actively seeking contrabands for service in the flotilla although they were still paid less than the other Sailors. He ordered the commander of the *Louisville* that "You will supply yourself with good contrabands wherever you can obtain them, but get none but first-rate young men. They are to be entered on the books at $9 per month, and a monthly return of them made to me."[73] A month later, in January, Porter informed Rear-Admiral Andrew Foote, Chief Bureau of Equipment and Recruiting, "Don't be astonished at the lists of niggers I send you. I could get no men, so I work the darkies. They do first-rate, and are far better behaved than their masters."[74] However, even with contrabands, the Navy was continually short of men throughout the war, and they were not a significant part of the flotilla prior to the Battle of Memphis. When the *Cairo* sunk in December 1862, the boat's records show only four men with black skin, and all were seamen, so they could not have been contrabands, as they were not authorized at that time to be that rank.[75]

Manpower shortages continued to have an impact on the Western Flotilla throughout the war and, upon occasion, negatively affected operations. In addition, a continual struggle took place between the Army and Navy for recruits as well as between the needs of the Western Flotilla and the Atlantic squadrons. In May 1863, when men were needed for the recently commissioned *Osage,* Captain Alexander Pennock, Commandant of the Cairo Station, was informed by the Chief of the Bureau of Equipment and Recruiting Rear-Admiral Andrew Foote, the flotilla's former commander, that "The Bureau regrets to inform you that it has no men to send." The message went on to state, "The Bureau must request of you and the officers to use every exertion to obtain men without relying on the Eastern rendezvous, which can not keep up to the demands of the service here."[76] Because of this shortage, the Navy refused to allow the Army to open a recruiting station at the mouth of the Red River in 1864, informing the Army officer who had requested the permission, "Please state to your commanding officer my regret at not being able to permit you to open a recruiting station here [mouth of the Red River]. This place is the principal recruiting station for the Navy, and we do not get sufficient for our wants [sic]."[77]

The manpower shortage negatively impacted the flotilla's initial operations. "[F]or want of men," Foote was to take only the three timberclads and four of his nine ironclads in February 1862 when he went to attack Fort Henry. Out of the five ironclads left behind at Cairo, only one had a sufficient number of men to man her.[78] Foote reported:

> It is peculiarly unfortunate that we have not been able to obtain men for the flotillas, as they only are wanting to enable me to have at this moment eleven full-manned, instead of seven partially manned, gunboats, ready for efficient operations at any point. The volunteers from the army to go in the gunboats exceed the number of men required, but the derangement of companies and regiments, in permitting them to leave, is the reason assigned for not more than fifty of the number having been thus far transferred to the flotilla.[79]

A little over a week later, the situation had not improved when the flotilla prepared to attack Fort Donelson, and Foote was forced to transfer "men from the disabled [gunboats] to the other gunboats, as we were too short to man more than one-half of the boats."[80]

Transferring men had a negative impact on the flotilla, demoralizing the men and leading to at least twenty-eight men "running off."[81] The boats left behind were so short-handed that even when fifty Soldiers joined the *Mound City* on February 19, the boat was not fully manned. It was not until late February that the crew of the *Mound City* was brought up to strength. By then, the men who had been on the *Carondelet*, and survived the fighting at Fort Donelson, rejoined the *Mound City*, along with seventy-six men from Boston. These additional men allowed the captain to release men, such as Acting Master's Mate Symmes Browne, from gun drill so that he could attend to his regular duties.[82]

The challenge for the officers of the flotillas was that even though the boats would have appeared on paper to have a full crew, illnesses made a lot of the men unavailable for duty. William Hoel, commander of the *Pittsburg*, informed Rear Admiral David Porter in November 1862 that he only had enough men on board to man six guns, less than half of the boat's guns. Forty-five men had been sent to the hospital within the last three months, but only seven had been returned to duty. The men in the hospital included his executive officer and paymaster.[83] It is easy to imagine the illnesses that the men contracted given that they were stationed in the hot and humid Southern states, a malaria mosquito–infested region, and drinking dirty water from the rivers while being inside a very hot ironclad. The only surprise was that more men were not sick.

Training new recruits was an ongoing effort especially in the operation of the large guns. Consequently, the men drilled continuously on the guns. Commander Rodgers wrote the Secretary of that Navy in August 1861, that "The Western river men, I find willing and tractable, and I presume they will readily make good artillerist. Now, however, they know far less of their duties than I hope we shall be able to teach them."[84] Lieutenant-Commander Thomas O. Selfridge concurred with this sentiment, as he stated in his memoirs that when he took command of the *Cairo*, "The officers and crew of these vessels were recruited principally from Mississippi River steamboats, and while inherently excellent men, initially they lacked that degree of military efficiency to be attained only through intensive discipline and training."[85] In the end, the men became excellent Sailors and were an asset to the Union's war effort.

Pilots held a unique position; foremost, their knowledge was essential for the safe operation of a boat on the rivers. But pilots were exempt from the draft, and thus could not be forced to join the Navy.[86] Consequently, the Navy hired pilots and paid them wages—although less than what the pilots were used to earning. For example, William R. Hoel earned $250 in June 1860, for a twenty-four-day trip to and from New Orleans piloting the *Queen of the West*, a boat that would later become an Ellet ram.[87] Then, in January 1860, he received $300 for standing a twenty-six day watch to and from New Orleans. Hoel entered the Navy as a pilot at Saint Louis in October 1861 for $175 a month.[88] On February 1, he resigned his position as a pilot and became a First Master at $150 a month, as he wished for "a more active position."[89] However, he turned down a position as Acting Volunteer Lieutenant because his pay would have been reduced to $125 per month, and his commission would have read "on temporary duty."[90] Hoel finally accepted the promotion when his pay was not reduced. Hoel experienced a similar situation later as commander of the ironclad gunboat *Pittsburg*. Hoel had to write Rear Admiral David Porter that Second Master A. J. Wilson wished to resign, as "he feels qreatly mortified, that in accepting the commission of an Ensign he would not only be disrated in pay, but also in rank."[91] Obviously, the pay and status that the Navy was willing to offer did not meet the expectations of experienced riverboat officers and pilots.

From the very beginnings of the flotilla, pilots received more pay than their eastern counterparts. John Rodgers discovered this disparity, even though he was paying them $150 per month—only $75 less than a lieutenant at sea earned.[92] Rodgers reported to Secretary of the Navy Gideon Welles that

> I [Commander John Rodgers] have been forced by the rates of wages for pilots on the Southern rivers to exceed the rates in the East. The pilots here claim and receive from private parties $250 per month. This is the rate fixed by themselves before the war and made obligatory upon them by an association, of which the great majority are members, called the Pilot's Association. It was only with great difficulty, delay, and reluctance that they consented to take the less wages which I offered.[93]

Due to the increased size of the flotilla, Andrew Porter had even greater problems finding pilots. In his frustration, he suggested to Major-General John Frémont in September 1861 that he was having "great difficulty in obtaining pilots for the gunboats, and [thus] respectfully suggest that all licensed pilots be compelled, within a reasonable time, to report themselves at the office of the provost marshal. The pilots are, in fact, the officers of the Government, and their refusal to serve is an act of treason."[94]

The issue of getting and retaining good pilots did not decrease as the war continued. Acting Rear-Admiral David Porter was forced to write to Secretary of the Navy Gideon Welles asking for an increase in pay for the pilots while stressing how important they were to the flotilla. He urged:

> I must intrude upon the Department again in relation to the pay of pilots. We can not get any to accept appointments with the present pay.

> We have not more than 10 good pilots in the whole fleet, and most of them have tendered their resignations.
>
> The river pay is now from $300 to $400, and the Department will see the necessity of either paying the old river prices ($250 per month) or else have the vessels stop running for want of pilots.
>
> While the river was high we could get along with the flatboat men we have been obliged to hire, but now the water is falling so rapidly, and the bars are so continually shifting, it requires the best pilots on the river to manage those vessels which draw 2 or 3 feet more water than the river boats.
>
> I sincerely think that the pilots earn all that they claim; they are exposed at all times to sharpshooters and other shot; have to steer the vessels themselves, and can not even leave their posts, no matter how imminent the danger. In the late action at Grand Gulf I felt much the need of good pilots. Had we had even one pilot who knew the river well the vessels could all have been placed in still water, where a gun could not have been brought to bear upon us; as it was, the pilots (or those we have to use as such) informed me that shoals existed where I wanted to place the vessels. I have since found 7 fathoms there.
>
> When the pay is increased to river rates I can get the best pilots and be able to discharge those I have been obliged to take for want of better.[95]

The predicament with pilot pay extended beyond the Mississippi, stymying naval operations throughout the West. In early July 1863, Major-General William Rosecrans, during his maneuvers in Tennessee, requested that gunboats be sent up the Tennessee River to keep the Confederates from crossing it at Florence or Decatur. However, Captain Alexander Pennock was having "great difficulty in getting pilots, notwithstanding the high rate of pay that is offered to them." He had written to Major-General Ambrose Burnside asking him to send pilots to Cairo, as "gunboats are detained here for want of pilots."[96] This problem was widespread, as Lieutenant-Commander Le Roy Fitch, commander of the USS *Moose* at Smithland, Kentucky, reported to Rear-Admiral David Porter in mid November 1863 that "I regret to state that there is great dissatisfaction among out Cumberland and Ohio pilots in consequences of their pay. The pay of pilots from Cincinnati to Nashville has been increased to about $300 per month or $10 per day. This, I think, together with the lower first-class pilots getting $250 per month, has caused the dissatisfaction here."[97]

Another quandary the Navy had with its pilots was that they were paid much less than their counterparts on Army-contracted boats. By June 1863, Navy pilots' pay had increased to $250 per month.[98] This salary was substantial and exceeded that of a Navy Lieutenant-Commander at sea ($195.25 per month), although was still less than the pay for a Navy Captain at sea ($291.67 per month).[99] The high pay pilots received meant that, in most cases, they were paid more than the commander of the boat they were on. In 1864, pilots working for the Army earned $300 per month by order of Lieutenant-General Ulysses Grant, who was now commander of all Union armies. Consequently, the Navy's pilots petitioned Acting Rear-Admiral Samuel Lee asking that the pay for a first class pilot be increased to the same amount.[100] Lee endorsed the petition and forwarded it to the Secretary of the Navy, stating that the increase in pay was "just and economical." It was just and economical because commercial pilots were being paid $450 to $750 per month due to increased trade on the rivers.[101] Obtaining good pilots was a constant challenge throughout the war due to the danger, discipline, and lack of status; even though wages were steady and, for the Navy, generous.

Due to their skill in navigating the rivers and the danger associated with their duty station, pilots more than earned their money. The pilothouse was very exposed, and numerous pilots were killed or wounded during the war. Indeed, being in the pilothouse was so dangerous that it was known as "the slaughter-pen."[102] After the battle at Fort Henry—because of the deaths of the pilots on the *Essex* as well as realizations about how vulnerable the pilothouses were—the pilothouse on all of the ironclads was reinforced. Beyond the practicality of protecting the pilots and boat captains who would be in the pilothouse, the pilothouses were reinforced because the pilots threatened not to work if they were not better protected. Because the boats could not safely navigate the rivers without the pilots, their threat was effective. In March 1862, Foote acknowledged their threat when he telegraphed the Chief of the Navy's Bureau of Ordnance, explaining, "The gunboats have been so much cut up in the late engagements at Forts Henry and Donelson in the pilothouses, hulls, and disabled machinery, that I could not induce the pilot [*sic*] to go in them again in a fight until they are repaired."[103] Because steaming back to a fully functional shipyard took time, most of the needed modifications were made on the spot by the crews. Modifications to the *Mound City* by her crew included adding ten inches of solid oak to the front of the pilothouse.[104]

Even with all of the issues the Navy commanders had with their pilots, by the end of the war, the Mississippi River pilots had earned an excellent reputation. After the Red River Campaign of 1864, Rear-Admiral David Porter informed Secretary of the Navy Gideon Welles:

> There is a class of men who have during this war shown [*sic*] a good deal of bravery and patriotism and who have seldom met with any notice from those whose duty it is to report such matters. I speak of the pilots on the Western rivers. Without any hope of future reward through fame, or in a pecuniary way, they enter into the business of piloting the transports through dangers that would make a faint-hearted man quail.
>
> Occupying the most exposed position, a fair mark for a sharpshooter, they are continually fired at and often hit without so much as a mention being made of their gallantry.
>
> On this expedition [Red River Campaign] they have been much exposed, and have shown great gallantry in managing their vessels while under fire in this, to them, unknown river. I beg leave to pay this small tribute to their bravery and zeal, and must say as a class I never knew a braver set of men.[105]

* * *

The boats in the flotilla were as varied as the officers and men who served on them. Beyond the well-known ironclads, the flotilla included timberclads and a number of different auxiliary vessels such as hospital boats, supply boats, barges, and mortar rafts. Three of the timberclads were the first warships in the flotilla. These three warships, USS *Tyler*, *Lexington*, and *Conestoga*, were converted riverboats and are collectively known as "timberclads" because their only defensive protection was the extra planking that rendered their hulls bullet proof.[106] The three timberclads arrived at Cairo, Illinois, on August 12, 1861, ready for action.[107] Because the timberclads were not involved in the Battles of Plum Point and Memphis, details of these boats will not be included in this book. Although auxiliary vessels were crucial to the success of the Union effort, only one—the mortar boat will be described as it—played an important role in the Battle of Plum Point.

The arrival of the timberclads in Cairo made them an important part of American military history, as Major-General John C. Frémont thus became the first combined commander—an individual who commands components from two military departments—in American military history.[108] In October 1861, Frémont, as the departmental commander, ordered Captain Andrew Foote, who had not yet been appointed a flag-officer, to "Officer, man, and equip, with all possible dispatch, not only the twelve gunboats proper, designed for the Mississippi Flotilla, but in addition to them you will take charge of and prepare for immediate active service, likewise, the mortar boats, propellers, transports, etc., belonging to the entire floated expedition down the Mississippi; and you will consider yourself in charge of, and commanding this expedition."[109] John Frémont earned the honor of being the first combined commander in United States military history, even though Rodgers first reported to McClellan, as the timberclads were not ready until Frémont had assumed command. [110]

The ironclads became the backbone of the Western Flotilla, even though some in the Navy doubted that the ironclads would be practical. The previously mentioned John Lenthall, Chief of the Navy's Bureau of Construction and Repair, wrote to Brigadier General Joseph Totten, Army Chief of Engineers, in June 1861, "It does not seem to be practicable [*sic*] to make an armed steam vessel for the Mississippi that will be very efficient." Lenthall proceeded to discuss all of the problems of designing a warship for the rivers; however, in closing he acknowledged, "It is difficult for any one practiced in sea-going shipping to give precise instructions for river boats, as no doubt the experience of persons in this kind of work has led them to many things that are not to be reached in any other way." Consequently, Lenthall recommended calling upon Samuel M. Pook, a well-known naval architect and ship builder from Portsmouth, New Hampshire, for advice—which was duly heeded.[111]

Many of the problems that Lenthall foresaw plaguing the ironclads were realized. The Navy could not achieve the firepower, protection, speed, and shallow draft it would have liked without giving something up. In the end, shallow draft was the most crucial design feature, followed by firepower, with protection and speed relegated to a secondary feature. However, the ironclads' shallow draft limited where they could serve. When Rear-Admiral David Farragut asked Rear-

Admiral David Porter to provide him ironclads to assist in his operations against Mobile, Porter was unable to send him any, as his ironclads "are all smooth-water craft, and would only bring discredit on the Navy if they went to any place where they would encounter rough weather."[133] The next commander of the flotilla, Rear-Admiral Samuel Lee, must have believed differently, as the *Cincinnati* was transferred to the West Gulf Blockading Squadron in February 1865, and patrolled off Mobile Bay.[113]

Constructing the ironclads depended on the cooperation and resources of a number of different individuals. Pook designed the City Class boats; Commander John Rodgers, who was under Major-General George McClellan's command, initially supervised their construction; and the Army's Quartermaster Department paid the expenses. Credit for construction of the ironclads in such a short period of time belongs to James B. Eads, a St. Louis businessman, engineer, shipbuilder, and bridge builder. His knowledge of boat construction, organizational ability, and industrial contacts enabled him to construct seven "Pook" City Class ironclad boats and to convert the *Benton*, a salvage boat, into an ironclad in a period no one thought possible. Importantly, the City Class boats were only partially armored; in fact, the unprotected, exposed surface area exceeded what was protected. The *Benton* was somewhat better off, as only its deck and roof were unprotected while its sides were completely armored.

The contract Eads signed with Army Quartermaster-General Montgomery C. Meigs on August 7, 1861, for the construction of seven ironclad boats is very detailed, filling 16½ pages in the Army's *Official Records*.[114] The contract specified that each boat was to have fifteen water-tight compartments, three keels, and iron plating of sufficient thickness to protect the boiler and engines from "the effect of shot or shell."[115] Although the weight of these gunboats varied during the war—owing to the addition and removal of armor—the Navy's *Official Records* lists them as 512 tons.[116] Due to the shallow waters in the Mississippi and its tributaries, the boats had a relatively shallow draft of six feet when heavily laden. Even with this light draft, they ran aground when the river was low and sometimes, due to poor piloting, even when the river was high.[117] The boats were slow and only had a speed of four knots going upstream; however, their speed varied depending on whether weight was added or taken off, how clean the boilers were, the quality of the coal, and the strength of the current. The boats were very broad relative to their length, having a width of 51 feet and 2 inches

Construction of one of the City Class gunboats. Courtesy of the Naval Historical Foundation, 165-C-702.

with a length of 175 feet.[118] In the end, the City Class boats were partially armored, slow moving gun platforms.

As could be expected with any contract of this complexity, especially when warships like this had never been built before, problems and changes to the plans arose during construction. One major design change was that the original contract called for each boat to have twenty guns, but when completed they only had thirteen. Another change moved the steam drums to the top of the boilers, a change that would later have disastrous consequences for the *Mound City*.[119] One administrative problem was payment for work that had been completed. At one point, Captain Andrew H. Foote, who had taken over from Commander Rogers, wrote General Meigs, "Mr. Eads, the contractor, informs me that he shall stop his work tonight on the gunboats for want of funds. What shall I do in the premises?"[120] Fortunately, the funding issue was resolved and work was continued, but all of these problems delayed final delivery of the boats.

Transporting the boats from their construction sites to Cairo, Illinois, also created delays, even though they steamed from their construction site to Cairo without guns, making them much lighter. In early December 1861, the *Benton*, on its own trip to Cairo, ran aground

USS *Benton* in 1864. It was the only non–City Class ironclad involved in the Battles of Plum Point and Memphis. Courtesy of the Naval Historical Foundation, NH 56664.

due to the low level of the river. Fortunately, Eads was on board and used his knowledge to get the *Benton* off the sandbar.[121] However, its captain, John A. Winslow, was seriously injured when a chain that was being used to get the *Benton* off a sandbar snapped.[122] Even the lighter *Pittsburg* grounded on its way to Cairo in early December 1861.[123] If either boat had been equipped with its guns and ammunition, it would have been even heavier and deeper in the water, making it even more difficult to get back into the channel. This type of delay was expected on the rivers, as Commander Rodgers had faced the same delay with the timberclads in August 1861, stating that the delay was "an accident incident to the nature of navigation."[124]

Beyond changes made to the original specifications, the armament of the boats changed throughout the war. When they were first commissioned, all of the City Class boats had six smoothbore 32-pounders, three 8-inch smoothbores, four Army 42-pounder rifles, and—except for the *Cairo*—a 12-pounder rifled boat howitzer.[125] (The 12-pounder rifled boat howitzer would not have been kept inside of the boat; it would have been on the deck ready to repel boarders or to accompany a landing party.) By August 1862, the armament on the boats began to vary. By that time, only the *Louisville*, *Pittsburg*, and *Cincinnati* had the same armament, and they had one 12-pounder smoothbore howitzer, six smoothbore 32-pounders, two Army 42-pounder rifles, three

8-inch smoothbores, and two 30-pounder Parrott rifles.[126] The main reason for the change in armament was that some of the guns they had been given were worn out and dangerous. Symmes Browne wrote home on April 24, 1862, that Sailors on the *Mound City* threw two of the Army's rifled guns overboard and replaced them with a 50-pounder Dahlgren and a 30-pounder Parrott.[127] The *Mound City* was not the only boat to discard some of its guns; the *Benton*'s log states that on April 9, by order of Flag-Officer Andrew Foote, two 42-pounder rifled guns were thrown overboard, having been condemned as worthless.[128] Later in the war, in 1865, the number of guns in each ironclad was reduced probably because fewer heavy guns were needed and to alleviate the previously mentioned manpower shortage.

The *Benton* was very different from the seven contracted ironclads. It was a converted salvage boat, named *No. 7*, which had been owned by James Eads. The *Benton*, along with the *New Era*, was converted based on an order from General Frémont.[129] Even though Foote had difficulties with Frémont, he probably wanted to thank him later, because the *Benton* became Foote's flagship, as he considered it to be superior to all of his other ironclads. As Foote wrote to Quartermaster-General Meigs, "The *Benton* is worth any three of the new gunboats. She will draw a foot less water and works better, but she also wants a tug or propeller. Every officer here pronounces her the best gunboat in the Union. She will stand a good hammering."[130] The *Benton* was the most heavily armed gunboat in the flotilla because it carried three more guns than the City Class gunboats, and all of its sides were protected by iron, although its deck and roof were not; however, the *Benton* was even more underpowered than the City Class gunboats. Because he was suspicious of the *Benton*'s speed, Foote ordered Commanders Alexander Pennock and Roger Stembel to test its qualities. They reported to Foote that "We are decidedly of the opinion that her machinery is insufficient to propel the boat in such a manner as to make her an efficient vessel in action, or even to propel her against the current of the Mississippi River in many places in an ordinary stage of water."[131] As a result of their report, Foote was not willing to accept the *Benton* as it was built, and recommended that a new engine and boiler be placed in her.[132] However, the cost and time involved to make these changes was too much. Consequently, the option of raising its wheel 18 inches and increasing the size of the rudder at the surface of the water was considered as these two changes would improve the *Benton*'s speed and maneuverability. In addition, the cost would be less than $2,000, and

USS *Cairo*. All of the other City Class ironclads would have looked very similar. Notice how exposed the pilothouse was, as it was located on top of the boat in front of the smokestacks. In addition, the gray stripe, identifying the boat as the *Cairo*, can be seen on each of the smokestacks. Photograph courtesy of the Vicksburg National Military Park.

Bow view of the USS *Cairo* as seen at the Vicksburg National Military Park. Photograph by the author, March 2010.

Interior view of the *Cairo*'s forward starboard gun. It would have been a hot, smoky, noisy, claustrophobic location during battle. Photograph by the author, March 2010.

Starboard side of the *Cairo*. Notice that only part of the boat is protected by armor. Photograph by the author, March 2010.

The *Cairo*'s vulnerable unarmored stern with a view of its paddlewheel. Photograph by the author, March 2010.

the work could be done in less than three weeks.[133] The issue had to be taken to President Lincoln, who authorized the changes on January 28, 1862, as long as they could be completed by February 22.[134] Although the changes probably improved the *Benton*'s speed and maneuverability, it was still slow, and Flag-Officer Andrew Foote informed the Navy Department in early March that "The Benton is underway and barely stems the current of the Ohio, which is 5 knots per hour in this rise of water, but hope, by putting her between two ironclad steamers tomorrow, she will stem the current and work comparatively well."[135] Later in the same message, Foote wrote, "As the current in the Mississippi is in some places 7 knots per hour, the ironclad boats can hardly return here [Cairo]."[136] Unfortunately, lack of power would be an issue that would plague the flotilla throughout the war.

Fortunately for the Union, all of the construction and delivery issues were resolved, and the USS *Carondelet* was commissioned on January 15, 1862, becoming the first ironclad warship built in the United States.[137] All of the *Carondelet* 's sister warships (*Cairo*, *Cincinnati*, *Louisville*, *Mound City*, *Pittsburg*, and *St. Louis* [later renamed the *Baron De Kalb*]), known as the City Class Gunboats, were commissioned by the end of January 1862.[138] The *Benton* followed on February 24, 1862.[139] The addition of these eight ironclad gunboats—even though they were not completely ironclad—provided the Union Navy with a powerful river fleet, one far superior than the opposing Confederate fleet. The flotilla became very formidable and, by November 1862, after the Battle of Memphis, the squadron, as it was then designated, consisted of ten ironclad steam gunboats, eight wooden gunboats, two steam rams, and thirteen steam tugs, not including the mortar boats and other auxiliary vessels.[140]

Although they were partially ironclad, the Union river gunboats had five major weaknesses. First, they were all vulnerable to plunging fire. This weakness became well known to the Confederates due a report of the battle from Brigadier General Lloyd Tilghman, commander of Fort Henry. In his report, Tilghman stated that "the roof, is in every respect vulnerable to either a plunging fire from even 32-pounders or a curved line of fire from heavy guns."[141] In addition, the City Class boats were vulnerable to direct fire on their sterns and on their sides between their ironclad-protected engines and their ironclad-protected bow. This weakness forced the City Class gunboats to attack with their bow facing the enemy. Presenting their broadside gave Confederate gunners an opportunity to hit their vulnerable stern; however, a bow-first approach only allowed them to fire three guns rather than the four a broadside would have allowed.

The second major weakness of the gunboats was the previously mentioned slow speed. The speed for the *Carondelet* was reportedly four knots, or 4.6 miles, per hour going upstream.[142] Although the Navy's *Official Records* do not list the speed for all of the City Class boats, it is safe to assume that all had comparable speeds. Even with this ideal speed, the City Class boats were so slow going upriver that the *Carondelet* had to be towed up the Cumberland River by the steamer *Alps* when Brigadier-General Ulysses Grant requested that it be brought to Fort Donelson to cooperate with the Army. Just before leaving for Fort Donelson, Commander Walke, commander of the *Carondelet,* wrote Flag-Officer Foote, "I [the *Carondelet*] am very slow."[143] Although the Navy's *Official Records* do not list an official speed for the *Benton*, it can be assumed that it was slower than the City Class boats due both to its greater weight and that it took two boats to tow it upriver. In a letter, Flag-Officer Davis stated that when traveling upriver from Vicksburg, the *Benton* needed the "powerful side-wheel boat *Switzerland* tugging at her on one side and the *General Bragg* on the other" to make adequate headway up the Mississippi.[144]

The lack of speed did not present a problem going downriver. The additional speed gained from the river current made the boats very difficult targets for artillery. However, going upriver, the current worked against them, and their very slow speed made them easy targets, which is why—when Admiral Porter was considering the proposal to run past the Vicksburg batteries he informed General Grant, "I am ready to co-operate with you in the matter of landing troops on the other side, but you must recollect that, when these gunboats go below, we give up all hopes of ever getting them up again."[145]

Another result of the gunboats' lack of power and design was their inability to develop enough thrust to efficiently back up.[146] A number of experiments, to include using anchors to stabilize the boat, were tried to remedy this situation, but none were successful.[147] The problem was that, in most cases, the gunboats had to approach the Confederate fortifications from upriver to attack them. If the boats were going upriver, as at Forts Henry and Donelson, the problem solved itself, but in the case of Island No. 10 or Fort Pillow, the challenge remained. In either circumstance, if the boats' protected bow was presented to the enemy and they had to retreat, the boats would be forced to turn around, thus giving the Confederates an opportunity to fire at their unprotected stern. Moreover, if they were disabled, they would drift with the current into Confederate lines and be captured. One result of this lack of power was that commanders of the flotilla were very careful when and where they exposed their boats to fire from heavy Confederate cannons. The problem was that if a heavy projectile hit the boat, it could become disabled. If it were disabled and captured and then reused by the Confederates, the Confederates could possibly use the captured boat or boats to gain control of the river. Fear of this scenario was so great that Foote specifically ordered Commander Walke, commander of the *Carondelet*, that if he met with disaster in trying to pass the batteries at Island No. 10, he would "as a last resort, destroy the steam machinery, and, if possible to escape, set fire to your gunboat or sink her, and prevent her from falling into the hands of the rebels."[148]

Lack of power, along with their weight and shape, made the ironclads very unmaneuverable, even though they had two rudders. In designing the boats, a tradeoff had to take place between maneuverability and the ability of the boat to carry a large number of heavy cannon. In the end, firepower trumped mobility. The City Class boats were 175 feet long and had a beam of 51 feet 2 inches—a ratio of approximately 3.4:1.[149] The *Benton* was even longer and wider, having a length of 200 feet with a beam of 75 feet—a ratio of 2.7:1.[150] In contrast, the more maneuverable USS *Monitor* was shorter and narrower, with a length of 172 feet and a beam of 41 feet 6 inches—a ratio of approximately of 4.1:1.[151] However, the *Monitor* only carried two guns in a turret—a sharp contrast to the thirteen guns on the City Class gunboats and the sixteen guns on the *Benton*—although the *Monitor* had a more efficient propeller than the paddle wheels on the Mississippi River gunboats.

Lastly, the guns on the ironclads had limited elevation, which would not have been a concern in ship-to-ship combat or when fighting a fort at water level—as with Island No. 10—but did become an issue when fighting Confederate guns that were located on a high bluff. On the other hand, when Confederate batteries were positioned on high bluffs, the ironclads gained an unforeseen advantage: The advantage was that a battery placed on a high bluff could not fire at a gunboat that hugged the the same side of the river on which the battery was located. The reason for this was that the Confederate guns could not be depressed far enough to fire at these boats . However, batteries located on a high bluff could place plunging fire upon any gunboat exposed to its fire, and plunging fire was responsible for the damage done to the *Mound City* in June 1862 and what sunk the *Cincinnati* at Vicksburg in 1863.[152]

One easily solvable identification concern was how to tell one City Class gunboat from another. The solution was to paint identifying stripes near the top of each boat's smoke stacks. The *Cairo* had a gray stripe; the *Carondelet* had a red stripe; the *Cincinnati* had a blue stripe; the *Louisville* had a green stripe; the *Pittsburg* had a light brown stripe; and the *St. Louis* had a yellow stripe. There is some confusion on how the *Mound City* was marked, as it was suppose to have an orange stripe but a photograph of the boat shows a five-pointed star.[153] In addition, each boat in the flotilla flew an ensign, explicitly coded for it; and at night each boat had a specified lamp signal.[154]

The ironclads were far from perfect, but considering all of the constraints under which they were designed and built, they were good warships. All of the weaknesses were well known or became known to the Union commanders as Foote wrote to the Chief of the Navy's Bureau of Ordnance in March 1862:

> The iron-clad boats cannot be held when anchored by stern in this current, on account of the recess between the fantails forming the stern yawing them about, and as the sterns of the boats are not plated, and have but two 32-pounders astern, you will see our difficulty of fighting down-stream effectually. Neither is there power enough in any of them to back up-stream. We must therefore tie up to shore the best way we can and help the mortar boats. I have long expressed to General Meigs [the Army's Quarter-Master General] my apprehensions about these boats' defects. Don't have any gunboats for rivers built with wheels amidships. The drift-wood would choke the wheel, even if it had a powerful engine. I felt it my duty to state these difficulties, which could not be obviated when I came here, as the vessels were modeled and partly built.[155]

Unfortunately, none of the Union ironclads that survived war survived the peace. The Navy saw no reason to have an inland squadron, and monitors were considered the best warships to protect the harbors. Once the war ended, the surviving river ironclads were quickly decommissioned and sold.[156] Although the ironclads had significant problems, they and their crews accomplished their missions of controlling the Mississippi River and its tributaries while providing needed support to the Army.

* * *

Charles Ellet Jr. was a brilliant individual who was extremely difficult to work with because he believed that he always knew what was best. Prior to the war, he had established a reputation as a talented engineer, designing and constructing canals, railroads, and bridges. The iron suspension bridge he designed and built across the Ohio River at Wheeling was completed in 1849 and, at the time, had the longest single span in the world.[157] However, Ellet was difficult to work for, and even more difficult to supervise. As such, he eventually found it hard to obtain jobs.

Ellet became interested in the military potential of steam rams after learning about larger ships being sunk by smaller ones that had accidently rammed them. One of the most famous of these incidents was the sinking of the wooden-hulled SS *Artic* after being rammed by the much smaller iron hulled SS *Vesta*.[158] Ellet so firmly believed in his idea about steam rams that during the Crimean War he offered to build a Ram Fleet for the Russians that could be used against the British and French fleets. However, the Russians declined his offer, at which point he made the same offer to the British, who also declined.[159]

When the Civil War started, Ellet was quick to write to government officials advocating a ram fleet. In June 1861, he wrote to Secretary of the Navy Gideon Welles; the tenor of his message offers a good example of his persistence and how he approached high-ranking individuals:

> Sir: I addressed a communication to you some weeks since, calling your attention to the value of steam rams as a formidable means of defending the coasts and harbors of this country against a foreign naval attack.
>
> Although I failed to obtain your serious attention, or that of either of your two predecessors in the Department, I think it proper to say to you that after the publication and distribution of my views to Congress six years ago, the very plan which I recommended was adopted, on a gigantic scale, both by the British and French governments.
>
> My purpose in addressing you again on this subject is, that I am induced, by a vague hint in a New Orleans paper, to suspect that they [Confederates] have now in preparation on the Mississippi a plan of this sort for running into and sinking some of the blockading vessels in the Gulf.

> I am of the opinion that it would be worth while to put our naval commanders there on their guard against that particular danger, and am, sir,
>
> Respectfully, your most obedient, Charles Ellet, *Civil Engineer.* [Italics in the original message][160]

Ellet advocated to everyone he possibly could that a ram fleet be built to use against the Confederates. Further, he argued that he should be in charge of it. Beyond the ram fleet, Ellet submitted numerous plans to President Abraham Lincoln, Major General George McClellan, and many other people in public office.[161] Most of his plans guaranteed that a crushing defeat would be inflicted upon the Confederates in a very short period of time, provided he was in charge of the operation.[162] When officials would not listen to him, Ellet published pamphlets. One pamphlet was written in late 1861 and entitled *The Army of the Potomac and its Mismanagement; Respectfully addressed to Congress.* However, at this time Major-General McClellan was still held in high regard. Ellet became so infamous that *Harper's Weekly* published a caricature of him holding numerous plans and ringing the bell to McClellan's headquarters, threatening that if he were not let in he would publish a pamphlet.[163]

The panic created by the CSS *Virginia*'s attack against the Union squadron at Hampton Roads, Virginia, on March 8, 1862, changed everything, as it convinced many people that steam rams could be an effective naval weapon and possibly the only effective means of sinking an ironclad. As a result, Secretary of War Edwin Stanton, who had replaced Simon Cameron in January 1862, took immediate action and, on March 23, the steamer *Vanderbilt*, owned by Cornelius Vanderbilt, was at Fort Monroe, Virginia, prepared to act as a ram against the *Virginia*.[164] By March 28, seven steamers were available at Fort Monroe ready to ram the *Virginia* if it should come that far down the James River.[165]

Although there was no need for Ellet's service on the East Coast, Federal officials feared that the Confederates would build an ironclad for use on the Mississippi River. Major-General Henry Halleck informed Stanton on March 25 that he had received a report that the Confederates were building ironclads similar to the *Virginia* at New Orleans. Halleck dreaded that "Such a river boat could pass any of our batteries, destroy Commodore Foote's flotilla, and burn the steamboats in the Western Waters. This is a very serious matter, which requires immediate attention." Stanton replied the same day that he had received similar information from other sources and that a meeting had been held to "consider the best mode of meeting the rebel boat."[166] Stanton further stated that "The universal opinion among naval and military engineers in the East is that a floating ram striking and sinking the iron-clad vessel is the best mode of encountering it." Stanton closed his message by asserting, "Charles Ellet, a distinguished engineer, has given the subject much attention. I will send him to-morrow to see and consult you, and with authority to act as you may deem best. He is a man of courage and energy, and willing to risk his own life upon his own job."[167]

With very little regard to bureaucracy, Stanton acted quickly after receiving Halleck's message, contacting the Presidents of the Board of Trade of Pittsburgh, Pennsylvania; Cincinnati, Ohio; and New Albany, Indiana, on March 26, asking them to appoint three of their "active members most familiar with steamboat and engine building, who would act in concert with this Department and under its direction, and from patriotic motives devote some time and attention for thirty days in purchasing and preparing such means of defense on the Western waters against iron-clad boats as the engineers of this Department may devise." They were also asked to "designate one of your most capable and substantial citizens who would accept the temporary appointment of assistant quartermaster, and in that official capacity make such contracts, audit and adjust such accounts, as the Department would authorize in the above business."[168] The Board of Trades for Pittsburgh and Cincinnati responded positively on the same day and recommended individuals for appointment as assistant quartermaster.[169] On March 27, New Albany's mayor personally responded to Stanton—as New Albany did not have a Board of Trade—stating that the city was willing to help. The mayor also sent a name forward for consideration as assistant quartermaster.[170]

Beyond the fact that he was a politician and wanted to spread the wealth and support for the war, Stanton's reason for contacting the three river ports was "to avoid the imputation of local favoritism, and also to bring out the whole mechanical energy of the Ohio Valley."[171] However, not everyone was completely patriotic. Stanton had to inform Joseph Butler, President of Cincinnati's Board of Trade, that "The Department [War Department] will submit to no speculative prices. If not, then I will authorize the quartermaster to seize such boats as may be needed as other property is taken for military purposes, leaving the parties to seek remuneration from Congress."[172] Stanton was not interested in delays, and informed Alexander Burnett, the major of New Albany, that "I want Pittsburg, Cincinnati, and New Albany skill, economy, enterprise, and patriotism to compete against each other. Will give each an equal fair test, and then choose between them for future work. Time is a great element of choice."[173]

The day after contacting the three cities, Stanton instructed Ellet to "proceed immediately to Pittsburgh, Cincinnati, and New Albany and take measures to provide steam rams for defense against iron-clad vessels on the Western waters."[174] Ellet was in continuous communication with Stanton, moving from city to city asking Stanton to authorize both the purchase of various riverboats and the right to modify the boats as needed. Stanton's system worked. At the end of May—about two months after Stanton's original instructions were issued—Ellet was able to assemble his fleet at Plum Point, where the Western Flotilla was located.[175] Although it was substantially cheaper than the flotilla, the Ram Fleet was not inexpensive, as the appropriations for the Ram Fleet for the 1862 fiscal year were $400,000.[176]

Along with authorizing Ellet to build a ram fleet, Stanton proposed making Ellet an Army Colonel to formalize his relationship to the military. With his characteristic modesty, Ellet replied that he "would much prefer that it should be a grade higher."[177] However, once Stanton explained that Army Colonel was the highest grade he could make Ellet without action by the Senate—which would cause a delay—Ellet accepted the rank. Along with making Ellet a Colonel, Stanton promoted Ellet's brother, Alfred W. Ellet, from Captain to Lieutenant Colonel, with the appointment of second in command of the Ram Fleet. Alfred Ellet was also authorized to "take with him a limited number of reliable men from the regiment he is now serving."[178] As such, the Ram Fleet was an Army operation because all of the officers and men were in the Army, although none of them was a regular.

Ellet created his Ram Fleet with a very different notion of how it was to be used in contrast to the Navy's ironclad flotilla. Ellet wrote Stanton that to be successful, the Ram Fleet would be required to "run down below the [Confederate] batteries, after which they [the rams] will be isolated, unable to return, and compelled to command the Mississippi or be sunk or taken." Ellet estimated that by using his method, command of the Mississippi would be accomplished within a month.[179] Unfortunately, Ellet's plan did not mention what was to be done about the Confederate batteries located along the river after his fleet had passed them.

Ellet's Ram Fleet. From a drawing by Alexander Simplot. Each boat has the first initial of its name between its smokestacks. Courtesy of the Naval Historical Foundation, NH 59007.

Many people disagreed with Ellet's mode of operation, including some of his crew. Ellet, "for the purpose of testing the temper of a doubtful crew," took the *Queen of the West* under the guns of Fort Pillow in an attempt to attack a Confederate boat lying there. Ellet was correct about his crew's lack of enthusiasm for his plan, as the captain, two of his three pilots, the first mate, all of the engineers, and nearly all of the crew "declined" to attempt the mission and left the boat. Ellet's crew members were not the only ones who were not enthusiastic about his plans. When he became aware of Ellet's proposed operation, Commodore Charles Davis, commander of the Western Flotilla, stated that he was not in favor of Ellet's attack; however, Davis conceded that Ellet's "mode of warfare is novel, and the service is peculiar."[180]

Based on Ellet's plan of operation, many believed that Ellet was suicidal— but he was not. In fact, he had designed his boats so that they could survive ramming a Confederate boat. Also, if Ellet had been suicidal he would have run his fleet past Fort Pillow without any assistance, but he waited. Still, if Ellet's fleet had run past a Confederate fort, most of his rams would have survived due to their speed. Ellet was a risk taker, but he was an excellent engineer and, having calculated the odds, firmly believed that he would be successful.

Stanton's creation of the Ram Fleet further confused Union command and control on the Mississippi. The problem was that command and control of the Ram Fleet went directly from Ellet to Stanton. Ellet wanted an independent command. He justified his need for an independent command because "the concurrence of the naval commander on the Mississippi might embarrass me much."[181] Ellet further wrote that he feared the naval commander might not concur with his plan to run past the batteries and would force him to remain idle. Stanton gave Ellet what he wanted, but in doing so further confused an already complex command structure, telegraphing Ellet on April 26, 1862, "There ought not to be two commanders on the same element in war operations, but as the service you are engaged in is peculiar, the naval commander will be so advised and will be desired not to exercise direct control over your movements unless they shall manifestly expose the general operations on the Mississippi, to some unpardonable influence, which is not, however, anticipated."[182] However, two days later, Stanton telegraphed Halleck that Ellet "will be subject to the orders of Commodore Foote,"[183] who in turn was subject to Army command. Ellet interpreted Stanton's message to his own benefit. When asked by Commodore Davis "how far you consider yourself under my authority," Ellet replied, "I do not consider myself at all under your authority." Ellet's response included a tacit insult of both Davis and the Navy. Ellet informed Davis that the Ram Fleet "was sent forward in great haste, in the hope that it might be here in time to contribute to avert such a disaster anticipated at the Department as that which recently befell two of the gunboats when assailed by the rebel rams." Ellet did let Davis know the limitation Stanton had put on his operations that the Ram Fleet "shall not move against the enemy without your concurrence, provided you consider the particular movement which I propose as bearing hurtfully upon the general operations which you are conducting." Ellet tried to temper his message when, in closing, he stated, "It is my intention to continue, as I have done, to communicate all my plans to you in advance, and to keep prepared to aid in the execution of all yours as soon as you deem it proper to intrust me with them; to do nothing contrary to your wishes, but to move against the enemy the moment you intimate that you are yourself ready, or that my advance will not interfere with your own program."[184]

Ellet wanted to be independent, but at the same time wanted the cooperation and aid of the Navy and was willing to collaborate with the Navy as long as it recognized his independence. Davis wanted Ellet's cooperation but wanted it on his terms, based on his point of view as a regular Navy officer. One *New York Tribune* newspaper reporter, writing after the surrender of Memphis, explained:

> Col. Ellet, by-the-by, though an energetic and able officer has made himself unpopular by arrogating to himself, be-

> cause the rams belong to neither branch of service, powers that are not his, and the exercise of which has place him more than once in a ridiculous position. Assigning the rams to neither the army nor navy give rise to much misunderstanding and confusion, and ought to be remedied at once. Such independence is anomalous and absurd in the extreme, as an experience at Fort Pillow, Randolph and Memphis has proved.[185]

Fortunately, for the Union, this dual command structure, lack of co-operation, and divergent methods of naval warfare did not negatively impact its operations.

The crews on Ellet's rams were either riverboat men or volunteers from the Army, and Ellet wanted to be sure that they were informed it would be dangerous duty.[186] Ellet was not interested in having naval officers on board, although Stanton offered to provide some. In reply to Stanton's offer, Ellet replied, "I prefer daring and skillful river men, if they can be got, to handle the boats; but will apply for naval officers if there is any difficulty in procuring the proper men, which I do not expect."[187] Beside the crews, Ellet had a number of volunteer Soldiers on each boat whose duty was to provide small arms protection.[188] Ellet so firmly believed that it would be a short mission that he felt the men would only need to be paid for one month. However, due to the hazardous nature of the mission, Ellet proposed that the crews be given an extra month's pay for every fortified Confederate position they passed, although Stanton turned down this request.[189] In addition, Ellet did not expect to take any prizes because he planned on destroying any Confederate shipping the fleet encountered. As a substitute for prize money, he asked Stanton to determine what the just compensation should be for the damage they inflicted.[190] In the end, Ellet's organization lasted much longer than a month, Confederate boats were captured, and prize money was awarded, but no extra money was given for passing Confederate fortifications.

Ellet had seven rams and two noncombat auxiliary vessels in his fleet. The two auxiliaries, *T.D. Horner* and *Dick Fulton*, kept the fleet supplied and played a crucial role in its success. The supply boats were also reinforced so that they could be used as rams in an emergency.[191] Ellet's auxiliary boats will not be described here; only the rams that participated in the Battle of Memphis will be discussed in detail (None of the rams was present for the Battle of Plum Point.) Out of the seven rams—*Lancaster*, *Lioness*, *Mingo*, *Monarch*, *Queen of the West*, *Sampson* (also spelled *Samson*, and renamed on October 24, 1862, as the *Pansy*[192]), and *Switzerland*—only the *Queen of the West* and the *Monarch* participated in the Battle of Memphis.

Each ram was unique, as they were all converted river steamers. Their conversion to rams followed one pattern, although they were a mix of stern and side wheelers. Ellet transformed his civilian boats into rams by placing

> three heavy, solid, timber bulkheads, from 12 to 16 inches thick, fore and aft from stem to stern, placing the central one directly over the keelson; in bracing these bulkheads one against the other, and the outer ones against the hull of the boat, and all against the deck and floor timbers, and staying the hull from side to side by iron rods and screw bolts; in fact, making the whole weight of the boat add its momentum to that of the central bulkhead at the moment of collision.[193]

In addition to making his rams capable of sinking an enemy boat, Ellet made sure that their boilers and machinery were held by iron stays in all directions. This added measure was so that the machinery would not be wrenched out of place when the ram struck another boat. Beyond offensive measures, Ellet provided protection to both the pilothouse and the engines and boilers from small arms fire, but not from cannon fire.[194] Ellet was aware that if he were to maintain the speed necessary to create massive damage to an enemy boat, he could not adequately protect either the crew or vital machinery from cannon fire without adding so much weight to the boat that its speed would be substantially reduced. The rams were fast, with an estimated speed of at least eighteen miles per hour down river or almost sixteen knots.[195] None of the rams was armed with cannon until after the Battle of Memphis, as Ellet believed that speed was much more important than armament; however, the rams were not defenseless. Each ram was well supplied with hand grenades and had between eleven and fifteen sharpshooters armed with breech-loading carbines that could be fired through loopholes. A hose was also attached to the boilers for the purpose of spraying any boarders with scalding hot water.[196]

Following the Civil War, the Navy did not think highly of these vessels. Only descriptions of four (*Mingo*, *Queen of the West*, *Sampson/Samson*, and *Switzerland*) can be found in the Statistical Data of Ships in the Navy's *Official Records*, although all of the Confederate boats that were at the Battles of Plum Point and Memphis are included. Further confusing the issue is that the Navy already had a sloop named the *Lancaster*. Even so, the Ellet's *Lancaster* did not have its name changed, probably because the Navy did not consider it a ship. In contrast, the name of the ironclad USS *St. Louis* was changed to the *Baron De Kalb* when it became part of the Navy. Because of this bias, very little technical data is available on the Ellet's rams compared to the City Class gunboats. As a further insult, the Navy does not give the *Sampson* credit for being the first ship named *Sampson*; instead, it refers to it as the *Samson* in its *Dictionary of American Naval Fighting Ships*. The same reference states that the *Switzerland* was never a Navy vessel even though it was transferred to the Navy in the autumn of 1862, at least six months before it was sunk. The Navy has also never seemed interested in the technical details of Ellet's rams. Interestingly, as much—if not more—technical information on the rams can be found in the Army's *Official Records*, which makes sense because the Army paid for the boats. Fortunately, Ellet's rams are easy to identify in any wartime photographs or drawings, as each ram had the first letter of its name placed between its smoke stacks.

The *Queen of the West* was a side-wheeled steamer built in Cincinnati, Ohio, in 1854,was 406 tons, had a length of 180 feet, a beam of 37 feet 6 inches, and drew eight feet of water. Purchased by the Federal government for $16,000 in Cincinnati in May 1862, and converted to a ram. Converting the Queen of the West cost $23,113.69. As with all of the rams, it was fitted out in Cairo. The Navy rated it as a fourth class vessel.[197] Ellet thought so highly of the Queen of the West that he personally commanded her.[198] The *Queen of the West* was also the name of a cargo ship in the Atlantic, which can create some confusion when researching the boat.[199]

Even less information is available on the *Monarch*, a 400-ton sidewheel steam towboat that worked in the Cincinnati area. It was purchased by the Federal government for $14,000 on April 20, 1862, and was converted at New Albany, Indiana, at a cost of $17,411,17.[200] Like most of the other boats, was shallow draft, drawing only six feet. Even then, it would run aground.[201] The *Monarch* is another boat whose name causes confusion as there was a Union hospital steamer on the Mississippi with the same name.[202]

Army Captain James Brooks believed that Ellet, "who felt to some extent responsible for the success of the experiment, spared no pains in getting the fleet out with the least possible outlay of money."

This statement was in response to a request from General Meigs, Quartermaster-General, to send to his "office without delay a report of the vessels composing the ram fleet under my direction, specifying their names and capacity, where and how received, and where and to whom transferred." Brooks also reported that "The prices paid for labor and materials I thought very high, but the committee explained that they had been obliged to submit to some extraordinary charges to enable them to get the work done in the short time allowed." Brooks went on to state:

> The principle adopted by him to strengthen the hulls of the boats to enable them to stand the severe shock to which they were subjected in action it will be hard to improve upon. His skill as a civil engineer of large experience shows itself prominently in the simple and efficient means adopted for that purpose, and should it be thought advisable to construct other boats to be used as rams it will be desirable, as far as practicable, to incorporate the same principle, by which the whole weight of the boat, without the spring which an ordinary boat would have, may be brought to bear with crushing effect upon the boat struck.[203]

Brooks may have been biased because he had been in Ellet's command, and his report was written in November 1862, after Ellet's victory at Memphis and subsequent death.

In the end, the Ellet's rams played a vital role in the conquest and control of the Mississippi River and its tributaries. They were assigned many tasks that the ironclads could not fulfill, such as transporting troops, providing escorts to convoys, and patrolling where their superior speed was required. Ellet's rams were an asset that increased the flexibility and capabilities of the Union ironclad flotilla. But the Ellet rams and their crews paid a heavy price during the war, as only three of the seven rams survived the war to be sold when it was over.

* * *

Another set of boats that warrants description are the mortar boats, or scows, as one of the mortar boats played an important role in the Battle of Plum Point. It should be noted that there were two very different types of mortar boats used by the Union during the war. One, the type built at St. Louis, was much more of a scow or barge than a boat. The other was a sailing ship capable of ocean travel. Both types were used on the Mississippi River. The scows were built and manned by the Army while the mortar schooner was a converted ship manned by the Navy. The former were rectangular barges that needed to be towed, and were used to bombard Confederate forts on the upper Mississippi as well, as Vicksburg, and played an important role in the Battle of Plum Point. The latter, although capable of sailing themselves, normally had to be towed into position.[204] These mortar ships, or bomb vessels, were used to bombard Fort Saint Philip and Fort Jackson prior to the attack on New Orleans.

Thirty-eight mortar boats/scows were built by the Army at St. Louis by Mr. Theodore Adams.[205] As Commander of the Department of the West, Major General John C. Frémont ordered their construction.[206] The boats were built of solid timber and carried a single 13-inch mortar. They were not named but given numbers from 1 to 38. (In contrast, the Navy's mortar ships were named.) Although the boats were built in St. Louis, the mortars and mortar beds were cast and constructed in Pittsburg, with the final outfitting done at Cairo. [207] Each mortar boat was armed with a 13-inch sea-coast mortar that could fire a 200-pound exploding shell 4,325 yards (2.457 miles).[208] However, the actual range was much farther, as tests conducted by the Navy had the shells being thrown three to three and a half miles.[209] The rate of fire for these mortars was significant. They could continuously fire twelve rounds an hour and could, if necessary, fire more rapidly, a factor that would be put to use during the Battle of Plum Point.[210]

There is a sketch of a mortar boat in the Navy's *Official Records* in a report from Captain Henry E. Maynadier, Commander of the Mortars. Although it does not indicate a scale, the sketch shows that the boat was flat bottomed, and approximately two-thirds of the boat was below the waterline. Maynadier also states in his report that the shape of the mortar boats made "it impossible to tow them without running them under the water, whilst their construction is, as I shall endeavor to show, very badly adapted to resisting the effects of firing."[211] In addition, the mortar boats could be run aground and, due to their design, were very difficult to get back afloat.[212] At best, the mortar boats were small barges that were poorly designed and constructed. In addition, due to a "want of money, of credit, and of material for building purposes," they were not "completed within the time specified by contract."[213]

Foote, being a blue water sailor, was not enthusiastic about the mortar boats. He wrote a private and confidential report for President Lincoln in January 1862, stating the following:

A mortar boat and the timberclad USS *Tyler*, as drawn by J. Muller, *ORN*, series II, vol.1., p. 227.

> With reference to the mortar boats, I only wish that you could see them; their magazines are merely square holes in the timbers banded together forming the boat, and of course most of them leak. The mortar boats would require, if all fitted out, about 800 men. There are no conveniences for living aboard. They will leak more and more. Some of our best officers have no better opinion of these rafts or boats than I; still this is unofficial. It is my business to let the Government judge, and I am to obey orders, and while I can not consider these boats as well adapted to the purposes for which they were designed, still, as I said to General Meigs, so much has been expended upon them, they ought not to be cast aside, or words to that effect, and I certainly would not presume to throw obstacles in the way of having them fitted, armed, and equipped.[214]

Even earlier, in December 1861, Foote had informed Quartermaster General Montgomery Meigs, "It is a pity that the mortar boats were built without the supervision of some officer or person experienced in such matters."[215] Contrary to what Foote reported, the magazines were lined with copper (a nonsparking metal),[216] but the boats were continually wet, as they leaked and were frequently waterlogged. Other costs were incurred because of the design; the mortar boats had to be towed by tugs, and steamers had to be purchased to accompany them to provide sleeping and living quarters for the officers and men who served the mortars.[217] As with the other two fleets, operating the mortar boats was not cheap. Captain Henry Maynadier estimated that it cost $2,000 a day to operate sixteen mortar boats, which included the cost of the crews, but not the cost of the projectiles. The projectiles were expensive, as each one cost $15.00 and, as of August 2, 1862, 8,000 shells had been fired, for a total of $120,000.[218]

The Army was expected to provide the 800 men (Foote later increased that number to 1,000[219]) needed to man the mortar boats, because the fleet was short-handed and did not have anyone who was familiar with mortars.[220] This shortage was especially true for officers. Captain Robert A. Constable, a former Major in the British East India Company, was the original commander but was reassigned by General Halleck.[221] Later, with the assistance of President Lincoln, Captain Henry E. Maynadier, Tenth US Infantry, assumed command with the title of Ordnance Officer of the Mortar Rafts, Mortar Division of the Western Flotilla, later receiving the title Commander of the Mortars.[222] Foote kept the Mortar Division a separate entity from his gunboats because he wanted it officered, paid, and clothed by the Army.[223]

Even with Foote's skepticism, the mortar boats had their supporters. In December 1861, Assistant Secretary of the Navy Gustavus V. Fox wrote Foote, "I have no doubt but what you will reduce Columbus without them [mortar boats], but if you leave them you leave the most efficient arm you possess."[224] Even one of Foote's own captains, Lieutenant Commander S. Ledyard Phelps, US Navy commander of the USS *Conestoga*, believed in the mortar boats and wrote to Foote on January 21, 1862, "Effective mortar boats must prove the most destructive adversaries earth forts can have to contend with." The advantage of mortar boats over gunboats was that they could be placed so that they were masked from the gunners in the fort and could bombard the fort without fear of counter artillery fire. Gunboats—with their direct fire guns—had to be in view of the fort and, thus, subject to counter artillery fire. It was also very difficult to seriously damage an earthen fort with direct artillery fire. Mortars, firing indirectly, created damage and destruction in the interior of the fort. Still, even after reading Phelps's report, Foote did not want the mortar boats on his expedition up the Tennessee and Cumberland Rivers due to the difficulty of towing them up river. Foote believed "that the gunboats would accomplish any service required there [Tennessee or Cumberland Rivers], independently of the mortar boats."[225] Foote was fighting a losing battle on using the mortar boats, since one of their strongest champions was President Lincoln, who took a personal interest in getting the mortar boats operational and wanted daily updates and results.[226]

Eventually, mortar boats proved their worth to Foote, who wrote during the fight for Island No. 10, "The mortar boats do well, and had we a place to put them out of the sight of the forts we could soon shell out the rebels. They have done good execution as it is."[227] The press also had a high opinion of the mortar boats, probably because, at times, they were the only boats fighting the Confederates. The sight of the mortar shells streaking across the night sky was a spectacular image for drawings being sent to the various newspapers and periodicals.

In the end, the effectiveness of the mortar boats was questionable. Even the commander of the mortars, Captain Henry E. Maynadier, did not think highly of them, and wrote a scathing report to Flag Officer Davis in August 1862.[228] In his report, Maynadier stated that he felt that the mortars were a great annoyance to the Confederates at Island No. 10, had very limited success at Fort Pillow, and at Vicksburg were credited with creating great destruction in the city but that most of the Confederate batteries were out of range. Maynadier also stated that there were numerous problems with the design of the mortar boats. Some of the design problems Maynadier detailed were that it was "almost impossible to tow them without running them under water," and that the design of the boat caused it to settle in the middle when the mortar was fired, which opened the seams and allowed the boat to fill with water. Maynadier concluded by stating that "the mortars have contributed as much as was in their power or could be expected of them toward the result of the campaign, still their services have not been near equal to their cost."[229] A Navy Board of Officers tasked to examine the condition of six of the mortar boats reported in August 1862, that they were "all water-logged, and the spaces left for the magazines are filled with water." Their final recommendation was that the mortars and their carriages be removed as they were in an almost perfect condition, but that the boats be broken up or sold.[230] Consequently, Admiral Porter requested in October 1862, that fifteen new mortar scows be built.[231]

Although they were not as successful as desired, the mortar boats provided a means of striking at the Confederates when no other weapon could do so. The harassing fire by the mortar boats always had the potential to create devastating damage to the heavy Confederate guns and their ammunition—besides disrupting the sleep of the gun crews. An additional advantage was that the Confederates had no effective means of striking back at them. Without the mortar boats attacking the Confederate forts, Union commanders, especial Foote and Davis, would have come under much greater pressure to prematurely attack them with potentially disastrous results. In this respect, the mortar boats were a success.

Chapter 4

The Situation

As you are aware our gunboats are not well adapted to fighting downstream, for want of steam power and other causes; while the exposed state of the river above, in case of defeat, would prove extremely disastrous.

—Message from Flag-Officer Andrew Foote to
Quartermaster-General Montgomery Meigs,
April 23, 1862[1]

I have the honor to acknowledge the receipt of your letter of the 12th, relative to Montgomery's expedition. The evacuation of Columbus overturns his original intentions of destroying the enemy's fleet at Cairo, and, in my judgment, they can now be used only as assistants to the land and naval forces in defending our own positions [New Orleans].

—Message from Major-General Mansfield Lovell to
Secretary of War Judah P. Benjamin,
March 22, 1862[2]

As discussed in Chapter One, no warships were on the Mississippi River or any of its tributaries at the start of the war. The Confederacy acted first to create a river fleet. A converted tug, the CSS *Jackson*, entered Confederate service at New Orleans in June 1861.[3] The Union was not far behind; in May 1861, it started converting three riverboat steamers into timberclad warships. These three warships arrived at Cairo, Illinois, on August 12, 1861, ready for action.[4] However, it took longer to build an ironclad flotilla, and the seven City Class ironclads were not commissioned until the end of January 1862. The more heavily armored *Benton* was started later and not ready until February.[5] These eight ironclads provided the Union Navy with the necessary force to start contesting the control of the Mississippi and its tributaries.

The Union Navy's mission was to assist the Army in securing the Mississippi River and its tributaries. But before that could be done, the

Union had to secure the Ohio River upriver from Cairo. The problem was that Confederate boats could enter the Ohio River by either the Tennessee or Cumberland Rivers and disrupt Union shipping between St. Louis and cities such as Cincinnati and Pittsburgh. An advance down the Mississippi would be pointless if control of the Ohio River was lost. Map I shows this situation quite clearly. In addition, both the Tennessee and Cumberland Rivers were highways leading into the heart of Tennessee and down into Alabama. However, both rivers were guarded by forts—Forts Henry and Donelson—respectively, which had to be captured before an advance up the Tennessee and Cumberland Rivers could continue.

Although the Union flotilla, especially the wooden gunboats, had seen action prior to the attack on Fort Henry, there were doubts about the value of the ironclads and mortar boats. These doubts were amplified when Foote used deployment difficulties—such as the lack of men—to explain why the flotilla could not undertake missions the Army wanted it to do. The Army interpreted this reluctance as an indication of the Navy's unwillingness to take risks. The situation became so bad that Major General Henry Halleck wrote to Major General Don Carlos Buell four days before the attack on Fort Henry, "The mortar boats are a failure; they cannot be taken up the river, and it remains to be determined whether the gunboats are worth half the money spent on them."[6]

Fort Henry was located on the east bank of the Tennessee River about sixty river miles upriver from the junction of the Tennessee and the Ohio Rivers. Due to a lack of Sailors, Foote was only able to take a portion of the flotilla—three timberclad boats and four ironclads—into the battle. Fortunately, Fort Henry was an ideal battle for the Federal flotilla. The boats could approach the fort going upriver with their armored bows facing the enemy's guns. Any disabled vessel would drift away from the fort and back into Union lines. Then, high water in the river flooded portions of Fort Henry. Another advantage was that the Confederate guns would be firing at the same level as the guns on the fleet. This configuration forced the Confederate gunners to fire directly at the ironclads' armor, depriving them of them the advantage of plunging fire.

At the cost of two disabled ironclads, one totally and one partially, and fifty-one casualties (eleven killed, thirty-five wounded, and five missing), the Navy captured Fort Henry on February 6, 1862. In one blow, the Union opened the Tennessee River south into Alabama.[7] The quick and relatively easy victory gave the Union—or, at least the

Army—a false sense of the abilities of the ironclads. Brigadier General Ulysses Grant informed his headquarters in Cairo, "The gunboats have proved themselves well able to resist a severe cannonading."[8] This victory also convinced many of the Confederate generals that the ironclads could defeat any open earthworks. General Albert Sidney Johnston informed Confederate Secretary of War Judah Benjamin, "the best open earthworks are not reliable to meet successfully a vigorous attack of iron-clad gunboats." Johnston went on to say that he believed that the Union gunboats would be able to take Fort Donelson without help from the Army.[9]

However, the battle was not as one sided as Grant and Johnston believed, and not everyone considered the ironclads invincible. One Union ironclad, *Essex*, was completely disabled and had to be towed to Cairo, while a second, the *Cincinnati*, suffered enough damage that almost two weeks were needed to repair her. The *Essex* was disabled when its boiler was hit, forcing it to leave the battle.[10] Because of this damage, ten men died immediately—including both of its pilots—twenty-seven men were scalded—including its captain, William D. Porter—and five men were missing.[11] The number of men who died as a result of being scalded was more than ten, as the five missing men had probably jumped overboard due to the steam and drowned, in addition, some of the men who were seriously scalded died later.[12] The *Cincinnati* was badly damaged, but was able to continue fighting—although its chimneys and pilothouse were completely riddled.[13] In addition, two of its cannon were disabled.[14] Along with the physical damage to the boat, one man was killed and eight were wounded.[15] However, it took thirty-one hits on the *Cincinnati* to cause this damage, but only fifteen hits on the *Essex*. Neither the *St. Louis* nor the *Carondelet* suffered any major damage, although the *St. Louis* was hit seven times and the *Carondelet* was hit six times. However, neither the *St. Louis* nor the *Carondelet* suffered any casualties.[16] The three timberclads, *Conestoga*, *Tyler*, and *Lexington*, participated in the battle, but did not have any Confederate artillery fire directed at them and, thus, did not suffer any damage or casualties. Confederate casualties, excluding prisoners, were fewer than those suffered by the Union Navy, with five killed and sixteen wounded, and some of the men were killed when their cannon exploded. The Confederate commander, Brigadier General Lloyd Tilghman, was aware of the weak points on the ironclads and informed the Confederate authorities in Richmond about them in his report. As he wrote:

> The weak points in all their vessels were known to us, and the cool precision of our firing developed them, showing conclusively that this class of boats, though formidable, can not stand the test of even the 32-pounders, much less the 24-caliber rifled shot, or the 10-inch columbiad. It should be remembered that these results were principally from no heavier metal than the ordinary 32-pounder, using solid shot, fired at point-blank, giving the vessels all the advantages of their peculiar structures, with planes meeting this fire at angles of 45 degrees. The immense area, forming what may be called the roof, is in every respect vulnerable to either a plunging fire from even 32-pounders or a curved line of fire from heavy guns.[17]

However, it is unknown how widely distributed this report was and whether this information was passed on to Confederate artillery units that were on the Mississippi. The next battle the ironclads were involved in—Fort Donelson—would prove both Brigadier General Grant and General Johnston wrong, and Brigadier General Tilghman right.

Although the fighting at Fort Henry was fierce, the war at this time was considered one between gentlemen. This perception is illustrated by the fact that Brigadier General Lloyd Tilghman was allowed to write his report while he was a prisoner and send it on to Richmond, although he arrived there in August 1862, before his report.[18] In addition, Tilghman saw a copy of Foote's telegram announcing the fall of Fort Henry and sent a message to him asking him to correct his statement that there were seventeen mortars in the fort. The same day that Foote received Tilghman's letter, he wrote to Secretary of the Navy Gideon Welles informing him about Tilghman's letter, that he had not addressed mortars in his message to Welles, and that the error must have been made at the printer's office. Foote did inform Welles that there were some errors in his message, though, such as overestimating the number of barracks and tents, and that he had overstated the number of guns in the fort. Foote concluded his message by saying, "I make this statement cheerfully, as I always want to have matters represented in accordance with facts; but, in this instance, General Tilghman fought so gallantly, and his bearing being that of a high-toned gentleman, my respect for him induces me to make this full statement. I see nothing about him but admirable points of character, except his perverted notion about his duties to the Union."[19]

Although Foote thought very highly of Tilghman, the war went on, and about a week later, on February 14—after some needed repairs and additional men—the flotilla, with four ironclads and two timberclads, attacked Fort Donelson and learned some painful lessons. Fort Donelson was located on the west bank of the Cumberland River about seventy river miles from its junction with the Ohio River. Although Fort Donelson was only a few miles overland from Fort Henry, the flotilla had to travel back to the Ohio River, and then steam up the Ohio for about five miles before it could enter the Cumberland River. Fort Donelson's location was very different from Fort Henry's, because some of its protective batteries were situated on a bluff; thus, the Union flotilla lost all but one of the advantages it held at Fort Henry.

Foote's battle plan was the same as the one he had used at Fort Henry, calling for the two timberclads to stay behind the ironclads and fire exploding shells at the enemy. Under this covering fire, the ironclads were to close with the enemy and engage them at short range. But victory was to be denied and, by the time the flotilla withdrew, all four ironclads had been heavily damaged, with the *Pittsburg* in danger of sinking.[20] Even with this extensive damage, Foote believed that if the action had continued for another fifteen minutes, he would have captured both of the forts the fleet was engaging.[21] A very optimistic public belief, especially, as Foote's personal correspondence told a different story. Foote sent a letter to his wife about two weeks after the battle, writing that he "won't run into the fire so again, as a burnt child dreads it."[22] Foote had learned some valuable but painful lessons at Henry and Donelson; in the future, he would be much more cautious about risking his boats against well-placed Confederate cannon.

Foote's men also knew that Foote's public proclamations were not true. Acting Ensign Symmes E. Browne, whose ironclad, the *Mound City,* was not involved in the action, wrote home, "We received word last night from our gunboats at Ft. Donelson, and the news is not in every respect the most cheering."[23] Even Foote's senior officers knew better. After the war, Henry Walke, Captain of the *Carondelet* during the battle, stated in his autobiography, "The fleet did its best, but could not boast of victory, and no friend of the Navy should maintain such unworthy pretensions."[24] Securing the fort was left to Brigadier General Grant and his army, which captured it on February 16, 1862.[25] The capture of the fort, besides being another morale boost for the Union, opened the Cumberland River past Nashville, the capital of Tennessee, allowing the Union to easily capture the city.[26] In addition, the Union was now able to supply its forces in central Tennessee by boat and by railroad.

With the Tennessee and Cumberland Rivers secured, the Navy and Army could turn their attention to the Mississippi. The first significant challenge was a little over fifty river miles downriver from Cairo, where the Confederates had built strong fortifications at Island No. 10.[27] However, before the flotilla could join the Army in the fight, Foote's damaged boats needed repairs. The vulnerable pilothouses, in particular, needed attention. As stated in Chapter Three, strengthening the pilothouses was important because the pilots, whose knowledge of the rivers was crucial to the success of the Navy, refused to rejoin the fleet until the pilothouses were strengthened.[28] All of the boats were strengthened—even those that had not been involved at either Fort Henry or Fort Donelson. The *Mound City* is an example of the extra protection; it had ten additional inches of solid oak placed in front of its pilothouse and new stanchions added between its decks when its engines were repaired in early March.[29]

On March 14, a fleet of seven ironclads and ten mortar boats left Cairo, Illinois, and steamed down to Island No. 10. Foote was more cautious, due to the lessons he had learned at Forts Henry and Donelson. Foote realized that in a battle with shore batteries his boats could easily become disabled. Moreover, at Island No. 10, if boats were disabled, they would drift into Confederate lines and would either be captured or have to be scuttled to avoid capture. His fear of losing his ironclads to the Confederates was so great that, in one instance, he had three of his ironclads lashed together and opened fire from over 2,000 yards. Foote's fear was that if his boats approached closer, their vulnerable bows would be exposed since the rapid current made the boats too unmanageable.[30]

Because of his fears, Foote engaged in a long-range, futile bombardment of the Confederate fortifications. The ineffectiveness was due to faulty fuzes and old cannon. The Navy's fuzes were old and frequently caused premature detonation of the projectiles. Foote informed Gideon Welles, Secretary of the Navy, in one report, "Our shells bursting prematurely, we have to drown them before loading the guns. The fuzes, many of which I am informed were made before the Mexican war, ought to have been condemned." Many of the guns mounted in the ironclads were old guns and included some former smoothbores that had been rifled. These old cannon, especially the ones that had been rifled, had a propensity to burst. During the fighting for Island

No. 10, one rifled gun burst, on the *St. Louis,* killing or wounding fifteen officers and men.[31] It is easy to imagine the impact a bursting cannon would have in the interior of an ironclad boat. Once such an incident occurred, the gun crews would have a tendency to reduce the charges in their guns for their own preservation, even though it meant that the striking power of the projectile would be proportionally reduced.

The situation changed when the Army captured New Madrid, which was downriver from Island No. 10. The seizure of the city allowed the Army to develop a plan to capture Island No. 10. The plan was to cross the Mississippi below the Confederate defenses and to attack the fortifications from the rear. Crossing the river was not an issue, as small unarmed transport steamers were available to ferry the troops across the river. These transports were available because the Union Army had dug a bypass channel around Island No. 10.[32] The problem was that while the Army's artillery had forced Captain George N. Hollins's Confederate squadron to move farther downriver, U.S. Brigadier General John Pope was still concerned that the Confederates would quickly move field artillery batteries to oppose any crossing once they spotted Union preparations to cross the river.[33] Ironclads were needed to silence the Confederate batteries as the river was about a mile wide, and the Army's smooth-bore batteries were not accurate enough at that range to "cover the landing in the face of an enemy with artillery." The hope was that an ironclad would "lie near the opposite shore to prevent the establishment of batteries or the use of field guns against our boats in the crossing."[34] Unfortunately, the bypass channel dug by the Army was not deep enough for the ironclads.[35] As a result, the Army badgered Foote with requests to have at least one of his boats run past the Confederate batteries and join up with the Union Army at New Madrid.[36] Foote was cautious, informing Secretary of the Navy Gideon Welles that "The exposed state of the river above for want of gunboats and troops induces me to act with the greatest caution, as momentous consequences are involved in the issue."[37] On the same day that Foote expressed his concern to Welles, he finally relented, and Captain Henry Walke, commander of the *Carondelet,* volunteered his boat for this hazardous mission.[38]

Efforts were made to increase the odds in favor of the *Carondelet.* First, the Army conducted a successful raid on the night of April 1, spiking some of the Confederate guns.[39] Then, the Confederate floating battery was forced to change positions due to accurate mortar fire.[40] Nevertheless, the Confederate defenses were formidable, and the *Carondelet* would have to run a long and dangerous gauntlet.[41] There was also the problem of navigating the treacherous channel at night. Fortunately, the best pilot in the fleet, William Hoel, who had twenty-one years of experience on the river—with 193 trips to New Orleans—volunteered.[42]

Walke prepared his boat for the attempt by providing protection to the nonarmored sides of the boat, muffling the sounds of the smokestacks, picking a volunteer crew, and adding twenty-three sharpshooters from the 42nd Illinois.[43] On the night of April 4, the *Carondelet*, with a barge lashed to her port (left) side, which was protected by hay bales and loaded with coal, started down river.[44] This night was selected, as it was a dark night, thus decreasing the possibility of the Confederate gunners seeing and hitting the *Carondelet*.[45] The limited visibility had its disadvantages, and there was a very real danger of the *Carondelet* running aground, as Hoel's range of vision, and thus his ability to navigate, was limited. The hope was that frequent lightning would allow Hoel to keep to the channel but not provide sufficient light for the Confederate gunners to accurately fire at the *Carondelet*. The attempt was successful, and the *Pittsburgh* followed two nights later. In the opinion of the Confederate naval commander, Captain George Hollins, the *Carondelet* gave the Union naval superiority below Island No. 10, one that he could not contest.[46] This perceived superiority allowed the Union Army to cross the river and capture the remaining Confederate forces and fortifications on April 7.[47]

One issue left unresolved during the Battle for Island No. 10 was the difference between the Army's and Navy's perception of how the ironclads should be used. The Army understood that the ironclads existed to support Army operations, but the Navy believed that their primary mission was to gain and keep control of the river. This disagreement became a major point of contention when Pope asked that an ironclad run past the fortifications at Island No. 10 to support the Army's river crossing. After the *Carondelet* ran the gauntlet without being hit during the attempt, Pope asked that another ironclad be sent down river.[48] As part of his message to Foote, Pope wrote, "My best artillerists, officers of the Regular Army of many years' service, state positively that it is impossible in the night to fire with any kind of certainty the large guns [32-pounders] of our batteries, especially at a moving object. The guns fired at the *Carondelet* passed 200 feet above her." Pope continued by stating, "With the two boats all is safe; with one, it is uncertain. The lives of the men composing this army are in my keeping, and I do not feel justified in omitting any steps to fortify this movement against any accident which might occasion disaster not to be repaired. Certainly, the risk in a gunboat running down in the night is not nearly so great and involves no such consequences as the risk to 10,000 men crossing a great river in the face of the enemy."[49] Foote had an entirely different view of the situation and was concerned with the safety of his ironclads and his ability to keep Confederate boats from getting upriver past his flotilla. In his reply to Pope's message, Foote stated:

> I can not consider the running of your blockade, where the river is nearly a mile wide and only exposed to a few light guns [not correct as the Union Army had some heavy artillery that was attempting to blockade the Mississippi[50]], at all comparable to running it here, where a boat has not only to pass seven batteries, but has to be kept "head on" to a battery of eleven heavy guns at the head of Island No. 10, and to pass within 300 yards of thirty strong fortifications. If it did not sink the gunboat, we would, in the Navy, consider the gunners totally unfit for employment in the service, and therefore my responsibility for the lives of the officers and men under my charge induces me to decline a request which would, especially without protection to the boat, were the rebels at all competent to perform their duty, result in the sacrifice of the boat, her officers and men, which sacrifice I should not be justified in making-certainly now, when, by your own admission, it will be easy for the new rebel steamers reported to be on their way up the river to pass your batteries in the night, and if they meet my squadron reduced by loss, so as to be unable to cope with them, can continue up the Mississippi or Ohio to St. Louis or to Cincinnati.[51]

The fear of Confederate boats getting upriver from his flotilla was not new, as Foote had written the following message to Welles well prior to the *Carondelet*'s successful passage of Island No. 10: "I shall proceed with caution in our work here, being fully aware of our disadvantages. If, however, any disaster should occur from circumstances beyond my control, I have ordered the ironclad gunboats *Cairo* and *Louisville*, with the wooden boats *Tyler* and *Lexington*, to meet at Cairo, or as far down as Columbus, and even Hickman, to prevent the rebel gunboats from ascending the river beyond Cairo, which place is now so nearly overflowed as to render it necessary for us to remover all our ammunition."[52] This fear would remain a constant worry for all of the commanders of the flotilla as long as a Confederate fleet existed.

The Confederate Navy had not been idle during this time. A regular Navy squadron of six gunboats (*Polk*, *Ivy*, *McRae*, *Jackson*, *Calhoun*, and the floating battery *New Orleans*) was at Columbus, Kentucky, twenty river miles downriver from Cairo, in December.[53] Many of the junior Navy officers urged an attack on Cairo, but because the Union ironclads were not yet fully armed and manned, none was made until mid January, by which time enough ironclads were armed and manned to repulse the attack.[54] It was another lost opportunity for the Confederacy. Yet one more opportunity was squandered when the Union flotilla attacked Fort Henry, and later Fort Donelson, with all of its fully operational ironclads.[55] With all of the operational ironclads gone, Cairo was only defended by the incomplete *Louisville* and some lightly armed Army forts.[56] The Navy was so short handed at Cairo that the Army was expected to provide enough men to temporarily man the ironclads in case of an attack.[57] If an attack had occurred, how effective the soldiers would have been is unclear, as they would have neither been trained nor had any experience operating the heavy cannon on board the ironclads. Consequently, any vigorous attack by the Confederate Navy during this time period would have probably succeeded. Such a success would have had a tremendous impact on the Fort Henry and Donelson campaign as well as on Union shipping on the Mississippi and Ohio Rivers.

The loss of Forts Henry and Donelson made the Confederate high command worry about the safety of its forces at Columbus, Kentucky. The concern was that the Union would be able to isolate the Confederate forces at Columbus and force their surrender.[58] Consequently, it was decided that a stronger naval force was needed on the upper Mississippi, and Flag-Officer George N. Hollins was ordered to leave New Orleans on February 19. He was instructed to take all of his forces to Memphis and, if there were no orders for him there, to continue on to Columbus, Kentucky.[59] Hollins took the *Pontchartrain* and *Ivy* with him, although the *Maurapus* and *Livingston* would later join the squadron.[60] Even with these naval reinforcements, Major-General Leonidas Polk received orders to evacuate Columbus and establish a defensive position down river. The evacuation was completed on March 2, 1862, and Polk selected Island No. 10 as the Confederacy's next defensive position on the Mississippi.[61]

As a consequence of the loss of Columbus, the Confederate squadron was stationed at New Madrid, and assisted the Confederate Army in defending it. Once the Confederate commanders realized that New Madrid would fall, the Confederate fleet evacuated the Confederate troops located there.[62] Hollins stayed close to New Madrid until Union batteries were constructed to challenge the Confederate boats. After suffering some damage from these batteries, Hollins moved farther downriver to protect his boats from the Union guns. Hollins informed General Beauregard that he felt "the preservation of these boats is of the last importance to our country, and am therefore unwilling to risk their loss or being crippled by the guns of the land forces of the enemy except in the last extremity."[63] Naval commanders on both sides apparently felt that the preservation of their boats was one of their primary concerns—a perspective that Army commanders did not have.

Although Hollins's squadron was downriver from Island No. 10, he was still able to keep in contact and supply the Confederate units there by running one of his boats past the Union batteries to Tiptonville.[64] His wooden boats could manage this maneuver more easily than the Union boats could run the Confederate batteries. The difference was that the river was about a mile wide near Tiptonville—compared to the narrow channel near Island No. 10—and that the Confederate boats were faster than the Union ironclads.

Unfortunately for the Confederacy, Hollins did not take advantage of his superior numbers when the *Carondelet* ran past Island No. 10. This was another lost opportunity for the Confederate Navy as the Battle of Plum Point would clearly demonstrate that Hollins's boats were more than capable of sinking or capturing the *Carondelet*. The ability of the Confederate boats to sink or capture the *Carondelet* would have been especially true when it was isolated from the rest of the Union flotilla. Even the addition of the *Pittsburgh*, two nights later, would not have materially changed the odds. Although Hollins was a brave man, he was a former US Navy career officer who believed in the power of gunfire rather than ramming. What makes this lost opportunity even more ironic was that the bows of his boats were plated with iron.[65] Hollin's traditional naval background—along with the fear many Confederates had of the Union ironclads—prevented him from attacking the isolated Union boats, even though some of his officers encouraged him to do so.[66]

Stephen Mallory, Confederate Secretary of the Navy, also encouraged Hollins to act when he wrote to him on April 8, the day after Island No. 10 fell, stating, "Strike a blow when and where you can; the harder the better." Hollins justified his inaction in a return message to Mallory, in which he stated, "These boats of the enemy are heavy iron gunboats, either one of which is heavier than all of mine. Have passed Island No. 10. I see nothing that I can do against them in a fight."[67] Hollins also asked for permission to take his squadron to New Orleans based on messages from Captain William Whittle, CSN, about the threat to New Orleans. Mallory refused his request, informing Hollins that his "duty is to do all in your power to resist the enemy's descent of the river."[68] However, Hollins disobeyed orders, and steamed down to New Orleans on the *Ivy* on April 11, leaving Commander Robert F. Pinkney—who was on leave in Memphis—in command of the fleet with orders that the *McRae* was to join him at New Orleans once Pinkney rejoined the squadron.[69] Hollins felt that the enemy would not go past Fort Pillow, and that he could defeat the Union squadron threatening New Orleans once the squadron had entered the river. However, Mallory probably assumed that the Union squadron could not safely get past Forts Jackson and Saint Philip; therefore, he felt that Memphis was under the greater threat. As a result, neither New Orleans nor the upper Mississippi was adequately defended by the Confederate Navy.

After the capture of Island No. 10, Foote left New Madrid on April 12, and steamed about fifty miles down river, where he met General Pope and his army on the April 13. Later that morning, a short action took place against the Confederate squadron—now under the temporary command of Lieutenant Thomas Huger— ending with the Confederates retreating to the protective guns of Fort Pillow.[70] Following the retreating Confederates, the Union flotilla stopped before it came within accurate range of the heavy guns at Fort Pillow, and anchored between Plum Point and Craighead Point. Pope and Foote immediately began preparations for attacking the fort.[71]

At Fort Pillow, the regular Confederate squadron was joined by Montgomery's River Defense Fleet, with each ram arriving as soon as its conversion was completed. Montgomery was on the last ram, and he arrived on April 22. Although Montgomery's original plan of attacking the Union flotilla at Cairo was no longer feasible, the only real change to his plan was the location where the Union fleet was to be attacked. Montgomery made a reconnaissance of the Union flotilla on April 23, the day after he arrived at Fort Pillow, but, "discovered they were in an unfavorable position to attack."[72] He continued making reconnaissances, hoping to find an opportunity for his fleet to attack the Union boats. Montgomery's aggressiveness was in sharp contrast to the passive defense the regular Confederate Navy had been conducting.

Prior to Montgomery's arrival, General M. Jeff Thompson and his mixed force of artillerymen and infantry had joined the River Defense Fleet to man the guns and provide sharpshooters.[73] The extra men were needed because, until then, the crews were only large enough to operate the boats and, as previously stated, had no knowledge of operating artillery pieces. Thompson was a parallel commander to Montgomery, and corresponded directly with General Beauregard, Montgomery's superior. On May 4, Thompson updated General Beauregard, informing him, "We are patiently awaiting the turn of events, and do not see much prospect for a fight at the present time. The enemy have changed their position since I came here, and keep their gunboats on each side of the river in a position to command a long stretch, where we can not reach them without being under a cross fire for from forty to fifty minutes."[74]

Both Thompson and Montgomery tried to get Commander Robert F. Pinkney—the commander of the regular Confederate squadron—to join them in an attack. They wanted his boats, with their heavy guns, as they were afraid that Union boats would move into water too shallow for the rams to strike them. If the Union boats maneuvered in such a way, then Pinkney's boats could still engage them. Pinkney refused, stating that his boats were not strong enough to have a gunnery battle with the ironclads, and that it would be murder to make such an attempt. Pinkney's remarks spread throughout Montgomery's River Defense Fleet, adversely affecting morale. It took Montgomery and Thompson a few days to rebuild the morale of their men.[75] When news of the fall of New Orleans reached the fleet, morale was devastated once more, as many of the men were from New Orleans. Again, it took some days to rebuild the morale of the men; finally, by the end of the first week in May, the fleet was prepared to attack.[76]

Pinkney was uncooperative with the River Defense Fleet, refusing to acknowledge the coming battle and position his boats to provide assistance in case of disaster. He withdrew his boats downriver prior to the battle so that they were at Fort Randolph, about ten miles downriver from Fort Pillow when the battle occurred.[77] Then, at the suggestion of Major-General Gustave Beaurgard, he took the guns off the *Polk* and *Livingston* and mounted them in Fort Randolph at the beginning of May.[78] He also sent the *Maurepas* up the White River and the *Pontchartrain* up the Arkansas River.[79] Pinkney's command was in such disgrace that when Lieutenant Charles Read was ordered to join Pinkney's command after the fall of New Orleans and the loss of the *McRae*—the boat to which he was assigned—he was ashamed to tell anyone that he was on his way to join it.[80] When Read joined the fleet, he was given command of two of the heavy guns from the *Polk* and *Livingston* that had been mounted on a bluff below Fort Randolph.[81] Upon hearing that Fort Pillow had been evacuated, Pinkney immediately left, leaving his heavy guns behind.[82] Luckily for the Confederacy, Lieutenant Sardine Graham Stone disobeyed Pinkney's orders and saved two of the heavy guns, which were put to good use at St. Charles when one of them disabled the *Mound City*.[83] Read's contempt for Pinkney was so great that in his reminiscences he refers to him as the "Artful Dodger."[84]

Foote and Pope had not been idle during this time. Upon reaching Plum Point, the two men agreed on a replay of their successful maneuver at Island No. 10, but this time half of the ironclads would run past Fort Pillow during a dark and stormy night. Once past the fort, the ironclads would transport Pope's army across the river, where it would assault the fort from the rear. If this plan failed, then a canal would be cut on the Arkansas side deep enough for the ironclads to use. Neither plan was ever executed because General Halleck ordered Pope's army to join him for operations against Corinth, Mississippi, a few days before the Fort Pillow operation was to take place.[85] In many respects, this decision was a good one, for if Corinth fell both Fort Pillow and Memphis would become untenable. Foote was also not aware of the capabilities of the Confederate rams, and even informed Secretary of the Navy Gideon Welles that "With the exception of this latter vessel [CSS *Louisiana*], however, we have little to apprehend from the other rebel gunboats."[86] If any or half of his ironclads had run past Fort Pillow, they would have been extremely vulnerable to attack by the rams stationed there. The rams would have been especially dangerous, as they would have had the additional speed of the current from attacking upriver. However, the loss of Pope's men delayed the capture of Fort Pillow and Memphis as Halleck moved at a very slow pace, and Cornith was not captured until the end of May, after the Battle of Plum Point.

Halleck left Foote two infantry regiments.[87] These two regiments were neither sufficient for assaulting Fort Pillow nor had the skill or equipment to dig a canal for the ironclads to bypass Fort Pillow.[88] Also, the bluffs upon which the Confederate batteries were located were higher than the guns on the ironclads could be elevated when they were close to the fort. Foote was left with no real option but to bombard

Fort Pillow with his mortars. The north side of Craighead Point provided an excellent firing position for the mortar rafts. At that location, they could safely anchor out of direct fire from the guns at Fort Pillow while Fort Pillow would still be within easy range of the mortars.

By this time, Foote had become more cautious, and informed Secretary of the Navy Gideon Welles on April 26 that "The defenseless state of the river above leads me to be more cautious than I otherwise should be in the attack on Fort Pillow." However, Foote did add that while he would be willing to run past Fort Pillow, he was afraid that even if the Navy could force the Confederates to abandon their guns, there was still not enough Union infantry available to hold the fort.[89] Foote was also anxious for reinforcements, and ordered Lieutenant Wilson McGunnegle to go to Cincinnati and Pittsburg for information on the status of any boats being converted to gunboats or rams to include when they would be ready for service.[90]

Foote was well aware that the Confederates wanted to attack his flotilla, informing Secretary Welles on April 30 of this likelihood and of the other difficulties he faced:

> I have the honor to inform the Department that, from information deemed reliable, the rebels have thirteen gunboats and rams [note: Confederates actually had 12 boats, eight Montgomery rams and four regular CSA navy boats under Pinkney] a few miles below Fort Pillow, and that on the 27th instant, at 3 a.m., an attack was contemplated by those boats on the flotilla, and preparations made accordingly. The attack, however, has not taken place. The reason assigned for its delay, or abandonment, as given by several deserters, is that a council of war was held and the rebels concluded the attack was impracticable. We are prepared for an attack at any moment, but unless there is an additional number of rebel gunboats reinforcing them, I question whether the attack will be made. Should it be made, however, our position here is a bad one, as our slow steamers can hardly stem the current, and in grappling with the enemy we should drift under the guns of the fort, which are but 4 or 5 miles below the upper gunboats. In view of this, there are strong reasons for our taking the initiative, and in a dark night, by running the blockade, get below the fort and attack the rebel boats and rams with our seven ironclad gunboats. I should much prefer this course, and our officers and

> men are ready for the hazardous service, which if successful, would enable us to turn from below, after destroying rebel fleet, and attack the fort upstream, and afterwards proceed to Memphis.
>
> On the other hand, the objections are that in running the blockade we might leave one or two rebel steamers behind us, which would come up to destroy our transports, mortar boats, and command the river above us, soon leaving us without coal or ammunition below; and, added to this we have but 1,200 troops, a portion, or one regiment of which, a military officer of rank informs me, is not in all respects efficient, and thus the force is not equal to holding the place, while we should proceed on to Memphis; and again, if disaster should occur to us, the rebel gunboats would have complete possession of the river or rivers above us, as I believe that No. 10 is (has) not even yet had its guns mounted to command the river, although I have strongly urged it. Had General Pope not been ordered away with his 20,000 troops, we should, before this, humanly speaking, (have) been in possession of Fort Pillow and Memphis, and even had the general left a sufficient number of troops under General Buford, who so effectually cooperated with me at No. 10 and wanted to remain with me with his 2,000 men, we would have been able to do more than we can do now, although Colonel Fitch is an officer of the highest intelligence and gallantry, but wants more men.
>
> The Department will see from this statement the difficulties and embarrassment of my position.[91]

Foote was facing the same problems and fears that all of the future Navy commanders on the river would face: the ironclads' lack of power and a Confederate warship getting upriver of the Union flotilla. While the gunboats' lack of power was a problem that would not be solved, the solution to protecting the river was to leave warships behind to guard the navigable tributaries; however, this scenario would obviously weaken the offensive capability of the flotilla.

Because of all of the Confederate activity, at the beginning of May, Foote reemphasized General Orders No. 4: Commanders must ensure that their boats are ready for battle at a moment's warning.[92] His stress on readiness was justified, as on the morning of May 8, the *Sumter*,

Bragg, and *Van Dorn* steamed up river to attack the mortar boats, possibly hoping to capture some of them. Fortunately, the mortar boats had not yet moved into their normal position by Craighead Point and were still near Plum Point, where the ironclads were anchored. The *Sumter* remained near Craighead Point until late in the morning, as its captain, William Lamb, hoped that at least one of the mortar boats would to move to where he could attack it. However, the mortar boats did not move into firing position that day until after the *Sumter* had returned to its anchorage near Fort Pillow.[93] Union officers viewed this incident as a minor engagement because only a few shots were fired, and no damage was done to any of the boats.[94]

Confederate activity continued, and on May 9, a Confederate boat, under a flag of truce, steamed up to the Union flotilla to return two paroled Union surgeons. Although returning parolees was normal, many of the officers and men in the Union flotilla felt, in retrospect, that the real object was to determine the exact positions of the Union boats.[95] It is likely that the officers on board the Confederate boat did note the positions of the Union boats, although no such record exists in Confederate reports.

Foote was having additional problems, as he was still suffering from the foot injury he had received at Fort Donelson. His injury had become so severe that he requested temporary relief from command, asking that Captain Charles H. Davis—whom Foote felt was the best qualified officer to command the gunboats in his absence—replace him until he recovered.[96] Lieutenant-Commander S. Leyard Phelps, commander of the *Benton*, was considered, but Foote felt that because he was a young officer, officers who ranked him would get jealous.[97] Foote's request was approved and, on May 9, he temporarily turned over command of the flotilla to Captain Davis.[98]

The very evening that Davis took command, Montgomery and his commanders were discussing whether to attack. Thompson advocated steaming through the Union flotilla at night to attack its transports, but Montgomery's captains, as experienced Mississippi River steamboat pilots and captains, opposed his idea. They were against Thompson's plan, because they knew that the Confederate boats could easily ram each other or run aground as they went upriver in the dark—assuming they survived running the gauntlet of the Union ironclads.[99] After further discussion, they decided to attack the Union boats in a column formation with the fastest boats taking the lead, and the fleet leaving its anchorage at 6:00 the next morning.[100]

Chapter 5

The Battle of Plum Point

Hope ere long you will be able to test with success the efficiency of your boats, which are now the last hope of closing the river to the enemy's gunboats.

—Message from General Pierre G. T. Beauregard to General M. Jeff Thompson, 4 May 1862[1]

We had a smart affair this morning before breakfast.

—Letter from Commodore Charles H. Davis to his wife[2]

The Battle of Plum Point was the first naval squadron engagement of the war, and lasted somewhere between thirty and sixty minutes.[3] Because of the brevity of the battle and the relatively few boats involved, determining what happened is not difficult. Still, after any battle, conflicting reports emerge about what occurred, with frequent exaggerations of the amount of damage done to the enemy, especially in the newspapers. The Battle of Plum Point is no exception. In this case, the Confederate reports are more accurate, although substantially fewer in numbers, than Union reports. In addition, Union and Confederate veterans' memoirs provide information on the battle, although with variations on what happened. As with any battle, what happened at Plum Point depended on the observer's location and perspective. Also, controversy soon erupted around the actions various Union commanders did and did not take.

In *Life on the Mississippi,* Mark Twain describes the Mississippi River around Plum Point and Craighead Point as a formidable place to navigate.[4] Commodore Montgomery agreed with his opinion, writing prior to the battle, "The position occupied by the enemy's gunboats above Fort Pillow offers more obstacles to our mode of attack than any other between Cairo and New Orleans."[5] The problem was that the river made a number of sharp bends upriver from Fort Pillow, resulting in numerous sandbars and snags. At Plum Point, the channel had split in two creating an island, but after rounding the point, the two channels combined and moved to the Arkansas side. Then, after rounding Craighead Point, the channel shifted to the Tennessee side flowing past Fort Pillow. A Union newspaper correspondent on board the *St. Louis* described the area as "probably the most difficult place in the Mississippi to navigate. The channel here is constantly changing, and new bars are yearly thrown up in which immense amounts of drift collect and become imbedded, rendering navigation extremely difficult. The Arkansas shore makes a bold sweep here, running down to a narrow point, behind which is the first Chickasaw Bluff, six miles below us."[6] Any naval battle fought here would be one with limited maneuvering.

For the Union, the section of river between Plum Point and Craighead Point was a good one; here, the river offered a location where their mortar boats could fire at Fort Pillow and be protected from direct return fire from the fort. Plus, the gunboats and the support boats could tie up to the shore—upriver from where the mortars were firing—and be safe from Fort Pillow's heavy artillery, although Confederate gunners tried to hit them.[7] For the Confederates, as noted by Montgomery, the narrow channel and numerous bars restricted maneuverability while

Present-day location of the Battle of Plum Point. Photograph by the author, March 2010.

the shallow draft Union boats could utilize more of the channel. The location favored the Union.

The morning of May 10 was pleasant but hazy, with the sun rising shortly after 5:00.[8] It would have taken a while longer for sunlight to reach the boats, because the Confederate fleet had bluffs to the east, and the trees lining the banks would have blocked the light from the Union fleet. The morning haze limited visibility, in addition to making the smoke from the boats' stacks and gun smoke from the mortars hovered above the surface of the river. These factors, plus the fact that the Union lookouts would have been looking into the sun, gave the Confederate fleet the opportunity to steam closer to the Union fleet than it could have had it made its approach later in the day. Another problem for both sides was that the river was high, having overflowed its banks and flooded the surrounding land, which was thickly covered with timber and brush. The high water would have also increased the speed of the current beyond the five miles per hour noted in the reminiscences of Henry Walke, captain of the *Carondelet*. The increased flow would have made the Union boats less maneuverable and lessened the impact speed of the Confederate rams if they rammed going upriver.[9]

Present-day scene of how the flooded riverbank would have looked during the Battle of Plum Point. Photograph by the author, March 2010.

The men of the Union fleet started the morning of May 10 like most of the other mornings spent at Plum Point. Mortar Boat No. 16, commanded by Second Master Thomas B. Gregory, USN, was towed to its firing position, about four miles downriver from the rest of the flotilla, on the Arkansas side of the river just above Craighead Point.[10] It was accompanied by its guard boat, the *Cincinnati,* commanded by Commander Roger N. Stembel, with the *Cincinnati* moored just upriver from the mortar boat.[11] At 6:00 a.m., the mortar boat commenced firing at Fort Pillow.[12] The remainder of the ironclads stayed where they had spent the night with the *Benton*, *Carondelet*, and *Pittsburg* tied to the Tennessee side of the river, and the *Mound City*, *St. Louis*, and *Cairo* tied to the Arkansas side of the river.[13] The rest of the flotilla—all of the supporting boats—was moored upriver from the ironclads.[14]

The Confederates had spent the night preparing for the battle. Duties aboard each boat were divided between Montgomery's riverboat men and Thompson's Soldiers. Thompson's men would man the guns and serve as sharpshooters, allowing the steamboat men to operate the boats. Written instructions were given to each boat's captain covering possible contingencies, as they "were not experienced enough in Signals [*sic*] to rely upon them in the smoke of Battle [*sic*]."[15] Having excellent knowledge of the daily activities of the Union fleet, Montgomery ordered that the fleet was to start upriver precisely at 6:00 a.m., unless the picket boat signaled that the Union fleet had changed its position. The Confederate battle plan was "to cut out a gunboat which for the past two days has been guarding the mortar boat."[16] The boats were forced to go single file due to the narrowness of the channel at that part of the river. The order of the boats was based on the speed of the boat, with the fastest boats in the front: *General Bragg*, *Sumter*, *General Price*, *General Van Dorn*, *General Beauregard*, *Colonel Lovell*, and the *General M. Jeff Thompson*.[17] The *Little Rebel*, the flagship, did not have a fixed location, as it was expected to go where needed. It was probably positioned in the middle of the column, where Montgomery could best control the fleet. Montgomery probably put the fastest boats in front because he wanted to achieve surprise. He knew that if the slowest boats were in the lead, the Union boats would have more time to react.[18]

Sometime between 6:25 and 6:30 a.m.—after Gregory's mortar boat had fired five shells—men on board both the *Cincinnati* and the mortar boat saw the masts and smoke from the stacks of the leading Confederate rams before they came around Craighead Point.[19] Men on both boats were able to see the Confederate boats at about the same time because the taller *Cincinnati* was moored upriver from the much smaller and lower mortar boat. Confederate surprise was complete, as the crew of the *Cincinnati* was involved in doing routine tasks. Some of the *Cincinnati*'s crew were busy scrubbing the deck with soft sandstone, known as holy-stoning, while others were writing letters home.[20] It was a hurried beat to quarters. Besides the crew doing routine work, steam was not adequate to fully maneuver the boat, and the engineers were forced to throw "oil and everything else inflammable into her fires that the necessary head of steam might be obtained to handle the boat."[21] For their part, as soon as they rounded Craighead Point and saw the enemy, the Confederate captains ordered their engineers to open every valve on their engines so they could get maximum speed from their boat.[22]

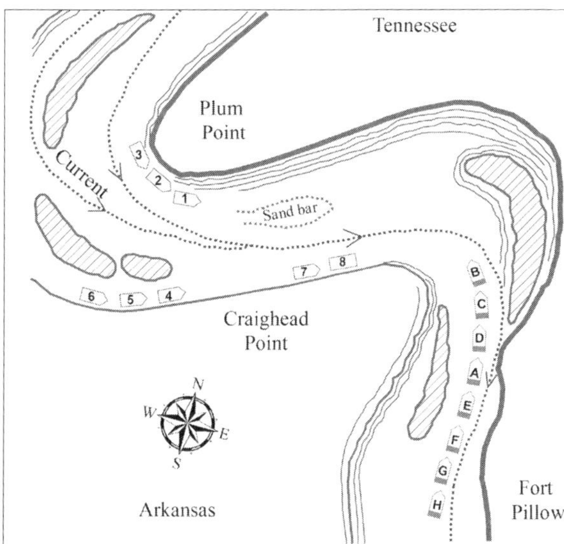

Not to Scale

	United States Boats		Confederate States Boats
1	*Benton (Flag Ship)*	A	*Little Rebel (Flag ship)*
2	*Carondelet*	B	*General Bragg*
3	*Pittsburg*	C	*Sumter*
4	*Mount City*	D	*General Price*
5	*St. Louis*	E	*General Van Dorn*
6	*Cairo*	F	*General Beauregard*
7	*Cincinnati*	G	*Colonel Lovell*
8	*Mortar Boat*	H	*General M. Jeff Thompson*

Battle of Plum Point: Sighting of the Confederate Fleet.

At about this same time, some of the men on the ironclads moored to the north bank saw the smoke from the stacks of the Confederate boats. Based on that information, the drums beat the men to quarters. Commodore Davis on the *Benton* ordered that the signal be passed to all boats to get under way.[23] There was some delay, as the boats—according to naval discipline—could not go into battle before the commanders received a signal from the flotilla commander, Commodore Davis, nor could they be in front of the flagship when going into battle.[24] Still, the *Carondelet*, commanded by Commander Henry Walke, having its steam up, quickly slipped its hawser and headed down river.[25] As the *Carondelet* passed the *Benton*, Commodore Davis ordered Walke not to wait but to go immediately to the aid of the *Cincinnati*.[26] However, not all of the boats were as quick as the *Carondelet* as, in disobedience of standing orders, neither the *Benton*, *Pittsburg*, and *St. Louis*, nor the

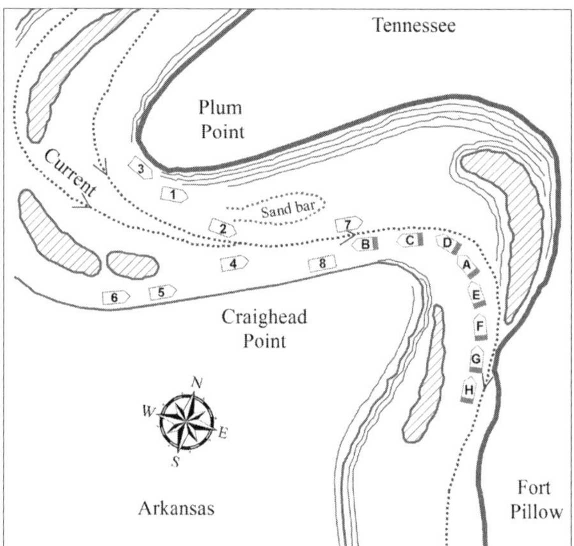

	United States Boats		Confederate States Boats
1	*Benton (Flag Ship)*	A	*Little Rebel (Flag ship)*
2	*Carondelet*	B	*General Bragg*
3	*Pittsburg*	C	*Sumter*
4	*Mount City*	D	*General Price*
5	*St. Louis*	E	*General Van Dorn*
6	*Cairo*	F	*General Beauregard*
7	*Cincinnati*	G	*Colonel Lovell*
8	*Mortar Boat*	H	*General M. Jeff Thompson*

Battle of Plum Point: Initial Phase.

Cairo had its steam up.[27] In addition, the signal could not be seen on the other side of the river due to the calm air and haze. Fortunately, someone on the *Mound City* spotted the Confederate rams, and the *Mound City* got under way about the same time as the *Carondelet*, even before its captain, Commander Augustus Kilty, saw the signal from Davis.[28] Richard Birch, first pilot on the *Benton*, used a speaking trumpet to hail the other boats to convey Davis' orders to their captains. [29] It was a bad start for the Union.

Commander Stembel reacted quickly, and the *Cincinnati* cast off, even before it had enough steam to maneuver, and drifted with the current to meet the onrushing Confederates. Once the Confederate rams were within range, the *Cincinnati* fired its bow guns—to no effect.[30] The *Bragg*, the leading Confederate boat, under the command of Captain William H. Leonard, steamed up the main channel on the Arkansas side of the river past the *Cincinnati*. Once there, Leonard turned his boat back toward the *Cincinnati*, maneuvering to avoid the *Cincinnati*'s cannon fire.[31] With General Thompson on board, the *Bragg*, going at full speed and assisted by the river current, struck the Union gunboat immediately after the *Cincinnati* had turned toward it to avoid being rammed in its vulnerable stern.[32] Due to this maneuver, the *Bragg* hit the *Cincinnati* on its starboard quarter (right rear of the boat) just behind the shell room, crushing in that side of the boat, filling the shell room with water, and knocking down all of the crew and anything loose.[33] The impact was so powerful that it spun the *Cincinnati* 180 degrees, with the *Bragg* following along. The *Cincinnati* was now headed toward the Tennessee shore, and the *Bragg* was headed toward the Arkansas shore.[34] While the boats circled each other, the crew of the *Cincinnati* went back to their posts and fired a broadside into the *Bragg* at point-blank range.[35] The projectiles went through the *Bragg* and, while starting a fire, only did superficial damage, although one man was killed.[36] However, one of *Cincinnati's* projectiles damaged the *Bragg's* tiller rope, and the boat drifted down river out of control until the rope could be repaired.[37] This loss of control, as well as the smoke coming off of the *Bragg* from the fire, gave Union officers the mistaken impression that the *Bragg* was mortally wounded.

Immediately after being struck by the *Bragg*, the *General Price* and *Sumter* rammed the *Cincinnati*. The *General Price*, commanded by First Officer Thomas Henthorne, received two broadsides from the *Cincinnati*'s two stern guns as it approached, but the damage was minimal, and the *General Price* struck the *Cincinnati* on the starboard side

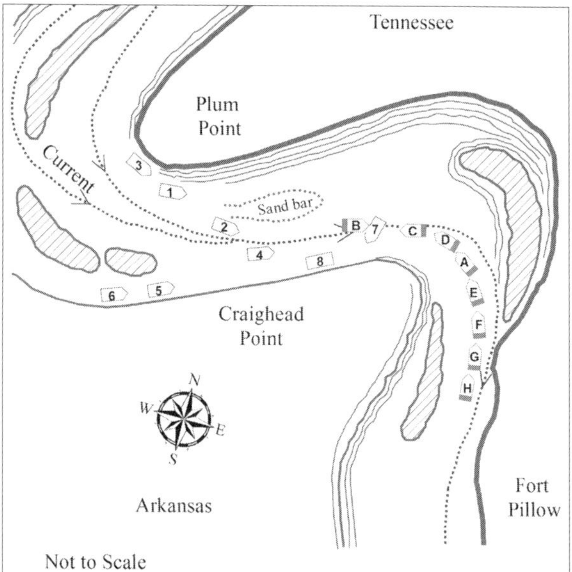

	United States Boats		Confederate States Boats
1	*Benton (Flag Ship)*	A	*Little Rebel (Flag ship)*
2	*Carondelet*	B	*General Bragg*
3	*Pittsburg*	C	*Sumter*
4	*Mount City*	D	*General Price*
5	*St. Louis*	E	*General Van Dorn*
6	*Cairo*	F	*General Beauregard*
7	*Cincinnati*	G	*Colonel Lovell*
8	*Mortar Boat*	H	*General M. Jeff Thompson*

Battle of Plum Point: Ramming of the *Cincinnati* by the *General Bragg*.

just behind where the *Bragg* had rammed it.[38] The damage was substantial, with one of the *Cincinnati's* rudders and part of its stern torn off.[39] The *Cincinnati* was rapidly sinking; as the *Sumter* approached, its commander, Captain William Lamb, offered to save the crew if they would haul down their flag.[40] The response was: "Our flag will go down when we do!"[41] The *Sumter* then rammed the *Cincinnati*'s port side of the fantail (left rear of the boat), inflicting additional damage. In the meantime, Stemble had been seriously wounded by a musket shot fired by one of the "skulking crew secreted behind the barricade of cotton bales" from either the *General Price* or *Sumter*.[42] With the *Cincinnati* rapidly sinking, Acting Lieutenant William R. Hoel, who had assumed command as Stemble was partially paralyzed, ordered that the Cincinnati be run aground on one of the sandbars on the Tennessee side of the river—the direction the boat was headed.[43] Although the *Cincin-*

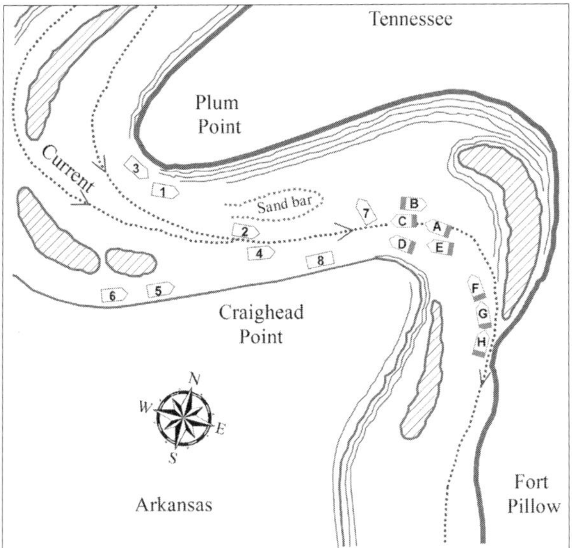

	United States Boats		Confederate States Boats
1	*Benton (Flag Ship)*	A	*Little Rebel (Flag ship)*
2	*Carondelet*	B	*General Bragg*
3	*Pittsburg*	C	*Sumter*
4	*Mount City*	D	*General Price*
5	*St. Louis*	E	*General Van Dorn*
6	*Cairo*	F	*General Beauregard*
7	*Cincinnati*	G	*Colonel Lovell*
8	*Mortar Boat*	H	*General M. Jeff Thompson*

Battle of Plum Point: The Union Flotilla Reacts.

nati did not get into water as shallow as Hoel would have liked, it was shallow enough that the hurricane deck remained above water, and it was there and on the wheelhouse that the crew found refuge.[44] Fortunately for the *Cincinnati*, the water was too shallow for the Confederate rams so the *Cincinnati* was not rammed againas; another ramming would likely have completed its destruction. In addition, the *Mound City* and the *Carondelet* were close enough to draw the attention of the Confederate rams.

Although the other ironclads were not able to immediately help the *Cincinnati*, Gregory and his crew did by continuously firing their mortar at the Confederate boats.[45] They were able to do so by adjusting the mortar so that the projectiles were being fired almost vertically. Although they would not have been able to fire at the boats that were close to them, Gregory and his crew could easily fire at the boats that

Battle of Fort Pillow, 1st Position. Confederate ships, seen at right, include (*left to right*) the *General Earl Van Dorn*, *General Sterling Price*, *General Bragg*, *General Sumter*, and *Little Rebel.* It should be noted that none of the Confederate boats had a bow gun in this battle. The Federal ironclads, in the center and left, are (*left to right*) the *Mound City*, *Carondelet*, and *Cincinnati.* A Federal mortar boat is by the riverbank in the lower right. Courtesy of the Naval Historical Foundation, NH 2049.

were a quarter mile or farther away. While the mortar shells did little damage to the Confederate boats, they had a psychological impact. Montgomery stated in his after action report that the mortar boat "was filling the air with its terrible missiles."[46] Although destroying the mortar boat was not one of the Confederate fleet's objectives, its firing drew attention to it, and at least the *Price* and *Van Dorn* fired at it. Captain Issac D. Fulkerson, commander of the *Van Dorn*, had kept close to the Arkansas shore—the same side of the river as the mortar boat. Consequently, he was able to fire his 32-pounder at close range a number of times at the mortar boat as the *Van Dorn* passed by. Two of the projectiles went through the lightly armored boat; surprisingly, neither the projectiles nor the small arms fire directed at the mortar boat injured any of the fifteen men on board.[47]

After ten to fifteen minutes, the *Mound City* and *Carondelet* got close enough to assist the *Cincinnati* and distract Confederate attention away from her, even though both boats had already been firing their bow guns at long range at the Confederate boats.[48] The *Van Dorn*, after firing at the mortar boat, charged toward the leading ironclad, the *Mound City*. The *Mound City* fired continuous broadsides at the *Van*

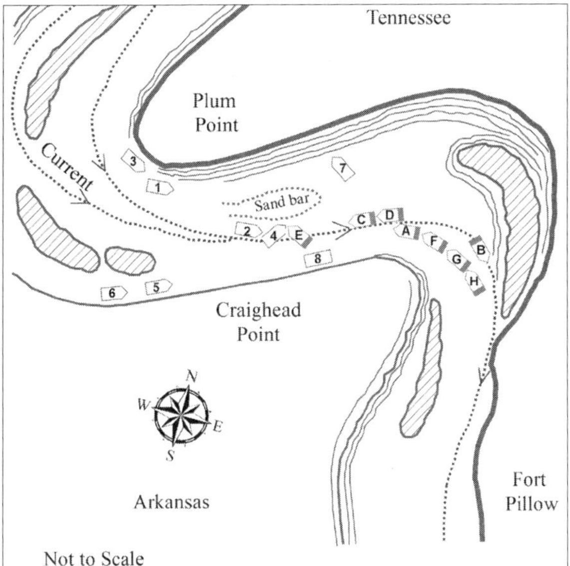

United States Boats		Confederate States Boats	
1	*Benton (Flag Ship)*	A	*Little Rebel (Flag ship)*
2	*Carondelet*	B	*General Bragg*
3	*Pittsburg*	C	*Sumter*
4	*Mount City*	D	*General Price*
5	*St. Louis*	E	*General Van Dorn*
6	*Cairo*	F	*General Beauregard*
7	*Cincinnati*	G	*Colonel Lovell*
8	*Mortar Boat*	H	*General M. Jeff Thompson*

Battle of Plum Point: Ramming of the *Mound City* by the *General Van Dorn.*

Dorn, but they did little damage, and at the last minute, the *Mound City* sheared away in an attempt to avoid being rammed by the *Van Dorn.*[49] The result of this maneuver was that the *Van Dorn* rammed the *Mound City* about four feet from the bow on the starboard side (right front). The impact was so great that the *Mound City* was turned around while the *Van Dorn* continued straight ahead and ran aground on the Tennessee side of the river.[50] The damage done to the *Mound City* was extensive, as its bow was almost completely wrenched off.[51] The Van Dorn was in trouble, too: While the crew of the *Van Dorn* was trying to free the boat, the *Mound City, Carondelet, Benton, Pittsburg,* and *St. Louis* were directing cannon fire at it, with some projectiles from the *Pittsburg* and *St. Louis* exploding above the other Union boats.[52] Luckily for the crew of the *Van Dorn*, the few projectiles that hit their

Battle of Fort Pillow, 3rd Position. Confederate ships, seen at left, include the *Colonel Lovell*, *General Beauregard*, *General M. Jeff Thompson*, *General Bragg*, *General Sumter*, *Little Rebel* and *General Earl Van Dorn*. The Federal ironclads, in the center and right, include the *Carondelet*, *Cincinnati*, *Mound City*, *Benton*, *Saint Louis*, *Cairo,* and *Pittsburg*. A tug is seen in the right foreground. Courtesy of the Naval Historical Foundation, NH 42755.

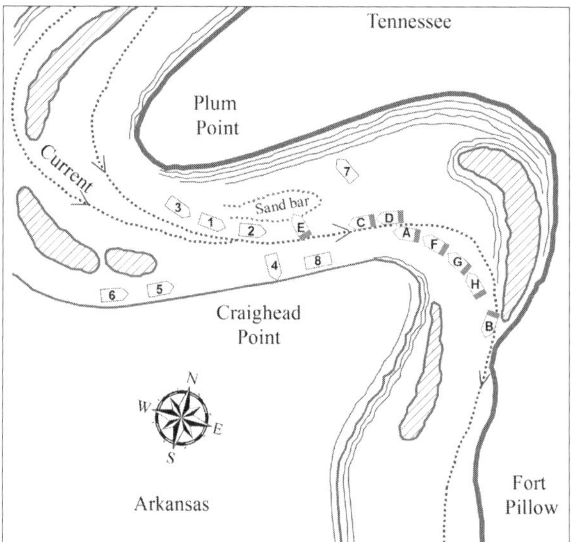

Not to Scale

	United States Boats		Confederate States Boats
1	*Benton (Flag Ship)*	A	*Little Rebel (Flag ship)*
2	*Carondelet*	B	*General Bragg*
3	*Pittsburg*	C	*Sumter*
4	*Mount City*	D	*General Price*
5	*St. Louis*	E	*General Van Dorn*
6	*Cairo*	F	*General Beauregard*
7	*Cincinnati*	G	*Colonel Lovell*
8	*Mortar Boat*	H	*General M. Jeff Thompson*

Battle of Plum Point: Arrival of the Main Union Force.

boat went through it, and only one man was killed and the captain wounded. By this time, the haze and the smoke created by the cannon fire made it very difficult to distinguish vessels more than a quarter of a mile away.[53] Once the *Van Dorn* was free of the sandbar, it retreated toward the rest of the Confederate fleet, because there were now four Union ironclads between it and the rest of the Confederate fleet.[54]

Commodore Montgomery, whose boat the *Little Rebel* had been in the thick of the action, observed that the Union ironclads were staying in water too shallow for his rams, and that the majority of the Union fleet was beginning to get into close range. Consequently, he signaled his fleet to fall back, even though his three heaviest and largest boats were just arriving. The Union boats and the mortar raft continued firing at the retreating Confederates as long as they were in range but, again, these shots did little or no damage.[55]

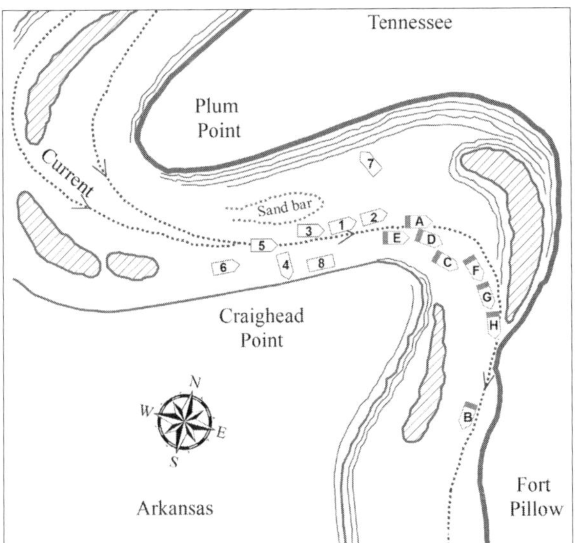

Not to Scale

	United States Boats		Confederate States Boats
1	*Benton (Flag Ship)*	A	*Little Rebel (Flag ship)*
2	*Carondelet*	B	*General Bragg*
3	*Pittsburg*	C	*Sumter*
4	*Mount City*	D	*General Price*
5	*St. Louis*	E	*General Van Dorn*
6	*Cairo*	F	*General Beauregard*
7	*Cincinnati*	G	*Colonel Lovell*
8	*Mortar Boat*	H	*General M. Jeff Thompson*

Battle of Plum Point: Withdrawal of the Confederate Fleet.

* * *

Gideon Wells, Secretary of the Navy, and Commodore Foote were quickly informed about the battle. The early reports were very optimistic and incorrect on the damage that had been inflicted on the Confederate fleet. Davis initially informed Wells that "Cincinnati sustained some injury from the rams, but will be in fighting condition tomorrow."[56] However, Davis later informed Wells that the *Cincinnati* and *Mound City* were damaged and needed repair. He optimistically stated that three enemy vessels were disabled, two of which had had shots put through their boilers, exploding them. Davis's only complaint was that he did not possess a vessel with adequate steam power for its size; if he had, all three disabled enemy boats could have been captured. Lieutenant Phelps, commander of the *Benton*, was even more optimistic. He informed Foote that the *Benton* had hit the boilers on two of the rams with its gunfire, and that the first one blew up with such an explosion that no one on board could have survived.[57] The Union officers' opinion of the damage they had inflicted on the Confederate fleet did not decrease with time, as Davis wrote his wife on May 21, "I cannot tell what damage I did to the rebel fleet. Two of their vessels dropped out of action, enveloped in steam and smoke, in the first fifteen minutes, and one appeared to sink as she rounded the point. The information given by the refugees (who are numerous) is, that she was kept afloat twenty-four hours and then sank, and that we killed one hundred and eight of the rebels."[58] Davis's account to his wife was far from reality.

Because honor was paramount to the regular Navy officers who served in the flotilla, it did not take much to foment resentment. Official reports had to be carefully worded, and newspaper accounts were closely read to make sure that no individual's honor was questioned and that officers received all of the honors they deserved. Thus, no mention was made in the Union reports about commanders not obeying General Orders No. 4 nor—except for Walke's report—was there any mention of gunboats accidentally firing on each other. Other reports were more controversial. The report from Lieutenant Seth Ledyard Phelps, commander of the *Benton*, stated that the *Benton* was the third boat to come to the assistance of the *Cincinnati* and that the *Benton* was responsible for the destruction of two of the Confederate rams. Phelps also stated that he interposed the *Benton* between one of the rams and the *Mound City*, and that this ram, "afraid to hit us, backed off, when he also blew up from a shot I fired."[59] While it was the third ironclad to come to the aid of the *Cincinnati*, the *Benton* could not have executed either of the other two actions because none of the Confederate boats blew up, and no other Confederate rams tried to ram the *Mound City*. While laudatory about his own boat, Phelps was critical of the *Pittsburg*, *Cairo*, and *St. Louis*, stating that "Neither the *Pittsburg* nor *Cairo* got into it [the battle], and the *St. Louis* can hardly be said to have done so."[60] Davis's official report provoked some bitterness, too, as he specifically mentioned Stembel, Kilty, and Phelps for "gallantry and good conduct," but not Walke.[61] Consequently, articles in various Northern papers, along with Davis's and Phelps's statements, created resentment among other officers that lasted long after the war had ended.[62] Luckily, this resentment did not materially affect future operations.

The Battle of Plum Point redoubled the Union's naval commanders' fear of a Confederate boat that was faster than their ironclads getting pass them and going upriver. Roger Stembel, the wounded commander of the *Cincinnati*, emphasized his dread in a letter to James Eads. Stembel wrote that, in his opinion, the object of the Confederates "was if successful in disabling our fleet, which I am sure they hoped to do, to proceed up the river, capture, burn, and destroy all that might fall in there [*sic*] way, and you [Eads] can readily conceive from your knowledge of the localities, etc., what a destructive raid they might have accomplished."[63] Fear of such an event clearly had an impact on all Union naval operations, because boats were left behind to guard tributaries, thus weakening the Union fleet. Even though it was not as easy to disrupt as wagon- or railroad-borne supplies, river transportation still could be thwarted, with far more serious impact. Foote and Davis had a similar opinion, as Stembel as Davis wrote to Gideon Welles that "Flag-Officer Foote thought it might be the intention of the enemy to pass the flotilla and ascend the river, and if they should attempt to do so, such is their vast superiority in speed, that pursuit would be hopeless."[64]

The Confederate commanders, Thompson and Montgomery, also quickly filed reports to their superior, General Beauregard. Thompson's was written on the day of the battle and Montgomery's two days later.[65] Both reports, rightfully so, were very complimentary to the men of the River Defense Fleet and the men from Thompson's command. Montgomery's report included information about a reconnaissance he had conducted on May 11, the day after the battle, during which he observed that the two damaged Union gunboats were still at the locations where they had sunk. Interestingly, Montgomery's official report was printed in the *Philadelphia Inquirer* on May 30, less than three weeks after Montgomery had written it.

Plum Point was a hard-fought victory for the Confederacy, in which it did not lose any boats; but it was a battle with no positive long-term results, as it did not slow down the Union advance or help delay the fall of Fort Pillow. However, the damage the Confederate rams inflicted on the Union fleet impressed the Union fleet's commander and officers. David D. Porter, future admiral and commander of the Mississippi Squadron, stated after the war, "Our iron-clads showed themselves unsuited in respect to steam power, to cope with swift river vessels that could ram them and then escape."[66] One result of the battle was that the ironclads were modified for better protection against rams. Davis also sent a messge to Gideon Welles, Secretary of the Navy, stating that if rams were being fitted out that "now is the time to make them useful". (Footnote ORN, Series I, Vol 23, 17. Consequently, the Union fleet would be better prepared for the Confederate rams the next time both fleets met. The Battle of Plum Point set the stage for the pivotal Battle of Memphis.

The *Cincinnati* and *Mound City* were quickly repaired and returned to duty. The *Mound City* rejoined the flotilla by May 22, with the *Cincinnati* ready for action during the first week of June.[67] The Confederate rams were repaired even more quickly, even though the "funnels looked like huge Nut-Meg graters, and the upper works were completely riddled, on the Boats [*sic*] that had closed with the enemy."[68] The battle proved that wooden rams could defeat heavily armed ironclads and escape with minimal damage, thus bolstering confidence among the Confederates and striking fear in knowledgeable Union commanders.

Casualties were light on both sides. The Confederates only had two killed and one wounded with a broken arm, along with some other minor injuries.[69] The Union fleet suffered four men seriously wounded (one of whom later died) and a number of other minor injuries.[70] The small number of casualties is surprising considering the amount of small arms fire and the number of projectiles fired. Thompson stated in his reminiscences that he "stood upon the hurricane deck where I could see everything until we got in range of the marines, and their minnie balls made me seek shelter."[71] Harry Browne on board the *Mound City* wrote to his parents describing the battle, stating, "Our pilot house is well marked with bullets in their attempts to shoot the pilots. The port holes are also well marked, some very close; but one entered, and that struck a gunner in the muscular part of the forearm, grazing the bone and passing through. I have frequently wondered that more of us were not shot, as we were exposed on deck. The bullets whistled thick, but didn't hit."[72] Considering the volume of artillery projectiles and bullets fired during this battle, many men on both sides were probably very thankful that they had survived uninjured.

The number of projectiles fired is also important, as it indicates the inaccuracy of smoothbore artillery fired from moving vessels, along with the disadvantages of using timed fuzes at close range against wooden boats, which projectiles could go completely through. Davis reported that the mortar boat fired eleven times during the battle, whereas Walke stated that the *Carondelet* fired sixty projectiles during the engagement.[73] Although reports could not be found on the number of projectiles fired by the other ironclads, one can assume that those in the heaviest action (*Cincinnati* and *Mound City*) fired at least the same number as the *Carondelet,* while the other ironclads that were not as heavily engaged (*Benton*, *Pittsburg*, and *St. Louis*) fired fewer, and the *Cairo*, which did not get into the action, fired none. These numbers mean that over 200 large artillery projectiles were fired at the Confederate boats, with most of those directed at the *General Bragg*, *Sumter*, *General Price*, *General Van Dorn*, and *Little Rebel.* Still, these 200 projectiles did not sink or seriously damage any of the Confederate boats. The lack of damage was a direct result of the inaccuracy of smoothbore artillery, the limited visibility the gunners were operating under, and the limitations of the fuzes they were using. Some commanders did not fully understand these limitations and blamed the poor results on lack of training. Porter stated after the war, "This was a small list of casualties for such a desperate brush, and would seem to indicate rather indifferent gunnery practice on the part of the Federals, who, with their heavy ordnance, ought to have swept the enemy from the face of the water, as his vessels were of wood and lightly built."[74]

Union commanders made a number of errors before and during the battle. First, they allowed themselves to be surprised, even though they had been warned that the Confederates planned to attack. Plus, no battle plans or general orders had been issued or discussed on what each boat was to do in case of an attack. Then, the damage inflicted by the rams was a shock, especially as it was discovered that cannon fire did not stop them. This shock was redoubled by the false impression that Commodore Hollins commanded the Confederate fleet, which probably gave them the idea that any battle would be a conventional one decided by cannon fire. Intelligence reports on the type of Confederate boats they were to fight were also incorrect. Union commanders thought that while some of the Confederate boats were rams, other boats were grappling boats, designed to capture their boats. Harry Browne, who was on the deck of the *Mound City* during the battle, wrote home that many of the Sailors on board the *Mound City* were afraid the Confederates would grapple the *Cincinnati* and drag it downriver. Another problem was the potential for fratricide. Walke stated in his after action report that, at times, they were "more in dread of her [*Pittsburg*] shot than those of the enemy," although no one was injured by these misdirected projectiles.[75] This problem was a direct result of the poor visibility and the haphazard deployment of the Union fleet. Indeed, visibility was so poor that Eliot Callender, who watched the battle from the wheelhouse of the sunken *Cincinnati*, stated after the war, "Soon the air was so full of smoke that little could be seen; every now and then a Confederate ram would rush past us within a stone's throw; then a shell would burst over our heads, or a solid shot plough up the water."[76] As poor as the visibility was, both sides were lucky that they did not ram one of their own boats. An almost fatal mistake on the part of the Union commanders was disobedience of General Orders No. 4, in that their boats were not ready for battle at a moment's notice. This negligence caused the Union fleet to engage the Confederates piecemeal, not have all of its ironclads involved in the battle, and allowed multiple Confederate rams to attack individual ironclads. The Union flotilla was very lucky to only have two boats seriously damaged. The Union was also fortunate that it had experienced and courageous officers who knew that to save their boats, they had to be run aground. In addition, the crews showed that even when surprised their discipline remained firm, and they were able to rapidly respond to orders and not panic when their boats were sinking.

The Confederate fleet achieved about the best results it could; however, greater damage could possibly have been inflicted on the Union fleet if the Confederate order of battle had been reversed, and the slowest boats had gone first. If such had been the case, the Confederate fleet would have been more compact, and, thus, more of its boats could have gotten into action. Nevertheless, considering the narrowness of the Mississippi at this location, questions remain about whether more Confederate rams would have had adequate maneuvering room. The officers and men on each of the Confederate boats—especially the crew of *Van Dorn*— displayed their courage as they gallantly fought at close quarters in wooden boats padded with cotton against ironclad boats armed with heavy cannons.

The victory the Confederate River Defense Fleet achieved at Plum Point raised false expectations that the fleet could not fulfill. On May 12, the *Memphis Avalanche* reported, "The impregnability of our cotton clad fleet is now considered to be fully demonstrated – the enemy's shot penetrating into the cotton only a few inches and not passing through. Therefore there is now no danger of the enemy reaching Memphis via Fort Pillow."[77] Two days later, the *Memphis Avalanche* reported, "The conviction seems to be in that quarter [Fort Pillow], that we can hold the Mississippi river with the fort, assisted by our fleet of cotton-clad boats."[78] However, the Confederate fleet, even with its tremendous effort at Plum Point, and the garrison of Fort Pillow, was not able to prevent the fall of Fort Pillow due to circumstances beyond its control. The campaign for control of the Mississippi River valley was a joint naval and land effort for both sides, and command of the river depended on each effort being successful.

Chapter 6

The Fall of Fort Pillow

> Arrangements were completed for a combined assault on the fort at 7 a.m. at a weak and accessible point, but the works were abandoned last night, and the guns and commissary stores destroyed. We are in possession, but propose proceeding to-day toward Memphis.
>
> —Message from Colonel Graham N. Fitch to Major-General John Pope, 5 June 1862[1]

> The evacuation of this place [Corinth] necessarily involves that of your present position [Fort Pillow], which you have so long and gallantly defended; hence I have this day telegraphed you that whenever the enemy shall have crossed the Hatchie River, at Pocahontas or elsewhere, on their way westward, you will immediately evacuate Fort Pillow for Grenada by the best and shortest route.
>
> —Message from General Pierre G. T. Beauregard to Brigadier General John B. Villepigue, 28 May 1962[2]

After the Battle of Plum Point, the Confederate fleet went back to its anchorage under the protective guns of Fort Pillow, and the men started to repair their boats. All of the damage inflicted on the boats was superficial, with the exception of the *Price*, which had been hit near the waterline. Damage to the *Price* was serious enough that it developed a leak, and some of its water supply lines were severed.[3] Still, all of the boats—even the more severely damaged *Price*—were easily repaired without needing to go to the repair facilities at Memphis. In fact, the damage to the boats was so minimal that only one day after the battle, all of the boats were once again ready for combat.[4] Once repairs were completed, the Confederate fleet waited for another opportunity to attack the Union fleet—an opportunity that never occurred.

Commodore Davis also immediately started repairing his damaged boats. The damage to the Union ironclads was too substantial to be repaired on site, and the boats had to be moved to the extensive repair facilities located in Illinois; however, before the damaged ironclads could be moved, they had to be raised.

Fortunately for the Union, Army Quartermaster George Wise had sent the salvage steamer *Champion* downriver, without authorization, the day before the battle to raise the *Grampus*, a captured Confederate boat.[5] The *Champion* was an excellent salvage boat for raising sunken vessels because its boats possessed high capacity pumps rigged to pump out sunken vessels.[6] As a result of Wise's unauthorized decision, the right boat was readily available to start pumping out the *Mound City*. In addition, Davis sent a request immediately after the battle to the captain of Bell-Boat No. 8 "to make all possible dispatch in reaching this squadron. The services of the boat are required for the Government use immediately, and whatever private engagements the boat may have they must be for the present disregarded."[7]

Davis had to act quickly to get the salvage boats to Plum Point, for if the river level fell too low, raising the sunken gunboats would become very difficult, if not impossible. Luckily, communications between the various Union commands on the Mississippi was rapid because fast boats carried the messages. Even without telegraph lines, river communications were so good that, in some cases, a message could be sent—and a reply received—in fewer than twenty-four hours, a factor that greatly benefited the Union war effort.

The *Mound City* was refloated one day after the battle because the watertight compartments limited flooding, and the rapid appearance of the *Champion*.[8] Once refloated, it left for the repair facilities at Mound City (a few miles up the Ohio River from Cairo), towed by the *Champion* and the *Brown*.[9] The *Mound City* arrived in Mound City on May 12, and when it was hauled out of the water, the damage was found to be worse than first supposed.[10] Work repairing the boat went on day and night, and it was able to rejoin the fleet on May 24, fewer than two weeks after the battle.[11]

Removing and repairing the *Cincinnati* took substantially longer, as the *Champion* was towing the *Mound City*, and the bell-boat did not arrive until May 14.[12] Davis was very concerned about this delay as the water level was falling and, as previously stated, if it fell too far it would be impossible to refloat the *Cincinnati*. In addition, Davis was forced to expose his other boats to cannon fire from Fort Pillow in order to protect the *Cincinnati* from additional attacks.[13] Working day and night, the men were finally able to raise the *Cincinnati* on the night of May 15, and immediately sent it upriver to be repaired.[14] Upon close examination, it was found to have "received a severe blow abaft [behind] the iron plating on her starboard quarter, which broke the tops of the head timbers for about 14 feet. She also received two blows on the stern, one on each side of the rudder, which did considerable damage." It was estimated that it would take two weeks of constant work "to put her in readiness for service."[15] Consequently, the *Cincinnati* was not back in the water until the evening of June 2 but still needed to be outfitted, as all of its stores and furniture had been ruined.[16] Still, within less than another week, the *Cincinnati* was ready for action.

The disabling of two of his ironclads forced Davis to ask for reinforcements. Shortly after the battle was over, Davis sent a message to Commander Benjamin Dove, commander of the *Louisville*, that "on receipt of this order you will immediately get underway with your vessel and make all possible dispatch in reporting yourself to me at this point or below."[17] Dove had anticipated Davis's order based on a conversation with Foote, who had stopped to talk with Dove on his way north. Unaware of the Battle of Plum Point, Dove sent a message to Davis on May 10, asking that his boat stay where it was so that he could support the Army in its efforts to fight Confederate raiders. Lieutenant-Colonel Harvey Hogg, commander of United States Forces at Hickman, Kentucky, also wrote Davis asking that the *Louisville* stay to support the Army at Hickman.[18] However, both letters were to no avail, as Davis replied on May 11 that, although he appreciated the importance of Dove's and Hogg's request, under the circumstances he was to join Davis "immediately upon receipt of this order."[19]

Davis also asked for rams on May 12, two days after the battle, when he wrote Secretary of the Navy Gideon Welles, "Everything indicates an intention on the part of the enemy to come up again; and if there are rams, as I understand there are, being fitted up under the direction of the War Department, at Pittsburg, Cincinnati, or elsewhere, for service in this river, now is the time to make them useful." Assistant Secretary of the Navy Gustavus Fox immediately sent a message to the Army's Quartermaster-General, Montgomery Meigs, "Can't the rams be hurried?"[20] Meigs had Peter H. Watson, Assistant Secretary of War, contact Ellet. Watson must not have seen the original message, for his telegram to Ellet stated that a telegram from Foote "indicates great anxiety for the immediate descent of your rams. How soon will you be ready to start?"[21] Ellet telegraphed back on May 15 that five of his boats should reach Cairo on the morning of May 16, and that his second in command, Lieutenant-Colonel Alfred Ellet, his brother, would take these boats down to the fleet. An additional boat would catch up with the fleet before it reached Fort Pillow, while another would be twelve hours behind. Ellet stated that he would be on the eighth boat, which should be at Plum Point by May 18, and that the last boat would leave New Albany, Indiana, on May 18 and go directly to Plum Point.[22] Meigs was then able to inform Welles, "Mr. Watson [Assistant Secretary of War] says that all that can be done to hurry up the rams is already done. Of the two heaviest vessels, one started for New Albany last night and the other will start to-morrow night, guns or no guns. These are the last."[23] The Union telegraph system again proved how quickly information could be transmitted, even with the bureaucratic involvement of a number of different individuals.

Ellet was a little optimistic in his timeline. His brother, after being delayed at Cairo trying to gather supplies and small arms, getting volunteers from the Army to serve as marines on board the boats, and waiting for additional rams, he arrived at Plum Point on the evening of May 18 with six rams. Coordination problems with the regular Navy started immediately, although Alfred Ellet conducted a demonstration requested by Commodore Davis for the purpose of the showing the Confederates that the Union flotilla had been reinforced.[24] Colonel Ellet arrived at Plum Point sometime on May 25, and from then on very little cooperation took place between the two fleets.[25]

In addition to asking for reinforcements, Davis ordered that each of his boats be modified to better protect them from ramming. Each boat had railroad iron put on its bow and stern, as well as having cypress logs slung from its sides.[26] The exception was the *Pittsburg*, whose captain, Lieutenant Egbert Thompson, had already strengthened his ironclad against ramming.[27] Lieutenant Phelps, commander of the *Benton*, went beyond what was required, stating:

> three bars of railroad iron secured between and along the fantails [the rear of the boat] so as to prevent cutting there, and the two runs have been secured by heavy frames enclosing rudders and ironed with railroad iron. Along the casemate where the iron is light, I have had one-half-inch plates flanged and firmly bolted to increase the strength of the angle at that vulnerable point. If we have time to secure the

> bows with three-quarter-inch plates already here, we will be able to split any boat that hits us there.[28]

Such protection came at a price, however. The iron increased the weight, and thus the draft of the boats, while the addition of the logs made them even less maneuverable. Although these measures were not tested in the Battle of Memphis, they were unlikely to have done much good based on the experience of the *Indianola* in February 1863 (see Chapter Nine, Rams versus Guns).

No one was censured for the Union defeat at Plum Point, probably because of the false reports of Confederate losses and the fact that the Confederate fleet withdrew. Beyond a general letter of congratulations from the Department of Navy for the flotilla, selected individuals were promoted due to their actions during the battle. Acting [Volunteer] Lieutenant William R. Hoel was appointed fourth master of the *Cincinnati*, based upon his performance after Captain Stembel became incapacitated.[29] Acting Master Thomas B. Gregory, who fired his mortar at the Confederate boats during the battle, was promoted to Acting [Volunteer] Lieutenant.[30] These promotions were an indication of the growing influence of the volunteers in the Union river fleet.

All this time, Davis was constantly considering ways of capturing Fort Pillow. Brigadier General Isaac Quinby arrived on May 20 with an additional six companies of infantry, four companies of cavalry, seven pieces of artillery, and some sappers and miners. Quinby reported that during his stay, Davis was "ready and anxious to co-operate with me in any plan that might seem to give reasonable promise of success." One suggestion—a repeat of the successful maneuver at Island No. 10—was to run at least part of the fleet past the fort and then land troops behind it. However, Davis was only willing to commit to this plan if a shore battery was placed down river from Fort Pillow on the Arkansas side to provide a refuge for any gunboat that became disabled.[31] This measure was important, as once the boats were downriver from Fort Pillow they would be unable to safely return upriver. The reason was that the current would slow the boats down so much that they would become all but stationary targets for the Confederates manning the heavy guns in Fort Pillow.

Quinby, in support of this plan, started his men working on a road that would be used to transport artillery across the levees. Unfortunately, one night, just when everything was ready to build the battery and emplace the artillery, the pickets who were guarding the proposed location of the battery accidentally shot one of their own men who refused to answer their challenge. Because of the noise, the Confederates sent a force across the river and drove in the pickets.[32] Quinby cancelled the operation under the assumption that the Confederates had discovered the levee road. In addition, a heavy rain fell, making it impossible to move the artillery. At the same time, Quinby learned of a Confederate threat to Hickman and Columbus, Kentucky, and returned with his force to protect those cities.[33] Without Quinby's troops, there were not enough Union Army units in the area to implement the plan.

Colonel Fitch, who was now the senior Army officer, and Commodore Davis continued to explore ways to get behind Fort Pillow. Luckily, the Union forces had good knowledge of the Confederate forces at this time. Most of the information they received was from deserters and escaped slaves. One piece of intelligence they received by the middle of May must certainly have disturbed the Union officers: that a "great craft" (CSS *Arkansas*) was being built in Memphis. They also knew the boat had been taken up the Yazoo River to be completed, and that they had to "catch her before she can be fitted out."[34] Having experienced first hand the damage that rams could inflict, they must have worried about what would happen if the rams were reinforced by an ironclad.

Colonel Ellet had his own ideas about Fort Pillow and the Confederate boats docked there, but cooperation between Ellet and Davis was all but nonexistent. The lack of cooperation poisoned the atmosphere between Ellet's Ram Fleet and the regular Navy fleet. The opinion the regular Navy officers had of Ellet's fleet was so negative that Lieutenant Phelps, commander of the *Benton*, wrote to Foote, "Colonel Ellet is here now with some half dozen rams. I am exceedingly glad that no naval officers were asked for to take those same rams. They serve to count as it is, and if we can get among the rebel fleet and by our fire prevent the use of their guns, these rams might be of service in sinking the rebel craft, which, on account of their being so stuffed with cotton, is a difficult thing to accomplish with shot alone."[35] Davis expressed a similar view in a letter to his wife: "They [Ellet rams] are not good for much in reality, but they are so formidable in appearance that they would strike terror to the soul of Kilhard."[36]

Ellet's view of the regular Navy officers was not very complimentary either. The day after he arrived at Plum Point, he wrote to Secretary of War Stanton that "I visited Commodore Davis immediately to obtain his views and offer cooperation. The commodore intimated an unwillingness to assume any risk at this time." Ellet went on to write, "To me, the risk is greater to lie here with my small guard and within an hour's march of a strong encampment of the enemy, than to run by the batteries and make the attack."[37] Unfortunately, Ellet and Davis had very different views about risks. Davis was very concerned about allowing any Confederate boats to get up river past his boats. In addition, he wrote his wife on May 21, "The service, which consists of standing and waiting, is suited to us, but not at all to the other side, to whom delay is the moth and rust that doth corrupt."[38]

On May 28, Ellet wrote Davis, asking him to join him or put under his command one or more gunboats to run below Fort Pillow in the "daylight and attack the rebel fleet wherever it can be found." Ellet stated that with Farragut's fleet moving up river, the Confederate fleet might disperse up the Mississippi's tributaries and, with the river falling, the Union boats might not be able to attack them. Ellet also stated that such a movement would assist the attack on Corinth by preventing the Confederate Army from crossing the Mississippi when it was defeated; and, even if the Union fleet were defeated, it could still cut Confederate supply lines.[39] However, Ellet did not explain how a defeated fleet could sever Confederate supply lines.

Davis replied to Ellet the following day. Although he did not discuss the possibility of running past Fort Pillow, he suggested a tactical arrangement for the two fleets:

> It will be most expedient and proper that the gunboats should take the front rank in a naval engagement with the enemy, and that the rams, coming up in the rear, should watch for an opportunity, either to take the enemy in the flank, to assail any straggler, to assist any disabled vessel of our squadron, and to pounce upon and carry off any disabled vessel of the enemy.
>
> The gunboats of the flotilla and the rams bear to each other the relation of heavy and light skirmishers; to expose the latter to the first brunt and shock of battle would be to misapply their peculiar usefulness and mode of warfare.
>
> It is my wish, therefore, in the event of a naval engagement, that the rams under your command should follow in the rear and on the wings of my squadron; particular instructions being given to their captains to profit from every opportunity of assailing a vessel of the enemy's flotilla, or making a prize of one of his disabled boats."[40]

This message was not well received by Ellet, who replied:

> Allow me to add, commodore, that almost the only efficient service these rams can render is that for which they were specially built, viz, to run into the enemy, with good speed and head on, and sink him. With that view my instructions which I have given have been to wait while we remain here until the enemy advances so far above the Point that he can not refuse the collision and retreat, and then go in each boat for itself, and strike wherever the blow can be delivered to the best advantage.[41]

Obviously, the two men had very different ideas about how to best use their respective fleets to attack the Confederates.

Ellet, tired of waiting and having postponed his attack in hopes of getting a gunboat to go with him, informed Davis on June 1 that he was going to send a tender, the *Dick Fulton*, down toward the fort on the chance that a Confederate ram would try to capture her. When the Confederate ram steamed upriver, the *Dick Fulton* would retreat and lead the Confederate ram into an ambush by four of the Union rams.[42] Davis replied to Ellet's message the next day, declining to participate and asking Ellet "how far you consider yourself under my authority; and I shall esteem it a favor to receive from you a copy of the orders under which you are acting." Ellet replied the same day, informing Davis that he did not consider himself under his authority. Ellet continued by disparaging the flotilla and emphasizing that his rams were at Plum Point to save the ironclads. In his words: "My fleet was fitted up under the orders of the War Department, and was sent forward in great haste, in the hope that it might be here in time to contribute to avert such a disaster anticipated at the Department as that which recently befell two of the gunboats when assailed by the rebel rams."[43]

The next day, June 3, Ellet sent Davis information on his instructions from Secretary of War Stanton. In his message, Ellet included verbatim transcripts of messages from Stanton, as well as Stanton's statement in response to Ellet's question about his needing to get the concurrence of the naval commander on the Mississippi River:

> The peculiarity of the enterprise which you [Ellet] have undertaken induced the expression "concurrence" instead of placing you distinctly under the command of the naval

> commander. There ought not to be two commanders on the same element in the war operations. But, as the service you [Ellet] are engaged in is peculiar, the naval commander will be so advised, and will be desired not to exercise direct control over your movements, unless they shall manifestly expose the general operations on the Mississippi to some unpardonable influence, which is not however anticipated.[44]

Ellet finished by stating, "From this you [Davis] will be able to gather the spirit of my instructions, which contemplate an advance beyond these fortified positions, whenever I may think it practicable or advisable to go by, with the single reservation that I must respect your objection to the movement, if, in your opinion, the success of your general operations will be jeopardized by that which I propose to undertake."[45] Davis replied that same day, acknowledging that Ellet was not under his command, and that his "undertakings do not necessarily require my concurrence or approval."[46] Davis promised to acquaint Ellet with the details of any plan of operations agreed upon by General Quinby and himself, and to invite Ellet to cooperate with them. Davis concluded by writing, "In the meantime I have no desire to oppose or circumscribe your movements. My opinion is unfavorable to your attack, as I understand it, but your mode of warfare is novel, and the service is peculiar; under the circumstances of the case I willingly defer to your judgment and enterprise."[47]

As discussed in Chapter Three, some of Ellet's men agreed with Davis and, on June 3, when Ellet ordered the *Queen of the West* to try to attack a Confederate steamer anchored under the guns of Fort Pillow, the "captain, two out of three of the pilots, the first mate, and all the engineers, and nearly all the crew, declined the service." Ellet informed Stanton of this incident : "Commodore Davis will not join me in a movement against them [the Confederate fleet], nor contribute a gunboat to my expedition, nor allow any of his men to volunteer so as to stimulate the pride and emulation of my own. I shall therefore first weed out some bad material and then go without him."[48] The day after receiving Ellet's message, Stanton sent a message to General Halleck, writing:

> I have a dispatch from Colonel Ellet, commander of the ram fleet at Fort Pillow, dated at that place yesterday. He informs me that he has been there a considerable time, and has made

> repeated applications to Captain Davis, commander of the gunboats, for leave to attack the enemy's fleet, but has been uniformly refused. Captain Davis not only refuses to join Mr. Ellet or give him the protection of a single gunboat, but also refuses to allow Ellet to attack on his own hook, nor will he allow any of his force to volunteer with Ellet. I regret the President would not place the fleet under your command. Ellet, however, made one demonstration, but the rebels slipped anchor and escaped. He says the strength of the rebel batteries is greatly overrated. He declares his intention to go on without the gunboats.[49]

At best Stanton's message is misleading; at worse, an outright lie. Stanton either misinterpreted Ellet's message, or there were additional messages not included in the records. Either way, Stanton knew that he, not President Lincoln, was responsible for the command arrangement. However, Halleck did not immediately act on the message, and the upcoming Union victories made the issue a moot point.

Stanton continued to make the situation worse by sending sympathetic messages to Ellet, stating in one, "Your several dispatches have been received and your proceedings cordially approved. The Department [War Department] regrets that you have had to encounter so much opposition in the employment of your force, and hopes that the obstacles will give way before your energetic purpose."[50] Although the Ram Fleet would probably not have been built without Stanton's support, his continual efforts to emphasize its independence and his control of it caused problems. At the same time, this weak command structure was probably the only way Ellet would have wanted it. The poor communications and command issues between Ellet and Davis produced other difficulties—although they turned out for the best.

Even with the continuing disagreements between Ellet and Davis, efforts continued to capture Fort Pillow. Colonel Fitch's men found an approach to Fort Pillow that would allow the Union infantry to avoid detection by the Confederates and get within thirty yards of the fort's outer works. On June 3, work began on the road that would allow infantry to move to the attack jump-off point. However, the same day, four of Ellet's rams moved down river, as previously stated, and the guns at the fort opened fire on them. Unfortunately, all of the rounds that overshot the rams landed in the vicinity of the Union troops working on the road. Consequently, work stopped for the day, delaying the attack, but started back up on the morning of June 4. Finally, everything was ready, and on the morning of June 5, Fort Pillow was to be attacked by the infantry and gunboats. However, at 3:00 a.m., Colonel Fitch discovered that Fort Pillow had already been evacuated, making the attack and the subsequent casualties unnecessary.[51] A communications race thus began between Ellet and Davis as to who would receive credit for the capture of Fort Pillow—a competition that would repeat itself at Memphis.

Chapter 7

The Battle of Memphis

> I am under the painful necessity of reporting to you the almost entire destruction of the River Defense Fleet in the Mississippi River in front of Memphis.
>
> —Report from Brigadier-General Thompson to General Pierre G. T. Beauregard[1]

> Thank God for this great success. If the gunboats had fled before me, as their speed easily enabled them to do, they would still have been a thorn in our side. Now they can give us no further trouble; and, moreover, the blockading force of the river by the rebels is destroyed.
>
> —Letter from Captain Charles H. Davis to his wife[2]

The Confederacy recognized the importance of Memphis early in the war, and quickly began fortifying it as well as constructing forts upriver. By May 1, 1861, Fort Wright (later renamed Fort Randolph), sixty-five river miles above Memphis, and Fort Harris (also know as Fort Harrison), six river miles above Memphis, already had some of their earthworks completed.[3] Although located on the high bluffs on the east side of the Mississippi, both forts had major defensive defects. Fort Wright had higher hills located behind it, whereas Fort Harris could be easily outflanked on its land-side.[4] Memphis itself was not initially neglected. By September 1861, two batteries had been constructed on its waterfront. The Jefferson Street Battery had six 32-pounders, and the Navy Yard Battery had two 32-pounders and two 63-pounders, with space for three more guns.[5] However, priority was given to the construction and arming of Fort Pillow. As a result, the defenses at Fort Randolph, Fort Harris, and Memphis languished.[6]

The Union capture of Corinth on May 30, and the cutting of the Memphis and Charleston Railroad, made the Confederate positions on the Mississippi north of Memphis untenable, including Forts Pillow, Randolph, Wright, Harris, as well as Memphis itself. The problem the

Confederacy faced was that it did not have sufficient troops to garrison the forts and oppose the advance of Halleck's army. Besides, the heavy guns necessary to defeating the Union ironclads were in short supply. As a result of the loss of Corinth and the planned evacuation of Fort Pillow, the regular Confederate fleet was dispersed by its commander, Commodore Robert F. Pinkney, while the River Defense Fleet retreated to Memphis, after assisting in the evacuation of Fort Pillow. However, before Fort Pillow was evacuated, General Villepigue, commander of the fort, gave Montgomery four 8-inch guns, which were placed on his largest boats—a welcome increase to his boats' armament.[7] This gain was offset by the loss of the services of General Thompson's sharpshooters and artillerymen when he withdrew his men from the boats and reorganized them back into their normal artillery batteries and infantry companies.[8] The absence of Thompson's men and their expertise with artillery and protective small arms fire would be sorely missed during the upcoming battle.

The loss of Thompson's men resulted from "a growing jealousy and misunderstanding" between Thompson's command and Montgomery's riverboat men.[9] Part of the problem was that Thompson was frequently away from the fleet, and without him present his men probably did not like taking orders from the captains of the boats. Another issue was how to use the rams. On June 3, a few days after the fall of Corinth, and the day before Fort Pillow was evacuated, Thompson wrote General Daniel Ruggles asking him, "If not already done, for God's sake, order the River Defense Fleet to defend every bend and dispute every mile of river from Pillow here. I am willing, and believe I am able, to hold the river, if Commodore Montgomery will co-operate, which I believe he will."[10] Thompson followed this message with another one, informing Ruggles, "If we are allowed to place the mortars on rafts and permitted to use the transports and play strategy back on the enemy, I will contract to hold this river above Memphis for a month."[11] Thompson was an aggressive, optimistic commander, but in this case, both his aggressiveness and optimism were misplaced, and neither suggestion was acted upon. Thompson also wanted to command, and the men he should have been commanding were scattered between the River Defense Fleet and various units in the Confederate Army. As a result of these issues, Thompson asked Ruggles on June 5 that his men and officers be relieved from their service in the River Defense Fleet, and that others be assigned in their place if Commodore Montgomery desired other men. His request was approved the very same day, and he informed Montgomery of the order.[12] However, one day later, General Beauregard telegraphed Thompson, giving him joint command of the river defense. Thompson immediately informed Montgomery, and asked him what was needed. Montgomery replied by requesting two companies of artillery to join the fleet the next morning—a day too late.[13]

While Thompson corresponded with Ruggles, the River Defense Fleet was not idle. Knowing that Fort Pillow was to be evacuated, Montgomery ordered that the boats be loaded with projectiles for their guns, including ones for their new 8-inch guns, along with commissary stores.[14] The fleet left Fort Pillow on June 4, arrived at Memphis midday on June 5, and immediately began loading coal aboard the boats.[15] Montgomery's plan, after replenishing his boats' supply of coal, was to steam upriver to Island No. 40 and engage the Union fleet there.[16] However, the Federal fleet advanced more rapidly than he expected, and that evening Captain James Delancy, commander of the *Lovell*, spotted the Federal flotilla approaching the city and fired a cannon to warn everyone.[17] Once the Federal fleet was spotted, Montgomery ordered his boats into a battle line in anticipation of an engagement; however, the Federal fleet did not continue its advance and anchored out of sight around a bend in the river.[18]

The surprise appearance of the Union fleet and its "overwhelming strength" made Montgomery decide to retreat down river.[19] However, another unexpected and unwelcome realization forced Montgomery to change his plans: there was only enough coal at Memphis to supply one boat with sufficient fuel to reach Vicksburg. The lack of coal was a surprise, because Montgomery had contracted for 20,000 barrels of coal to be transported upriver before he had left New Orleans. Unfortunately, General Mansfield Lovell refused to pay for it, and the coal remained in New Orleans.[20] Consequently, Montgomery asked the citizens of Memphis to bring any coal they had to the boats.[21] Although some fuel was collected, it was not enough, and Montgomery faced the decision of either destroying most of his fleet or fighting. Although he wanted to retreat to the safety of the guns at Vicksburg, the lack of coal forced him to stay at Memphis and fight as he rejected his other option—destroying his boats[22] Montgomery prepared for the upcoming fight as best as he could by ordering the tug *Gordon Grant* upriver as a picket boat so that all of his fighting boats could remain at anchor and minimize their use of coal. Unfortunately, the *Gordon Grant* ran aground and had to be burned.[23]

Immediately after the capture of Fort Pillow, Ellet steamed downriver to Fort Randolph with three of his rams. When he reached Fort Randolph, he sent his brother, Lieutenant-Colonel Alfred Ellet, ashore. Alfred confirmed that the Confederates had abandoned the fort. While Ellet's boats were anchored at Fort Randolph, the ironclad fleet passed by on its way down to Memphis. Later in the day, Ellet continued down river and anchored on the Tennessee side of the river about eighteen miles from Memphis.[24]

Davis also steamed downriver, after learning that Fort Pillow had been evacuated, with the *Benton*, *Louisville*, *Carondelet*, *Cairo*, and *St. Louis*. He left around noon on June 5, leaving the *Pittsburg* and *Mound City* behind. The *Pittsburg* was to help secure Fort Pillow, and the *Mound City* was to protect the troop transport convoy.[25] The flotilla steamed slowly downriver because each bayou or chute had to be investigated; as a result, the ironclads became separated. The *Benton*, which was in the lead, was well ahead of the other boats.[26] When the *Benton* got close to Memphis, daylight was fading, and the river became too dangerous to safely navigate. Davis decided to stop, and sent a tug back with a verbal message to the other boats not to proceed any farther. However, Captain Walke, commander of the *Carondelet*, was worried about the safety of the flagship and, disobeying orders, continued downriver. Once he reached the *Benton*, he was informed that Davis's order had been misunderstood, and a message was quickly dispatched to the other boats for them to join the flagship.[27] Finally, at about 8:00 in the evening, the fleet anchored at the lower end of Island No. 45, about a mile and a half upriver from Memphis, while the supporting mortar boats, towboats, and supply boats anchored at Island No. 44.[28]

At daylight on June 6, the flotilla formed up. The air was clear, and there were no clouds in the sky.[29] Davis deployed his boats in a line across the river, with the *Carondelet* on the left, by the Tennessee shore, then the *Benton*, *St. Louis*, *Louisville*, and *Cairo*.[30] All of the boats faced upriver so that they could maintain their positions, because, as previous experience had shown, they could not back up the river, and if they were facing downriver they would have had difficulty maintaining their positions. Davis was able to deploy his fleet in a line across the river due to the width of the river at Memphis. In addition, Davis probably wanted all of his boats to fight as a single unit rather than as individual boats, as they had at Plum Point. Plus, if a Confederate ram wanted to ram one of the ironclads, it would be forced to face the cannon fire of at least two of the Union boats. Obviously, there was a risk of friendly fire, but this was a risk Davis was willing to take.

Because Davis's view of Memphis was blocked by the bend in the river, he ordered his messenger tug, the *Jessie Benton*, to go downriver and determine if the Confederate fleet was still present. As the *Jessie Benton* went on its mission, the tug was slowly followed by the *Benton* and *Carondelet* as they drifted downriver stern first. Rounding the bend, the *Jessie Benton* discovered that the Confederate fleet was still at Memphis and beginning to leave its anchorage to move out into the river. Spotting the Confederate fleet, the captain of the *Jessie Benton* quickly turned his boat around and moved back to the fleet, followed by the *Benton* and *Carondelet*.[31]

Montgomery prepared his battle plan the night of June 5. Early the next morning, he received a message from Thompson stating that General Beauregard had given him joint command of the fleet and asking what he needed. Montgomery requested that Thompson's artillerymen join his fleet first thing that morning to man the guns.[32] Although Thompson may have known what was to happen, Montgomery failed to communicate his plan to his captains.[33] Montgomery's failure to communicate and the late notification by Thompson worked against him, as Davis, again, moved too fast. Once Montgomery saw the Union fleet moving toward the city, he knew that he could no longer wait and began to move his boats out into the river. Montgomery arranged his fleet in two columns, with the boats on the Tennessee side echeloned in front of those to their left. The two slowest boats, the *Jeff Thompson* and *Colonel Lovell*, were in the first rank, with the *Thompson* on the Tennessee side of the river and to the right of the *Lovell*. The *Sumter* and *General Beauregard* were in the second rank, with the *Sumter* on the Tennessee side of the river and to the right of the *Beauregard*. The *Van Dorn* and *Bragg* were behind these four, while the *Price* had orders to remain below the bend. The *Little Rebel*, being the flagship, had no assigned position.[34] This time, Montgomery was determined to get his entire fleet into the fight and not make the same mistake he had at Plum Point, where the fastest boats were first and outran the slower boats behind them. In addition, the leading four boats had the recently acquired large and powerful 8-inch guns on their bows, which fired a projectile that could penetrate the armor on the ironclads.

Union reports stated that the Confederate fleet was arrayed in two lines, but this was an optical illusion due to the Confederate's column formation and the bend in the river. In a column formation, with two boats in each rank, if the *Thompson*, the leading boat, rammed an ironclad any of the other boats could also ram it or ram a different ironclad, provided the opportunity presented itself. If the Confederate fleet was just in two rows, it would have been very difficult for more than two boats to ram the same victim. Although the Mississippi was wide at Memphis, the navigable channel for Montgomery's boats was much narrower than it was for the Union ironclads as the Confederate rams had a larger draft. Consequently, Montgomery had to keep his boats in a column for maximum maneuverability. If four of the boats had been in line, the ones closest to the Arkansas shore would have been in danger of running aground. Considering the strengths and weaknesses of his boats, Montgomery chose an excellent formation for his fleet.

Beyond Thompson and his few men who had just arrived, a large crowd of civilians gathered on the Memphis bluff and levee overlooking the river. The first ones came because they had been told that the Confederate fleet was not going to retreat, but rather battle the invaders. The later ones came once the Union fleet had been spotted, and people were sure that there was going to be a battle. Some of the viewers had relatives on board the Confederate boats, and many more knew the men personally. Although there were Union sympathizers in the crowd, most witnesses assumed that it would be a Confederate victory based on the results from Plum Point. Consequently, the crowd was quite large. Union reporters estimated that from 15,000 to 40,000 people watched the battle, while Lieutenant Phelps, commander of the *Benton*, estimated the crowd at 15,000.[35] Even if these estimates are high, as the total population of Memphis in 1860 was slightly over 22,500, the upcoming battle would be the second most civilian viewed battle of the war after the bombardment of Fort Sumter in April 1861.[36] It was as if the battle were taking place in an arena, for the crowd could look down on the action while cheering on its team; however, this game was a life and death struggle.

For both fleets, the Mississippi River at Memphis created a different situation from that at Plum Point. Whereas the current was the same—about four to five miles per hour—the upper bend in the river was much sharper. As a consequence, the main channel was deeper and wider and flowed against the bluffs on the Tennessee side of the river. The Wolf River, where the former Navy Yard was located, also had an impact. It joined the Mississippi downriver from where the Union fleet anchored, but upriver from the port of Memphis.[37] The wider channel gave both fleets more maneuvering room, but presented the risk that any boat that was damaged and could not quickly get out of the main channel would be lost. Thus, due to the location of the channel and the steep bluff, all of the captains of the boats that were disabled during the battle tried to seek the safety of the shallower Arkansas shore, where they could run their boats aground and allow their crews to safely wade ashore. The wider channel helped Davis because he was able to deploy his boats in a single line, where they could avoid firing over each other. It also helped Montgomery because he could deploy his boats in two staggered columns. This scenario presenteda true squadron action, with all of the boats on each side involved in the battle and plenty of maneuver room.

After being informed by the tug *Jessie Benton* about the Confederate fleet, Davis ordered it, as well as the *Benton* and *Carondelet*, to rejoin the main Union force.[38] Once the *Benton*, *Carondelet*, and *Jessie Benton* were back with the flotilla, Davis ordered that breakfast be served as he believed that men fought better on a full stomach.[39] While the men were eating, the Confederate fleet began to move upriver.

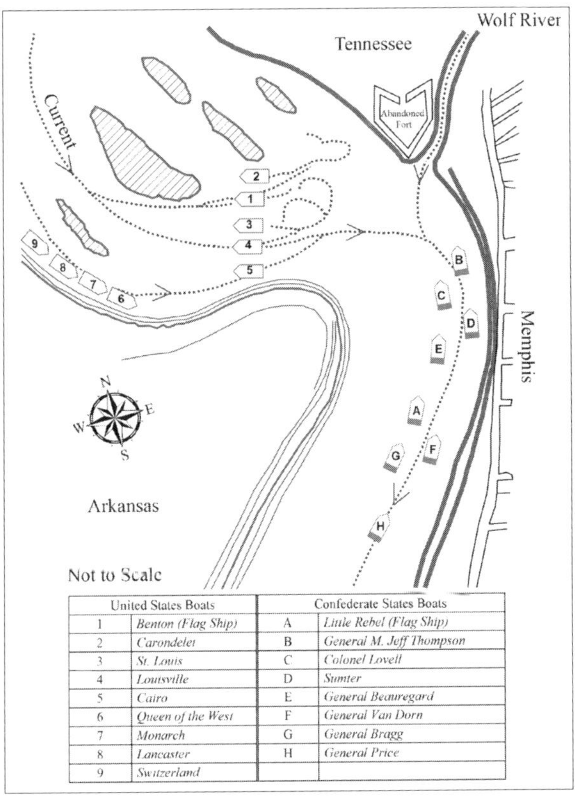

United States Boats		Confederate States Boats	
1	*Benton (Flag Ship)*	A	*Little Rebel (Flag Ship)*
2	*Carondelet*	B	*General M. Jeff Thompson*
3	*St. Louis*	C	*Colonel Lovell*
4	*Louisville*	D	*Sumter*
5	*Cairo*	E	*General Beauregard*
6	*Queen of the West*	F	*General Van Dorn*
7	*Monarch*	G	*General Bragg*
8	*Lancaster*	H	*General Price*
9	*Switzerland*		

Battle of Memphis: The *Thompson* and *Lovell* Open Fire.

When the *Jeff Thompson* was in the vicinity of where the Wolf River meets the Mississippi, Captain John Burke fired his 8-inch gun at the *Benton*, starting the battle.[40] After the *Thompson* fired, the other Confederate boats opened fire as they steamed into range. The Union boats received the Confederate fire for a few minutes, until about 5:40, when they began returning fire from their stern guns, with the *Cairo* firing first.[41] Due to the Union formation and the bend in the river, the *Cairo* was closest to the Confederate boats, even though, based on naval protocol, all of the Union boats stayed behind the *Benton*, the flagship.[42]

Union gunfire only did superficial damage to the Confederate boats during this initial, relatively long-range duel. During this part of the battle, each Union ironclad could only bring its two stern guns to bear on the Confederates—at best, a 32-pounder smoothbore gun and a 30-pounder rifled Parrott and, at worst, two 32-pounder smoothbore guns.[43] The 32-pounder smoothbore was notoriously inaccurate at long range, andthe gunners firing the Parrott would have been handicapped in having to deal with the sun in their eyes along with a glare off the water. Adding to their problem, the air was still, and smoke from the guns would have quickly obscured their already limited view.[44] The Confederate gunners were much more successful, even though their guns were also smoothbores. They scored some hits on the ironclads, although none of the Union boats received any serious damage.[45] The Confederate gunners' superior accuracy can be attributed to having the sun at their back and better visibility, as they were higher off the water. In addition, their guns were in the open, which allowed them to better determine where their shots were hitting. However, their better visibility came at a price, as they were more exposed to shell fragments and small arms fire than their Union counterparts. Unfortunately for the Confederacy, the accuracy of the Confederate gunners did not improve as the range decreased, probably due to the inexperience of the riverboat men who were manning the guns and to their exposed positions. The reporter for the *New York Tribune* wrote, "The enemy fired very wildly, either from excitement or discouragement, and had in some instances, as in the case of the rams, shot at a distance of less than 30 yards without hitting their object. The Rebels never, within my knowledge, fire so poorly."[46] More accurate fire would have well served the Confederate cause, as their 8-inch projectiles would easily penetrate the unprotected sterns of the City Class ironclads. Such a hit would, in all likelihood, disable any of the City Class ironclads, as the projectile would have smashed through the paddlewheel and possibly hit the boiler.

During this part of the battle, Montgomery and his men, as well as the civilian spectators, must have thought that the battle was going to be a Confederate victory. The Union fleet appeared to be retreating upriver with their unarmored sterns exposed to cannon fire from the advancing Confederate boats. Even though the Union ironclads were returning fire, Davis had been hoping to delay the battle, in part because he was waiting on Ellet's rams to arrive. He knew they were upriver from him, but did not know how far away they were. In one respect, this scheme worked in favor of the Union fleet, giving the Confederates the impression that the Union fleet was wavering due to variable currents that made it impossible to keep the battle line steady.[47] However, Montgomery did not close with the Union fleet because he hoped to draw the Union boats off of a sandbar they were over.[48] In addition, he realized that as long as the Union line remained unbroken, he would not be able to engage isolated ironclads. Consequently, he ordered his fleet to back down the river, with the hope that the solid line of ironclads would break up as they moved downriver and off the sandbar to pursue his boats.[49] The Confederate boats only withdrew a short distance as the leading Confederate boats stopped opposite Beal Street, well within view of all of the people watching the battle, and waited to see what the Union boats would do.[50]

Ellet had not been idle during this time period. His instructions to his captains the on the night of June 5 were that they were to start at daylight. The order was to be *Queen of the West*, *Monarch*, *Lancaster*, *Switzerland*, *Dick Fulton*, *Horner*, *Mingo*, and *Lioness*. All boats were to keep a half-mile apart and to avoid crowding.[51] Ellet only expected the first four boats to be involved in any action, as the *Dick Fulton* and *Horner* were auxiliary supply boats towing barges, whereas the *Mingo* and *Lioness*, although rams, were also towing barges. As the *Queen of the West* approached Memphis, Ellet saw Davis's boats in line across the channel, and signaled all of his boats to land. Ellet secured his boat to the Arkansas shore with the intention of conferring with Davis; but before he could leave the *Queen of the West*, a projectile from the *Jeff Thompson* passed nearby. Realizing that a battle was imminent, he ordered that the lines securing the *Queen of the West* be cast off, and hoisted the signal to his fleet that they were going into action.[52] Quickly gathering speed, the *Queen of the West* sped forward, staying in the main channel and passing close to the *Benton*, about fifteen to twenty minutes after the first shots had been fired. However, this maneuver exposed the *Queen of the West* to cannon fire and ramming from

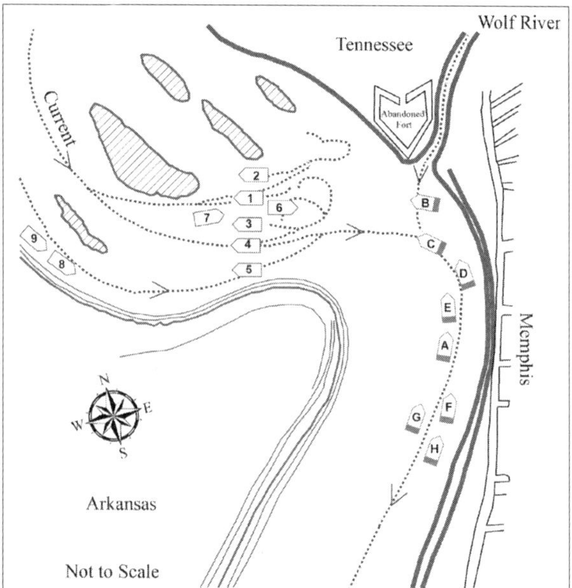

United States Boats		Confederate States Boats	
1	*Benton (Flag Ship)*	A	*Little Rebel (Flag Ship)*
2	*Carondelet*	B	*General M. Jeff Thompson*
3	*St. Louis*	C	*Colonel Lovell*
4	*Louisville*	D	*Sumter*
5	*Cairo*	E	*General Beauregard*
6	*Queen of the West*	F	*General Van Dorn*
7	*Monarch*	G	*General Bragg*
8	*Lancaster*	H	*General Price*
9	*Switzerland*		

Battle of Memphis: *Queen of the West* and *Monarch* Charge the Confederate fleet.

the Confederate boats, as well as cannon fire from the Union ironclads. Still, neither Ellet nor his brother, Lieutenant Colonel Alfred Ellet, hesitated, and the *Queen of the West* was followed by the *Monarch*. Neither the *Lancaster* nor *Switzerland* followed the two leading rams. The *Lancaster* did not get into the battle due to human error—the boat was backed into the shore, disabling its rudder. Then, the commander of the *Switzerland* followed his orders to the letter, and maintained his position a half-mile behind the disabled *Lancaster* until after the battle.[53]

The sudden appearance of Ellet's rams was probably a surprise to Davis, even though he had been expecting them. Immediately after the rams steamed through his line, Dave signaled his boats to follow the flagship's motion to turn about and steam toward the Confederate

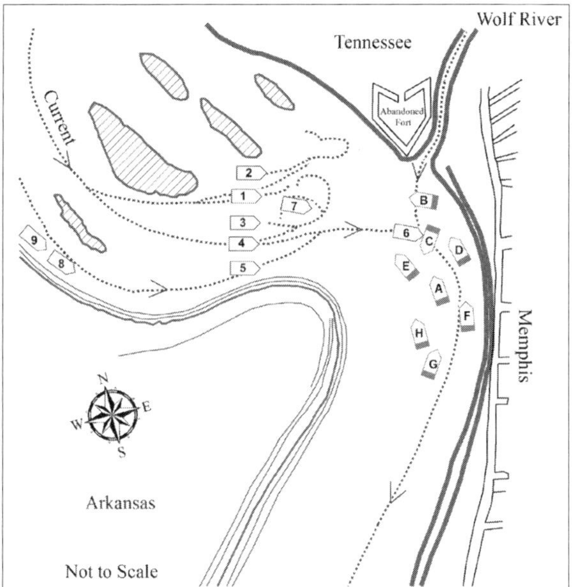

United States Boats		Confederate States Boats	
1	*Benton (Flag Ship)*	A	*Little Rebel (Flag Ship)*
2	*Carondelet*	B	*General M. Jeff Thompson*
3	*St. Louis*	C	*Colonel Lovell*
4	*Louisville*	D	*Sumter*
5	*Cairo*	E	*General Beauregard*
6	*Queen of the West*	F	*General Van Dorn*
7	*Monarch*	G	*General Bragg*
8	*Lancaster*	H	*General Price*
9	*Switzerland*		

Battle of Memphis: *Queen of the West* Rams the *Lovell.*

fleet.[54] Davis probably decided to turn about for the purpose of closing the range, bringing more guns to bear on the Confederate boats, presenting each boat's armor-plated bow to the enemy, as well as supporting the attack by Ellet's two rams. However, this operation took much longer than normal, as the logs suspended from the sides of the ironclads severely reduced their ability to maneuver. In contrast, Ellet's boats were very navigable and fast—even faster than normal, as running with the current increased their speed by about a third. Consequently, they were able to close with the Confederate fleet well before the ironclads.

Ellet's charge must have surprised the Confederates, too. Although they knew about the Union rams, the *Queen of the West* suddenly appearing out of the thick smoke—steaming toward them at a very high

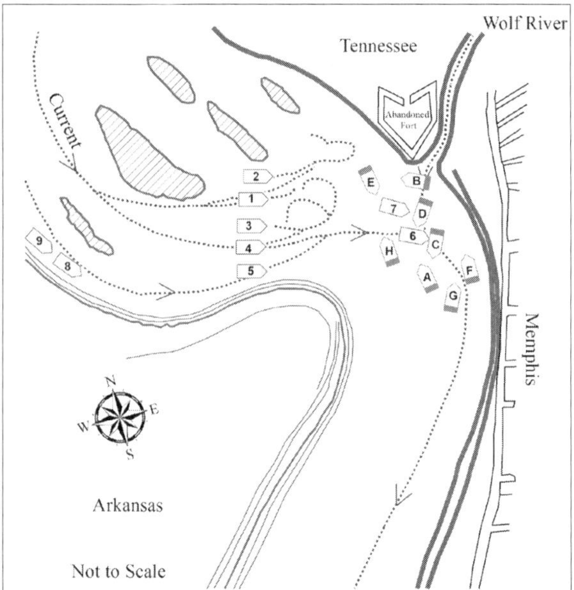

United States Boats		Confederate States Boats	
1	*Benton (Flag Ship)*	A	*Little Rebel (Flag Ship)*
2	*Carondelet*	B	*General M. Jeff Thompson*
3	*St. Louis*	C	*Colonel Lovell*
4	*Louisville*	D	*Sumter*
5	*Cairo*	E	*General Beauregard*
6	*Queen of the West*	F	*General Van Dorn*
7	*Monarch*	G	*General Bragg*
8	*Lancaster*	H	*General Price*
9	*Switzerland*		

Battle of Memphis: The Confederate Fleet Reacts to the Attack of the Ellet Rams.

rate of speed—must have been a shock.[55] The captains of the Confederate boats would have realized the immediate danger this one ram presented, causing them to quickly redirect their attention. Due to the bend in the river and the tight Confederate formation, the *Queen of the West* appeared to many to be attempting to ram the lead Confederate boat, the *Thompson*. Consequently, the *Thompson* maneuvered to avoid the collision, and Ellet selected the *Lovell* because it appeared to be closer to him.[56] His choice resulted in the *Queen of the West* and the *Lovell* racing toward each other at a speed that would destroy them both. However, at the last minute, the *Lovell* veered, presenting its broadside to the oncoming *Queen of the West*. To Ellet, and everyone who could see what was happening, the captain of the *Lovell*, James C. Delancy, seemed to have lost his nerve.[57] In reality, one of the *Lovell*'s engines stopped working at this crucial moment, causing his boat to lose power to one of its paddlewheels.[58] Still, the *Lovell* was not defenseless; as the *Queen of the West* closed on its intended target, the gun crews of the *Lovell* fired grapeshot at her. However, they missed due to their boat being out of control, the high speed of the *Queen of the West*, and anyone exposing themselves on the deck of the *Lovell* was targeted by the *Queen of the West*'s sharpshooters. When the *Queen of the West* rammed the *Lovell* just forward of its wheelhouse, the impact was tremendous. Although both boats were damaged, the *Lovell* was almost cut in half. The hull was crushed in, and its smoke stacks threatened to fall into the river.[59] The damage to the *Lovell* was extensive enough that only five out of eighty men survived the sheer speed at which the boat sank.[60] Although the damage to the *Queen of the West* was not as extensive, everything not secured was thrown about, including its crew. In addition, the impact drove the bow of the *Queen of the West* so far into the *Lovell* that the two boats were wedged together. Consequently, the *Lovell* threatened to take the *Queen of the West* down with it, a frequent problem when two vessels rammed.[61]

The rest of the Confederate fleet quickly responded to this new threat. The *Sumter* turned to port and rammed the *Queen of the West* on its port side before it could get free of the *Lovell*.[62] The *Sumter*'s impact broke the *Queen*'s tiller rope, and crushed in its left wheel and hull, leaving *Queen* nearly helpless. Fortunately, the crash also broke it free from the grasp of the rapidly sinking *Lovell*.[63] Immediately after the *Sumter* rammed his boat, Ellet left the wheelhouse to inspect the damage and was shot about two to three inches above the knee by Signal Quartermaster J. Sullivan.[64] Even though he was disabled, Ellet was able to order the *Queen of the West* to steam toward the Arkansas shore.

By now, the *Monarch* had steamed into the fight, but by this time the battle had become a confused melee with decreasing visibility. In addition, the *Queen of the West*, *Sumter*, and the sinking *Lovell* blocked part of the main channel. Still, the captain of the *Beauregard*, James H. Hurt, was able to see the *Monarch* and turned his boat downriver to ram it. At the same time, the captain of the *Price*, Thomas E. Henthorne, steaming upriver to join in the battle, also picked the *Monarch* as his target.[65] The *Monarch*, although grazed on the stern by the one of the Confederate boats, was able to avoid being directly struck by either boat.[66] Unfortunately for the Confederates, visibility was so limited that the two Confederate boats collided with each other. As a result, the *Beauregard* knocked off one of the *Price*'s wheels and disabled her.[67] The two ram fleets had been in contact for much less time than

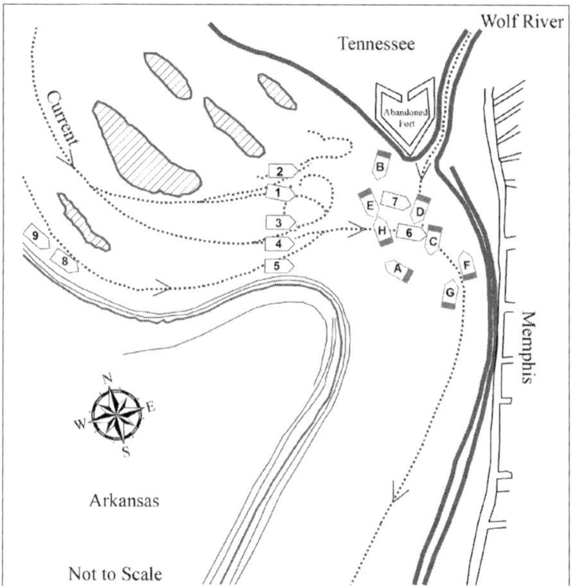

United States Boats		Confederate States Boats	
1	*Benton (Flag Ship)*	A	*Little Rebel(Flag Ship)*
2	*Carondelet*	B	*General M. Jeff Thompson*
3	*St. Louis*	C	*Colonel Lovell*
4	*Louisville*	D	*Sumter*
5	*Cairo*	E	*General Beauregard*
6	*Queen of the West*	F	*General Van Dorn*
7	*Monarch*	G	*General Bragg*
8	*Lancaster*	H	*General Price*
9	*Switzerland*		

Battle of Memphis: The Confused Melee.

the preliminary gunfire, yet three Confederate boats—almost half of the fleet—and one Union boat were already out of action.

The swirling, obscured action continued with worsening visibility. Although conflicting reports exist on what happened during the initial sequence of events, even more conflicting reports were produced about what occurred after the *Beauregard* and the *Price* accidentally rammed. What happened next varies tremendously depending on which report, newspaper account, or reminiscence is read. Ellet summarized this issue in one of his reports, stating:

> Many versions differing from each other entirely have been given by eyewitnesses of these occurrences, who stood in plain view on the levee at Memphis, in our own gunboats, and on the Arkansas shore. These discrepancies are attributed to the fact that there were three rebel rams and but

> two of our own mingled together and crashing at hand. In this confusion the different boats were mistaken for others, and the steamer struck by the *Queen* disappeared from view beneath the surface of the river. This uncertainty of view was doubtless increased by the accumulation of smoke from the chimneys of so many boats and the fire of our own gunboats.[68]

To show the improbability of some of the accounts, Ellet stated in one report that the *Monarch* rammed and sank the boat that had rammed the *Queen of the West*; then was rammed by one of the Rebel rams, but was not injured. After that, the *Monarch* rammed the *Beauregard* and burst open its side at the same time that a projectile hit the *Beauregard*'s boiler, scalding a number of men. Next, the *Monarch* pushed the *Little Rebel* to shore; then towed the *Beauregard* to shoal water, where it sank; and finally pursued the remaining Confederate gunboat and transport.[69] Considering how long the battle lasted—fewer than two hours—and that the *Monarch* was not involved in the first twenty to thirty minutes, it could not have possibly accomplished all of these feats. Ellet had a very high opinion of the abilities of his rams and this probably clouded his memory. Ellet wrote his wife after the battle that "Had the other two [rams] come up gallantly we should have destroyed the entire rebel fleet, and left nothing for our own gun boats to do."[70] In contrast, Lieutenant Phelps, commander of the *Benton*, wrote in a letter to Foote that "The rebels were evidently disconcerted by this move [Ellet's rams charging through the ironclads], and the *Queen of the West*, failing to hit the *Beauregard*, made a pass at the *Colonel Lovell*, cutting her through, and that vessel sunk in a few minutes, many of her crew going down with her, and she is entirely out of sight. This is all the rams did, except the confusion created by them gave us better chances at the rebel craft."[71] Phelps later stated in his letter, "If the rams had done their duty she [*Van Dorn*] would have been captured also, but after the first dash we saw no more of them."[72] The truth is probably somewhere between these two versions, and the following account is based on my judgment after having read all of the conflicting documents.

The *Monarch*, after successfully dodging the *Beauregard* and the *Price*, went to the aid of the *Queen of the West*, and rammed the *Sumter*. Although this damage was not fatal, the cumulative damage to the *Sumter* forced it to leave the battle and attempt to escape by steaming downriver. However, the *Sumter* failed to escape because it inadvertently ran aground.[73]

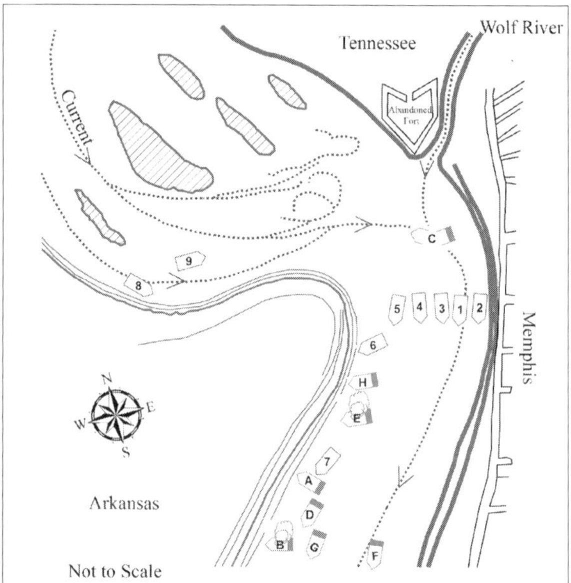

United States Boats		Confederate States Boats	
1	*Benton (Flag Ship)*	A	*Little Rebel(Flag Ship)*
2	*Carondelet*	B	*General M. Jeff Thompson*
3	*St. Louis*	C	*Colonel Lovell*
4	*Louisville*	D	*Sumter*
5	*Cairo*	E	*General Beauregard*
6	*Queen of the West*	F	*General Van Dorn*
7	*Monarch*	G	*General Bragg*
8	*Lancaster*	H	*General Price*
9	*Switzerland*		

Battle of Memphis: Defeat of the Confederate Fleet.

By this time, the Union ironclads had completed their turning movement and closed with the Confederate fleet, with the *Benton* in the lead. The *Jeff Thompson* became caught between the confusing action of the six rams immediately downriver from it and the advancing Union ironclads. As the range had significantly closed between the ironclads and the *Jeff Thompson*, the Union ironclads were able to hit its superstructure a number of times with exploding shells. As a result, the cotton bales, put around the superstructure to protect it, were set on fire, just like the fires that had started on the *Bragg* during the Battle of Plum Point. However this time, the fires got out of control because General Thompson's men were not on board to man the guns and help put out the fire. Captain John H. Burke, the commander of the *Thompson*, tried to steam downriver, but eventually realized that his boat was lost and ran it aground on the Arkansas side below Memphis. The fire continued to burn, and after the battle was over the fire reached the magazine, and the boat blew up.[74]

Meanwhile, the *Little Rebel* had steamed up to engage the Union ironclads. Before it could ram any of them, it was hit by a cannonball below the waterline, which passed through the engines leaving it totally disabled. The *Little Rebel* turned toward the Arkansas shore, but was rammed by the *Monarch* before reaching the shore and sank in shallow water.[75] The *Beauregard* suffered that same fate because it lost a lot of speed when it rammed the *Price*. Consequently, the Union ironclads were able to get close enough to it to bring it under effective cannon fire. One of these projectiles—probably fired by the *Benton*, as it was in the lead—hit its boiler, disabling the boat with the escaping steam, killing a number of its crew.[76] Fortunately for the crew, by using the river current and its remaining momentum, the badly damaged *Beauregard* was able to reach the Arkansas shore. As soon as it did, the crew abandoned ship and escaped into Arkansas.[77]

The captains of the two remaining Confederate boats, the *Bragg* and the *Van Dorn*, saw that the battle had turned against them and

The Great Naval Battle before Memphis, June 6, 1862. Engraving after a sketch by Alexander Simplot and published in *Harper's Weekly*, June 28, 1862, depicting the action between the Confederate River Defense Fleet and Federal warships off Memphis. In the center foreground, the CSS *General Beauregard* is being rammed by the Federal ram *Monarch*. On the left side is the disabled Federal ram *Queen of the West* and the Confederate boats *General Sterling Price* and *Little Rebel*. Other Federal boats are in the center and left distance, with other Confederate boats in the center and right middle distance. Courtesy of the Naval Historical Foundation, NH 58891.

View of the "battlefield" from the Memphis's bluff. The bridge is part of I-40. Mud Island can be seen on the right side of the photograph. Photograph by the author, March 2010.

turned downriver to flee. Unfortunately for the *Bragg*, it ran aground on a sandbar when turning downriver. The crew was not able to free it before the Union gunboats arrived and shattered the boat's upper works and hull by cannon fire.[78] The *Bragg* then caught on fire, but it is unknown whether the fire was started by the crew in an attempt to prevent the Union from using the boat or by exploding Union projectiles. However, Lieutenant Joshua Bishop and some of the crew from the *Benton* boarded the *Bragg* and were able to extinguish the fire before it got out of control. This effort was fortunate for Bishop, as later that day he would be given command of the *Bragg*.[79]

The *Van Dorn*, along with the store boat *Paul Jones*, which was carrying an important cargo of powder, shells, and cannonballs, avoided the sandbars and wrecked boats and started their escape downriver.[80] The Union ironclads attempted to pursue, but were not fast enough to catch the fleeing Confederate boats, even though some of the captains had ordered that the logs protecting their sides be cut off to increase their speed and maneuverability.[81] Davis also requested that Ellet send his rams in pursuit of the *Van Dorn* and *Paul Jones*.[82] Consequently, the *Monarch* and *Switzerland*, whose commander had decided to go past the damaged *Lancaster* and join the battle, pursued the escaping boats. However, both the *Van Dorn* and *Paul Jones* successfully avoided their pursuers. By 7:30 in the morning, about two hours after the first shot had been fired, the battle was over, and the Navy had won one of its most decisive and pivotal victories.

Chapter 8

The Aftermath

For my first and special duty was to retain command of the river.

—Commodore Charles Henry Davis, 8 June 1862[1]

Joint resolution of thanks to Commodore J. E. Montgomery and the officers and men under his command, for gallant and meritorious services on the 10th of May and 6th of June, 1862.

—Confederate States House of Representatives and Senate[2]

Immediately following their decisive victory, the Union commanders quickly moved to secure Memphis. Ellet, assuming that the city had surrendered, acted first and sent his son, Medical Cadet Charles R. Ellet, along with Lieutenant Warren D. Crandall of the 59th Illinois Volunteers and two Soldiers from the *Lioness*'s boat guard into the city.[3] Cadet Ellet took a message from his father to the Memphis authorities stating that he was instructed to raise the United States flag over the customs house and post office. The mayor replied that although the city had not surrendered, it had no force with which to oppose the raising of the flags.[4] Based on that reply, Cadet Ellet and his group proceeded to the post office to raise the flag. On their way, young boys threw pebbles at them, and they were followed by a small group of men. At the post office, the mayor and a couple of policemen met them and accompanied them to the roof of the building where they raised the flag. Quickly, an angry mob surrounded the building and fired pistols and threw rocks at them. The local civilians took a Confederate flag up to the trap door leading to the roof but were unable to open it, as a policeman was standing on top of it.[5] Once word of the situation reached Ellet, he notified the mayor that if the men were not speedily and safely returned to the boats and the flag were not kept flying, then the city would be bombarded.[6] Ellet issued this threat without informing Commodore

Davis, even though he could not have enforced it himself as none of his boats had cannon. However, Davis probably would have taken severe action if the men had been injured.[7]

Davis was much more formal, sending a message to the mayor of Memphis requesting that the city be surrendered. The mayor, John Park, replied that "the civil authorities have no resources of defense, and by force of circumstances the city is in your power."[8] Upon receiving the reply from Mayor Park, Davis informed him "that Colonel Fitch, commanding the Indiana brigade, will take military possession of Memphis immediately."[9] The city was occupied peacefully at 11:00 a.m. on June 6, and remained in Union control for the remainder of the war.[10] That same day, Davis informed Secretary of the Navy Gideon Welles that the city had surrendered to him, although Ellet's son had already raised the United States flag over the city.[11]

There were a number of casualties during the battle. Remarkably, there were no civilian casualties, although some of the projectiles from the Union ironclads landed in the city. Davis believed that the Confederate fleet fired at his flotilla with the city behind it in the belief that the Union ironclads would not return the fire for fear of hitting the city and the civilians on the riverbank. Davis stated in a report that "The fire was returned on our part with care in this regard."[12] Still, a few projectiles hit the city and more probably would have except for the fact that the city is on a bluff and the gunners were aiming low to hit the Confederate rams below the waterline. Even with Davis's concern not to fire at the city, one young acting master on the *Benton* deliberately fired his cannon into Memphis. When asked why he did it, he replied "with a vacant smile, that he thought it would be a good thing."[13]

Union casualties were extremely light. Walke was the only ironclad captain whose official report appears in the Navy's *Official Records,* and he reported that only three men were slightly wounded. Lieutenant Phelps's unofficial report did not mention any casualties, whereas one of Davis's reports stated that only three men were slightly wounded and that only one boat was hit.[14] In the Ram Fleet, Ellet was the only one wounded, and his wound was not considered serious; however, he caught the measles, and his condition worsened.[15] Due to his incapacity, he turned command of the Ram Fleet over to his brother and steamed north on the *Switzerland* to recover.[16] Unfortunately, he died on June 21 when the boat was almost to Cairo.[17]

Confederate casualties were significant, although exactly how many died will never be known. An estimate at the low end would be at least one hundred killed, because seventy-five men went down with the *Lovell*, and a number of men were scalded when the *Beauregard*'s boiler exploded.[18] Along with the dead, there were probably about the same number wounded. Assuming that each Confederate boat had the same size crew as the *Lovell*—a safe assumption given that the *Lovell* was one of the larger boats—the strength of the Confederate fleet would have been 640 men. If one hundred men were killed and one hundred men were wounded, that number would represent a lose rate of 31%, an extremely high percentage.

A number of men became prisoners of war. Seventeen officers ended up at Johnson's Island Prison Camp, with most of them being from the *Price* and *Beauregard*. All of the men were listed as being in the Confederate Navy even though the River Defense Fleet was not part of the Confederate Navy. However, their ranks were a combination of Army and Navy ranks, as some of the men are listed as "2d Lieutenants," whereas others are listed as pilots, pursers, or assistant engineers.[19] Montgomery states in his report that the Federals claimed to have taken 161 prisoners, while a memorandum in the Navy's *Official Records* from the *Memphis Daily Avalanche* states that seventy to one hundred prisoners were taken.[20] Many more would have been taken prisoner, but they were able to escape into the woods and brush on the Arkansas side of the river, even though the Union boats fired at them when they refused to stop. Only the few survivors from the *Lovell* were close enough to the Tennessee side of the river to swim to shore, and most of them—including the captain of the *Lovell*, James C. Delancy—were taken prisoner.[21]

The survivors of the Confederate defeat finally assembled at Yazoo City, Mississippi. There, Montgomery was able to pay them on June 21 from $30,000 provided by General Lovell. Once they were paid, the men were discharged and, for all intents and purposes, the River Defense Fleet ceased to exist.[22] Lieutenant Issac N. Brown, commander of the CSS *Arkansas*, was very disappointed that Montgomery paid off and discharged his men. Brown was under the impression that some of them would join his crew on the ironclad *Arkansas*.[23] This was a tremendous loss for Brown, because Montgomery's men were experienced riverboat men, many of whom knew how to operate steam engines. However, Brown benefited from one of the Confederate boats that escaped, the *Paul Jones*, as it was a supply boat. The *Paul Jones* was carrying an important cargo of gunpowder, artillery projectiles, and commissary supplies. All of these supplies were turned over to Brown, who put them to good use.

Of the eight Confederate boats in the River Defense Fleet, four—*General Bragg*, *Sumter*, *General Price*, and *Little Rebel*—were captured, made into prizes, repaired, and became Union warships.[24] Prize money for these boats was awarded to the men aboard the ironclads and eventually to the men aboard the Ellet rams.[25] Three of the captured Confederate boats were not salvageable. The *Colonel Lovell* was sunk outright; the *General Thompson* caught on fire and blew up; and the *General Beauregard* was so badly damaged that it was not worth recovering.[26] Only one, the *General Van Dorn*, escaped; however, it quickly shared the same fate as other boats in the River Defense Fleet. It was burned, along with two other boats on June 26 in the Yazoo River by Commodore Pinckney, who panicked when the unarmed *Lancaster* and *Monarch* appeared in front of his position.[27] In addition to the four rams that the Union Navy was able to salvage, there were a number of civilian steamboats at Memphis. These eight boats were valued at $40,375 and seized as prizes.[28] The prize money and the honor of who was to be given credit for capturing the various boats quickly became a matter of contention between Davis and Ellet.

Ellet believed that the Ram Fleet should be given credit for capturing all of the boats into which it came in contact, and granted the right of adding them to his fleet. However, Davis quickly secured the *Bragg*, *Sumter*, and *Little Rebel*, and put Navy officers in command of them.[29] Securing the *Price* took longer, as there was competition on who was to raise it and which fleet the boat would join. Ellet made the first attempt, asking Davis for use of the salvage boat *Champion No. 3* to pump the *Price* out and raise it.[30] Unfortunately, the *Champion* broke its pump; thus, Ellet's attempt was unsuccessful. Lieutenant Le Roy Fitch, who was in command of the USS *Judge Torrence*, visited the site of the attempted recovery and informed Davis on June 9 that he did "not think there will be any great difficulty in getting her [*Price*] afloat, and if you [Davis] will sanction it I will move down here and endeavor to raise her."[31] Fitch, with help from the crew of the *Champion*, was successful; on June 15, the *Price* was afloat.[32]

Ellet was particularly incensed by the loss of the *Little Rebel*, and sent a number of messages to Davis about the boat, in addition to complaining to Stanton about it. Davis answered one of Ellet's messages on June 9 using wording similar to Ellet's instruction from Stanton that giving up any of the captured boats "would interfere with my general plan of operation."[33] Ellet did not relent and replied on June 10:

> Now, commodore, it was not from the enemy, but from this little prize crew that your tugs took this vessel [*Little Rebel*]; and I do not ask you to give her to me, as your note assumes, but merely to restore her to me as she was before she was taken from me. She is mine, commodore, the spoils of my first and, I fear, my last naval engagement. I may afford hereafter to give her to you, but I can not, until she is returned to my possession, consent to her surrender.[34]

Ellet never gained control of any of the captured boats. In a report to Stanton, he philosophically stated, "These facts [the sinking of the Confederate boats] go to show that ram fighting and prizes are scarcely compatible."[35]

Ellet and Davis continued having disagreements over matters beyond the fate of the captured Confederate boats. Davis appeared to be willing to cooperate with Ellet, offering to send a gunboat with Lieutenant-Colonel Ellet on an expedition downriver—an offer that Ellet informed Stanton he would not decline although he feared that "the slowness of the gunboat will impede the progress of the expedition."[36] The expedition was delayed, and Davis asked Ellet to provide three rams and a small tug for an expedition up the White River.[37] However, Ellet did not reciprocate Davis's cooperation as he did not send any of his boats on the White River Expedition. Ellet cited a number of reasons for not providing the requested support, the most critical of which was that he did not want any of his boats to be placed under the command of one of Davis's commanders. Ellet stated that he thought "it would be better to keep the two branches of the expedition entirely distinct, that emulation may be excited and that some men of spirit in the Ram Fleet who had not a chance to distinguish themselves at Memphis may have it on this occasion."[38]

Ellet was probably glad that he did not send any of his rams with the White River Expedition, as the expedition was a disaster for the Navy. During the battle with the Confederate batteries at St. Charles, Arkansas, an artillery projectile went through the unarmored roof of the *Mound City*, hitting its steam drum. The resulting explosion killed eighty-two men and severely wounded twenty-five more, some of whom later died. Out of a crew of 175 officers and men, only three officers and twenty-five men were not injured.[39] It was probably due to this disaster that Stanton questioned Ellet about his lack of cooperation, to which Ellet replied, "I did not send a detachment up White River to act in conjunction with the gunboats, as Commodore Davis requested, because the commodore was not willing to receive my cooperation unless I placed my vessels under the command of one of his officers. This, of course, I could not consent to do. Our successes at Memphis were gained by acting independently."[40] Even without Ellet's cooperation and the disabling of the *Mound City*, the expedition achieved its objective of capturing St. Charles when the 46th Indiana Infantry stormed and captured the Confederate batteries.[41]

Ellet's departure from his fleet, and subsequent death, improved relations between the two fleets. The increased cooperation was probably due as much to Alfred Ellet's personality as to a message from Stanton to Alfred Ellet when he assumed command of the Ram Fleet. Stanton wrote, "You will observe that by his [Charles Ellet] instructions the Ram Fleet was placed under the general command of the commander of the gunboat squadron. The President desires you to consider yourself in the same position, believing that cooperative action will be more likely to produce good results than independent action, and that the commander of the gunboats should have chief command."[42] Stanton's message had the desired effect: Alfred Ellet received praise from both Davis and Farragut for his willingness to cooperate. However, difficulties soon arose.

On July 16, 1862, the Senate and House of Representatives passed a resolution that the "Western Gunboat Fleet, constructed by the War Department for operations on the Western waters, shall be transferred to the Navy Department."[43] But, the transfer was not finalized until October 1. However, Davis did not stay with the squadron long after that. David D. Porter was informed by Secretary of the Navy Gideon Welles that command of the squadron was to be transferred from Acting Rear-Admiral Charles H. Davis to him no later than October 12. In addition,, upon assuming command, he would become an acting rear-admiral.[44] Stanton, still wanting the Ram Fleet to be independent and reporting directly to him, informed Alfred Ellet that "The Ram Fleet was not included in the transfer of the Gunboat Fleet to the Navy Department. Its disposition was left for further consideration. You will retain command, as heretofore, until further orders."[45] Ellet must have shown his instructions to Acting Rear-Admiral David Porter, as Porter informed the Secretary of the Navy that Ellet had not received any instructions to turn the Ram Fleet over to him. Welles wrote to Stanton about this issue, stating, "I had supposed that that act of July 16, 1862, included a transfer of all gunboats in the Western waters, the Ram Fleet among them."[46] Messages were passed between Porter and Alfred Ellet, with the former insisting that the Ram Fleet was under his command and the latter informing Porter that it was not and that he was "authorized to act on the river independent of the naval commander." Porter told Alfred Ellet that he "would recognize no organization within the limits of my command other than the one established by the Navy Department, and shall direct that all vessels acting without my orders be brought to and detained by any naval commander who might meet them operating on the river contrary to the general order for the organization of the squadron."[47] Luckily, none of Porter's captains ever had to fulfill this threat.

The issue of the Ram Fleet continued to fester. Porter wanted control of the Ram Fleet and continually badgered Welles and Fox about needing to add it to his command. In addition, he requested the formation of a naval brigade under the command of Colonel Alfred Ellet, which would be used to fight the guerrilla bands that interfered with shipping on the river.[48] Porter informed Welles that he recommended its transfer to his command most strongly, "provided that it is transferred without any of the personnel. The rams are the best vessels for certain purposes on the river, and there is not one of them that would not be useful to us, one way or another." Porter further stated that he proposed to retain some of the men giving " them an appointment in the Navy – nothing higher than ensign."[49] The issue was finally resolved at a meeting of the full cabinet on November 7, during which President Lincoln decided "That Brigadier-General Ellet report to Rear-Admiral Porter for instruction, and act under his direction until otherwise ordered by the War Department."[50] Stanton followed up with a message to Ellet, stating, "As soon as your brigade is organized [the proposed Naval Brigade] and ready for service you will report for orders and duty to Rear-Admiral Porter. The Ram Fleet, when ready for duty, will also be reported to him for orders."[51]

* * *

During the Battle of Memphis, the Union benefited from a number of factors, the first of which being that the Battle of Plum Point occurred first. The Battle of Plum Point taught Union Navy some tough but useful lessons that paid a dividend at Memphis. Based on what he learned at Plum Point, Davis made sure that the ironclad fleet fought as a unit.

He was helped in this regard at Memphis because the river was wide enough for all of his boats to be in a single line, allowing each boat to protect the sides of the ones adjacent to it. The initial location of the deployment of the ironclads was fortunate, as the river's deep main channel was narrow, and many of the ironclads were in water too shallow to allow an attack by the Confederate rams. This small geographic feature was crucial, because initially the ironclads were steaming upriver with their vulnerable sterns exposed to ramming. Had the Union boats been in deeper water, and the Confederates attacked before he ironclads had turned around to face downriver, they would have exposed their sterns or broadsides to ramming—an easier and more vulnerable target for the rams. Also, Union gunnery was much better than it had been at Plum Point, and Union gunners were able to achieve some disabling hits to the Confederate rams. Lastly, not enough credit can be given to the timely appearance of Ellet's rams. The *Queen of the West* and *Monarch* were responsible for completely disrupting the Confederate battle line, as well as for disabling more of the Confederate fleet than the Union ironclads had.

Everything went wrong for Montgomery and his fleet. The lack of coal at Memphis limited his options, forcing him to risk an engagement that would lack the element of surprise. There were no heavy guns emplaced on the bluffs, as at Fort Pillow, which could have helped the fleet by directing plunging fire onto the Union ironclads as well as providing a refuge if the battle went against the Confederates. Even with these issues, victory was still a possibility, until things went amiss during the battle. First, Thompson's experienced gunners were missing, and Montgomery's inexperienced riverboat men were only able to hit the ironclads a few times, even when firing at their vulnerable sterns. Then, the engine breakdown on the *Lovell* could not have happened at a worse time, having allowed Ellet's rams to completely disrupt the Confederate formation in addition to directly or indirectly putting out of action at least four of the rams. Fortune was not with the Confederate fleet on June 6.

In the end, the Battle for Memphis was a forlorn hope, as the city was doomed when Corinth fell because there were no significant defenses on the landside of the city. The defeat at Memphis also represented a significant reduction in communication capabilities between the Confederate forces on both sides of the Mississippi as well as decreased access to the resources west of the Mississippi. Memphis was also more important industrially than Vicksburg and Port Hudson combined, which meant that its loss further depleted the Confederacy's limited industrial base.

For both the United States Army and Navy, Memphis became an important river supply depot, whose supply route from the north was almost impossible for the Confederates to interdict. The Navy made maximum use of Memphis's port and repair facilities, making it possible for any damaged boat to be repaired there rather than having to make the long trip upriver to Cairo. Additionally, in the spring of 1863, a Navy hospital was established in the Commercial Hotel.[52]

The loss of the Mississippi River Defense Fleet was a greater blow to the Confederacy than the loss of Memphis. As long as the Confederates were able to maintain a significant naval threat on the river, a fleet in being, the options of the Union Navy were limited. If Montgomery's fleet had been able to retreat to the Yazoo River, the White River, the Red River—any of the other major rivers that flowed into the Mississippi downriver from Memphis—the Union Navy would have been forced to detach substantial forces to guard each river. Porter would have had even more serious reservations about running a large part of his fleet past Vicksburg knowing that if the Confederate fleet came out of the side rivers, he would not be able to steam upriver in time to help the boats that were left behind. Also, had Montgomery's fleet remained intact and sortied with the *Arkansas*, the damage his rams could have done to the stationary Union ships would have been significant. The Union admirals were well aware of the advantage the destruction of Montgomery's fleet gave them, as Davis wrote his wife, "Thank God for this great success. If the gunboats had fled before me, as their speed easily enabled them to do, they would still have been a thorn in our side. Now they can give us no further trouble; and, moreover, the blockading force of the river by the rebels is destroyed."[53] Farragut wrote Gideon Welles. "Captain Davis having destroyed the enemy's gunboats composing the Montgomery fleet, there remains nothing but the ram now building in the Yazoo River and two gunboats. They are up at Greenwood, and I do not think they will every venture out within our reach. As soon as Vicksburg surrenders the river will be clear from anything but occasional assaults by the guerrillas from the bluffs in passing some five or six points on the river."[54]

The Union victory at Memphis gave the Union unchallenged control of the upper Mississippi, with the exception of an occasional guerrilla attack. The results of this victory would impact the future course of the war in the west. The victory gave the Union a supply line that the

Confederates could not seriously interrupt, and secured access to a substantial supply of cotton that could be transported north by riverboat. But, most importantly, this victory allowed the Union Navy to provide unhindered support to the Army on the upper Mississippi, and, once the CSS *Arkansas* was destroyed, gave the Union Navy freedom of action that it would make good use of during the Vicksburg Campaign.

Chapter 9

Rams versus Guns

> The universal opinion among naval and military engineers in the East is that a floating ram, striking and sinking the ironclad vessel, is the best mode of encountering it.
>
> —Secretary of War Edwin M. Stanton, 25 March 1862[1]

> In conversations with the Secretary [Confederate Secretary of the Navy Stephen R. Mallory] I always have been under the impression that, for purposes of coast defense, he conceived that ironclad rams were the best vessels.
>
> —Commander John M. Brooke, 26 February 1863[2]

Rams have a long history and were effectively used by many countries, especially Mediterranean ones. Sailing ships and cannon eventually made countries consider rowing and ramming obsolete. Ramming also fell out of fashion as sailing ships were ill equipped for the tactic. Sailing ships did not deliberately ram an enemy ship because they had no effective means of backing away from their target. Sailing ships did grapple each other with the idea of sending a boarding party over to take control of the enemy ship. But the concept of ramming was revived when ships became steam powered, especially after the CSS *Virginia*—formerly the USS *Merrimac*—rammed and sank the USS *Cumberland.*

The CSS *Virginia* was the first fully ironclad ship built during the Civil War and, although it was armed with ten heavy guns, a protruding cast iron ram was affixed to its bow.[3] Great emphasis was placed on the ram as the order appointing Franklin Buchanan, commander of the CSS *Virginia,* included the statement, "Her [*Virginia*] powers as a ram are regarded as very formidable, and it is hoped you will be able to test them. Like the bayonet charge of the infantry, this mode of attack, while the most destructive, will commend itself to you in the present scarcity of ammunition. It is one also that may be rendered destructive at night against the enemy at anchor. Even without guns the ship would, it is believed, be formidable as a ram."[4] On March 8, 1862, Buchanan followed his instructions when he rammed the USS *Cumberland* rather than stand off and sink it with the *Virginia*'s guns. The *Virginia* almost went down with the *Cumberland* when its ram got stuck in the *Cumberland*. Luckily for the *Virginia*, the ram broke off when the *Cumberland* was sinking, thus saving it from the same fate. The next day during the battle with the USS *Monitor*, the *Virginia*, now under the command of Lieutenant Catesby Jones, tried to ram the *Monitor* because its projectiles were unable to inflict serious damage. Even without the *Virginia*'s ram, Jones must have assumed that his iron bow was strong enough to damage the *Monitor*. However, due to the *Monitor*'s superior speed and maneuverability, Jones was not successful. All rams have faced this problem. If the ramming ship's speed and maneuverability were not superior to its target and adequate maneuvering room was available, the odds of a ramming attack being successful were negligible.

All steam-powered ironclads could be considered rams, even if they did not have a protruding ram. They were rams, because their bow was reinforced by protective iron and strong enough to crush an enemy ship's hull—if it was struck with sufficient momentum. Commander John M. Brooke testified before a Joint Special Committee of both Houses of the Confederate Congress, which was investigating the affairs of the Confederate Navy Department, that he considered all ironclads rams, whether or not they had a beak: "When I speak of a ram particularly, then I should regard it as doubtful, whether she had armament or not; but when I speak of ironclad vessels, I intend to convey the idea that they are also rams, but carrying armament."[5] Brooke also informed the committee that

> Any strong ship can ram another down whether she has a beak or not, and the greater the weight and strength of the vessel, the greater the momentum. If a man spoke to me of a ram, I should infer that she had only a strong cutwater. I should not take it for granted that she had a beak. There are some persons who think that it is necessary for a vessel to have a beak in order to run another vessel down and sink her. Such is not the case; the stronger and heavier vessel, the advantages of collision being equal, will run the other down whether she has a beak or not. In the accidents which have happened demonstrating the power of ships to run each other down, the damage has been done by the stem or cutwater.[6]

Although iron ships could be considered rams even without a projecting beak, a wooden ship without a projecting beak or a reinforced bow could not. Wooden ships that were not sufficiently reinforced would normally inflict as much or more damage to themselves than they did to their victim. As wooden ships could not stand up to an ironclad when exchanging broadsides, ramming was about the only option available for a wooden ship to sink an ironclad, which is why all Mississippi rams had reinforced bows.

The Union fleet found out about self-inflicted damage when wooden ships—the bows of which had not been reinforced—rammed the ironclad *Tennessee* during the Battle of Mobile Bay. During that battle, Farragut ordered the USS *Monongahela* and *Lackawanna* to "run down the ram [CSS *Tennessee*]" when the *Tennessee* came out from the protection of Fort Morgan to challenge the Union fleet.[7] Although both the USS *Monongahela* and *Lackawanna* were able to ram the *Tennessee,* they suffered more damage than they inflicted upon the *Tennessee.* In fact, in a postbattle examination of the *Tennessee,* discerning where the *Lackawanna* and *Monongahela* had rammed it was impossible.[8] However, when the *Lackawanna* accidentally rammed the wooden *Hartford,* it crushed "half-way through, knocking two port-holes into one" and upset one of the Dahlgren guns. The damage to the *Hartford* was severe enough that its crew feared the ship would sink.[9]

The difficulty of destroying a fully ironclad ship by cannon fire was also demonstrated during this battle. Even though the *Tennessee*'s smoke stack was shot away, and many of its gun ports jammed shut, only one shot penetrated its armor. This one shot was a 15-inch solid shot projectile, fired at point blank range, from one of the monitors.[10] What finally forced the surrender of the *Tennessee* was that its exposed rudder chain was cut and she became unmaneuverable.[11] If a true ram with a projecting beak had been in the Union fleet, it would have been able to penetrate the hull of the *Tennessee* and sink it with relatively little damage to herself due to both the slow rate of fire of the large guns on board the *Tennessee* and the problems the *Tennessee* had getting its guns to fire reliably.

The slow rate of fire and the inaccuracy of the smoothbore guns used during the Civil War helped made ramming feasible. Even the adoption of large caliber rifled guns did not significantly change this fact. The problem was how to hit and disable a ram moving toward your ship at a high rate of speed when it presented a relatively small head-on target. During the Battle of Plum Point, the USS *Carondelet* fired "fifty-seven 64-pounder, 32-pounder and rifled solid shot, and three rifled shells," then, during the Battle of Memphis, the *Carondelet* fired "52 solid shot [rifled and round] and 10 rifled 15-second shell."[12] Because not as many ironclads were heavily involved at Plum Point, it can be estimated that the Union fleet fired about 200 projectiles during that engagement while at Memphis; with more boats involved, the fleet may have fired 300 projectiles. Although no Confederate boats were seriously damaged by gunfire at Plum Point, the Union ironclads were able to disable some at Memphis. One, the *Thompson*, was set on fire when its protective cotton caught fire. The fire got out of control, and the boat blew up when the fire reached its magazine. The *Little Rebel* was disabled when its engine was hit as it was trying to ram one of the Union ironclads. As a result, the crew ran it aground, and the boat was captured. The *Beauregard* was damaged after having accidentally rammed the *Price* and was all but stationary when projectiles from the ironclads hit her. The damage to the *Beauregard* was severe enough, that, although the it was captured, it was considered too damaged to be salvaged. The *Bragg* was also hit by gunfire from the ironclads, but at the time it was stuck on a sandbar and completely stationary. The *Bragg* was captured and put to use by the Union.[13] In summary, the five Union ironclads were responsible for taking out of action two moving boats and damaging two stationary boats at close range while firing about 300 projectiles. In contrast, the two Union rams sank the *Lovell*, disabled the *Sumter*, as well as assisting in damaging at least two others. In reality, both rams and Civil War–era heavy naval guns were only truly effective at close ranges.

Both the Union and Confederate Navies continued to use rams on the Mississippi and its tributaries throughout the war. After the CSS *Arkansas* made its famous run past the Union fleet to Vicksburg, the ironclad USS *Essex* and the ram *Queen of the West* were given the mission of destroying the *Arkansas*. The attack took place early on morning of July 22, 1862.[14] Because the *Arkansas* was anchored under the protection of the Vicksburg batteries, no Union boat, least of all the wooden ones, could stand the sustained fire of all of the guns and maintain its position while fighting the current of the river. Consequently, both the *Essex* and the *Queen of the West* attempted to ram the *Arkansas*, although the *Essex* fired on the *Arkansas* as well.[15] Although some damage was inflicted on the *Arkansas*, it was neither sunk nor permanently disabled.

Admiral Porter, commander of the Union Mississippi Squadron, was a firm believer in the capabilities of rams. In January 1863, he informed Lieutenant Commander Selfridge that the Confederates had a ram, the CSS *Pontchartrain*, up the Arkansas River, and that if it appeared, he should use the ram *Bragg* to ram and destroy her.[16] Then, Porter informed the Secretary of the Navy that the monitor being built at Cincinnati could sink the *Benton*—the most powerful ship in his fleet—with its beaked ram if he failed to sink it with gunfire.[17] However, in his enthusiasm for rams, Porter was mistaken about the monitor. What Porter saw as a beaked ram was actually an extension of the hull for the purpose of providing extra length and speed to the monitor. In addition, the anchor chain locker was located immediately behind the "beak," and thus would have made it a very structurally weak ram.[18]

Porter wanted to cut off river-borne supplies en route to Port Hudson or Vicksburg, hoping to starve the garrison at Port Hudson. To accomplish this, on February 8, 1863, Porter ordered Colonel Charles Rivers Ellet, who was already down river from Vicksburg, to take the *Queen of the West* and the *De Soto* on a mission to destroy "all you can of the enemy's stores and provisions and get your vessel back safe" to the mouth of the Red River.[19] However, Porter was worried that the Confederate ram *Webb*, which was known to be up the Red River, would attack and defeat the *Queen of the West* and *De Soto*. Consequently, he ordered the ironclad *Indianola*, under the command of Lieutenant Commander George Brown, to run past Vicksburg for the purpose of protecting the *Queen of the West* and the *De Soto* from the *Webb*. However, before he sent the *Indianola* down river, Porter had the ironclad strengthened so that it could act as a ram. Porter's instructions to Brown included the statement , "Don't forget that I had your vessel strengthened to perform the part of a ram; don't hesitate to run anything down."[20]

Porter ordered the *Indianola* past Vicksburg on this mission, even though he knew that it could not safely return. The problem was that the *Indianola* would have to run the Vicksburg gauntlet against the current to rejoin the squadron, and it could not make more than two knots against the current. This slow speed, even at night, would make the *Indianola* an all but stationary target for the Confederate gunners. However, going downriver, the force of the river tremendously increased the speed of the boat, and allowed the *Indianola* to successful run the Vicksburg gauntlet on the night of February 13.[21]

After successfully passing Vicksburg, Brown learned from Ellet, now aboard the captured *Era No. 5*, on the morning of February 16, about eight miles below Natchez, that the *Queen of the West* had been captured and the *De Soto* had been burned.[22] On February 18, Ellet decided to go upriver in the *Era No. 5* to inform Porter about the situation, and request that another boat be sent downriver to help Brown, who had decided to stay downriver. Brown's decision was based on the hope that an additional boat would be sent to help him and that, if the river rose another foot, Port Hudson would become unapproachable by land, making his blockade more effective.[23]

On February 22, Brown decided to go upriver, but kept two coal barges lashed to the *Indianola*, even though they severely slowed his speed to about two knots.[24] Brown kept them, thinking that it may be necessary to supply any boat that came to help him with coal. At about 9:30 p.m., on February 24, Brown realized that four boats were pursuing him.[25] These four boats were the rams *William H. Webb* and the recently captured *Queen of the West* along with the unarmed steamer *Dr. Beatty*, which had close to a 250-man boarding party on her, and the unarmed *Grand Era*.[26] Not all of the Confederate boats were fast as the *Dr. Beatty* was lashed to the *Grand Era* because it did not have enough power to keep up with the two rams.[27]

Upon seeing the Confederate boats, Brown immediately prepared for action, turning the *Indianola* around to face downriver. The *Queen of the West* was the first to ram the *Indianola;* striking one of the coal barges, but becoming stuck. The *Webb* then rammed the *Indianola*, an impact that helped free the *Queen of the West.* These initial rammings stripped the protective coal barges away from the *Indianola*, leaving it vulnerable. Then, in quick order, the *Queen of the West* rammed the *Indianola* twice, and the *Webb* rammed it once. After being rammed four times, the *Indianola* began sinking and surrendered. Even though the *Indianola* had fired its large guns at point-blank range at both the *Queen of the West* and the *Webb,* only three men on board these boats were killed and five wounded. The most serious damage done to either boat was from the impact of ramming the *Indianola*. This damage was severe enough that both boats needed repairs.[28]

This action was the most effective use of rams after the Battle of Memphis, and demonstrated the potential of rams during the Civil War. However, it needs to be noted, that the *Indianola* was very slow and not very maneuverable. In addition, the action took place in the dark, where the gunner's visibility was even more limited than during the day. Still, two wooden rams were able to sink and capture a heavily armed ironclad, one that was invulnerable to the guns on board the rams.[29]

The success of the Confederate rams during the war forced the Union Navy to take the threat seriously. Consequently, the new monitors, being designed by John Ericsson, were required to be ram proof at all depths and have a powerful butting instrument.[30] The danger rams presented based on their success during the Civil War—combined with the invulnerability of a heavily armored ship from all but the largest guns—created a dilemma for naval officers around the world. Many officers became convinced that rams were the only real effective countermeasure to ironclad ships—an opinion reinforced by the results of the Battle of Lissa in 1866.

The Battle of Lissa was part of the Austro-Prussian War in which Italy became involved due to a treaty with Prussia. The Italian fleet was not very active, and finally the Italian government forced it to take the offensive. As a result, the fleet besieged the island of Lissa. The Austrian fleet took the challenge and came to the aid of the island. Although inferior to the Italian fleet, the Austrian's fleet was more aggressive and attacked the Italians. The battle was a confused melee with limited visibility due to fog and smoke. The most dramatic action was when the Austrian flagship, *Ferdinand Maximilian*, rammed and sank the armored Italian *Re d'Italia*. This battle was invoked by ram advocates for years, as gunfire during the battle had not sunk any of the armored ships. However, ram advocates failed to mention that the *Re d'Italia* was stationary when it was rammed. There had been other attempts to ram during the battle, but the captains of those ships lost their nerve and did not complete the maneuver, or the intended target was able to maneuver out of the way.[31] The Battle of Lissa solidified the presence of rams in navies around the world, including the pre-eminent British Navy. However, ramming was seldom tested due to the infrequency of naval warfare between the European countries. As a consequence, "it was to prove far more of a potential danger in squadron manoervres [*sic*] during peacetime than a possible weapon in war."[32]

By the start of World War I, rams had fallen out of favor, but the Allies soon discovered that ramming was an effective tactic against the U-boat. Unfortunately for the Allies, any ship that rammed a U-boat normally suffered serious damage. Since the ships doing most of the ramming, which were generally destroyers and corvettes, were cheaper to construct than a U-boat, it was an economic solution. Even during World War II, when better technology was available to detect and destroy U-boats, ramming was still used when the opportunity presented itself.

In October 1942, Convoy SC104 was steaming to Great Britain when it came under attack by a number of U-boats. Due to the bad weather, many merchant ships had difficulty keeping position. Additionally, the escorts had trouble keeping their radar and sonar units working—besides getting false radar readings due to the high waves. U-boats were spotted, and the HMS *Viscount*, a World War I–era destroyer, rammed and sank a U-boat after it had missed ramming one the previous day. Unfortunately, the *Viscount* was so badly damaged that it had to leave the convoy and steam directly to its home port. The next day, the HMS *Fame*, a destroyer launched in 1934, started to ram a U-boat that surfaced after the *Fame* had depth charged it. However, the captain of the *Fame*, realizing that the U-boat was seriously damaged, changed course and stopped engines, only hitting the U-boat with a glancing blow. While the U-boat was sinking, the hydroplanes on the U-boat ripped open the side of the *Fame* below the waterline, forcing the *Fame* to leave the convoy, and reducing the protective escort to four corvettes. Shortly after the *Fame* had departed, the *Potentilla*, under the command of Lieutenant Commander Monsen, the new convoy escort commander, detected a U-boat and steamed at full speed toward it. The ships were steering straight for each other and, had they rammed, both vessels would have been heavily damaged. However, both ships veered, passing within thirty yards of each other. Even though it was hit by fire from the *Potentilla*'s guns, the U-boat escaped. Ramming a U-boat was a viable means of sinking one, but when it occurred, the ship doing the ramming was normally so badly damaged that it needed extensive repairs. Still, comparing the cost of a corvette or destroyer to that of a U-boat, the results were normally economically justified unless, of course, the convoy lost too much of its protection.[33]

The use of air and naval kamikazes by the Japanese during World War II was, in reality, a ramming tactic. These suicide attacks were probably the only means of successfully ramming an enemy surface ship in World War II due to the rapid and powerful guns then in use. Today, suicide ramming is still a threat and a low cost means of damaging or sinking an enemy ship. The best contemporary example is the USS *Cole*, which was seriously damaged from a suicide attack by a small explosive-packed boat—although the explosives and not the ramming did the damage. However, prior to the advent of high-powered, rapid-fire guns, ships were vulnerable to nonsuicidal ramming, and it was a tactic feared by commanders of armored ships that were invulnerable to gunfire.

Conclusion

The Impact of the Battle of Memphis

> But they [the press] should remember that if you expose that flotilla needlessly, though you may acquire [a] reputation, you will needlessly expose the possession of the great Mississippi and all its wonderful tributaries as well as all the magnificent cities on their banks.
>
> —Message from Flag-Officer Andrew H. Foote to Captain Charles H. Davis, 30 May 1862[1]

> From the result of this battle [Plum Point] I have no hesitancy in saying that had not the fleet been weakened by taking six of my fastest boats and sending them to Fort Jackson I would have destroyed the entire Federal fleet in the Upper Mississippi.
>
> —Message from Commodore Joseph E. Montgomery to Secretary of War George W. Randolph, 1 July 1862[2]

The Naval Battle Memphis was a pivotal battle during the Civil War because it meets three main criteria. The first criterion is whether it was necessary for the battle to have occurred, the second is what would have happened if the results of the battle had been different, and the third is how the results of the battle impacted future events. Although a battle does not need to meet all three criteria to be considered pivotal, the Battle of Memphis does.

For the Union Navy to gain naval control of the Mississippi River, the Battle of Memphis, or a similar battle, had to occur. If the battle had not taken place, Montgomery's Ram Fleet would have survived and remained an unremitting threat to the Union squadron. If the fleet dispersed, Davis and his successors would have been required to leave a strong force at all navigable rivers, so that fast Confederate warships could not slip back into the Mississippi and disrupt Union shipping.

If the fleet remained intact and went up the Yazoo River or came under the protection of the guns at Vicksburg, Porter's decision to run the Vicksburg batteries with a large part of his fleet would have been very risky—a gamble that Porter would probably not have made. The reason is that any ironclad that ran the Vicksburg batteries would have had a slow and difficult journey to safely return upriver. Thus, even if Porter had decided to take the risk, he would have been forced to leave enough warships behind so that the Confederate fleet could not have overwhelmed the remaining boats and headed north, severely weakening the force he took downriver. Consequently, the Confederate Ram Fleet had to be destroyed before the Union could gain control of the Mississippi River.

If the results of the Battle of Memphis had been different, and Montgomery had won a decisive victory, the impact upon future Union operations in the Mississippi River valley would have been tremendous. A Confederate victory was a real possibility considering the results of the Battle of Plum Point, the disabling of the *Mound City* when its boiler was hit during the White River Expedition, and the capture of the *Indianola* by Confederate rams. If all five Union ironclads had been lost, the Union would have been forced to rebuild its river fleet to include recruiting new crews, officers, and pilots. Such a loss was possible, as Davis and his captains were reluctant to abandon any disabled boat, and would have continued the battle even if they were being overwhelmed. Moreover, it would have been difficult for the ironclads to retreat, as they could not have outrun the Confederate rams.

Rebuilding five ironclads would have taken six months at a minimum. Although the Union had the industrial capability to rebuild the fleet, providing trained officers, crews, and pilots would have been more difficult. The Navy may have been reluctant to provide the number of required regular officers, the new crews would have needed extensive training, and experienced pilots may have been hesitant to serve in such a dangerous job. Such a time lag would have prevented Grant from moving south of Vicksburg in 1863, and would have allowed the city to remain in Confederate hands into 1864. If it had still been committed to capturing Vicksburg, Grant's army would not have been available to go to the rescue of the besieged Union Army at Chattanooga. The potential ramifications of a decisive Confederate victory at Memphis include surrender of the Union Army at Chattanooga and possible Confederate independence due to Union war wariness.

The momentous Union victory at Memphis gave the Union full control of the upper Mississippi. Davis's victory at Memphis, along with the dispersal of the regular Confederate Navy and the destruction of the *Arkansas* in August 1862, gave Porter freedom of action that he would exploit as he assisted Grant in taking Vicksburg. Grant fully understood this significance, stating in his memoirs that "The navy under Porter was all it could be, during the entire campaign [Vicksburg Campaign]. Without its assistance the campaign could not have been successfully made with twice the number of men engaged. It could not have been made at all, in the way it was, without such assistance."[3] Without the decisive victory at Memphis, Grant's plan to cross the Mississippi south of Vicksburg could not have happened. Memphis was one of the pivotal battles in the opening of the Mississippi River. The full significance of Davis's victory at Memphis can be summed up in a letter he wrote to his wife just after the battle:

> My situation was, I may now say, a very unpleasant one. I felt if fully. To attack the batteries [Fort Pillow] and rebel fleet with my own insignificant force would have been an extreme folly, a risk which nothing could have justified. For my first and special duty was to retain command of the river. This was the charge I had to keep, my particular trust. Losing that command, I exposed the long extent of country bordering on the Mississippi to St. Louis, bordering on the Ohio, the Tennessee, the Cumberland, and all their tributaries. I exposed the rear of General Halleck's army at Corinth; and, finally, I renewed the alarms of war throughout the West and Northwest, losing all the hard-won advantages of Foote and Pope.[4]

Unfortunately, the Battle of Memphis has been forgotten by many students of the Civil War, as the Union victory appears, in retrospect, to have been a foregone conclusion and is overshadowed by later events. However, it was one of the pivotal battles of the Civil War, and the key events in the Union's naval success on the upper Mississippi. The victory at Memphis was a Trafalgar-style victory that gave the Union absolute naval control of the upper Mississippi and continued the Union on the path to victory.[5]

Appendix A

History of the Boats

This appendix describes the history of each of the boats that fought at the Battle of Plum Point or the Battle of Memphis. It is not my intention to provide detailed physical information or armament for each of the boats. Such information, in many cases, is not available. In addition, the armament for most of the boats changed significantly throughout the war.

Benton

A converted catamaran snag-boat originally owed by James Eads. Named after Senator Thomas Hart Benton of Missouri. Commissioned by the Army on February 24, 1862. Although not fully armored, the *Benton* had more armor than any of the Pook ironclads. Involved in the capture of Island No. 10. Fought at Plum Point and Memphis. Transferred to the Navy on October 1, 1862. Ran past the Vicksburg batteries and participated in the bombardment of Grand Gulf. Was part of the Red River Expedition. Decommissioned on July 20, 1865, and sold in November 1865.[1]

Cairo

A Pook-designed ironclad. Named after Cairo, Illinois. Commissioned by the Army on January 25, 1862. First major action was the Battle of Plum Point. Fought at the Battle of Memphis. Transferred to the Navy on October 1, 1862. Was sunk on December 12, 1862, by a Confederate torpedo (known today as a mine) in the Yazoo River. Was raised in 1964, and is currently on display at the Vicksburg National Military Park.[2]

Carondelet

A Pook-designed ironclad. Named after Carondelet, Missouri, which is now part of St. Louis. Commissioned by the Army on January 15, 1862, it was the first ironclad, by one day, to be commissioned by the

United States. Fought at Fort Henry and Fort Donelson. Was the first ironclad to run past the Confederate batteries at Island No. 10. Fought at Plum Point and Memphis. Transferred to the Navy on October 1, 1862. Ran past the Vicksburg batteries and participated in the bombardment of Grand Gulf. Was part of the Red River Expedition. Decommissioned on June 20, 1865, and sold on November 29, 1865.[3]

Cincinnati

A Pook-designed ironclad. Named after Cincinnati, Ohio. Commissioned by the Army on January 16, 1862. Participated in the capture of Fort Henry and Island No. 10. Rammed and sunk during the Battle of Plum Point. Was raised, repaired, and returned to service. Transferred to the Navy on October 1, 1862. Took part in the White River Campaign. While fighting Confederate batteries at Vicksburg was hit and sunk for a second time. Was again raised, repaired, and returned to service. In February 1865, was transferred to the West Gulf Blockading Squadron and patrolled off Mobile Bay and in the Mississippi Sounds. Decommissioned on August 4, 1865, and sold on March 28, 1866.[4]

Colonel Lovell

Previously named the steamer *Hercules.* Named after Confederate Colonel William S. Lovell, who was a graduate of the United States Naval Academy and a colonel in the Confederate Army. Commissioned by the Confederacy in early spring 1862. Participated in the Battle of Plum Point, but was not actively engaged. Participated in the Battle of Memphis; was rammed by the USS *Queen of the West* and sunk in deep water.[5]

General Beauregard

Previously named the *Ocean* and used as a towboat in the New Orleans area before becoming a Confederate warship. Named after Confederate General Pierre Gustave Toutant Beauregard. Commissioned by the Confederacy in early spring 1862. Participated in the Battle of Plum Point but did not get into action. Participated in the Battle of Memphis and accidently rammed the CSS *General Price* while trying to ram the USS *Monarch.* Its boiler exploded when hit by an artillery projectile, probably fired by the USS *Benton.* As a result of the damage, the *Beauregard* sunk and was left as a wreck.[6]

General Bragg

Previously named the *Mexico*, it steamed between New Orleans, Vera Cruz, and the Isthmus of Panama before becoming a Confederate warship. Named after Confederate General Braxton Bragg. Commissioned by the Confederacy in early spring 1862. Participated in the Battle of Plum Point, ramming and heavily damaging the USS *Cincinnati*. Participated in the Battle of Memphis, running aground so that the crew could escape. Salvaged by the Union Navy and commissioned as the USS *Bragg*. In Union service, the *Bragg* spent most of its time patrolling the Mississippi. On June 15, 1864, the *Bragg* and some other boats engaged a Confederate battery near Tunica Bend, Louisiana. During that fight, the *Bragg* was disabled, but was repaired and returned to duty. Decommissioned at Cairo on July 24, 1865, sold on September 1, 1865, and renamed the *Mexico*.[7]

General M. Jeff. Thompson

Named after Confederate General M. Jeff Thompson. A tugboat on the Mississippi, was purchased by the Confederacy, converted, and then commissioned in early spring 1862. Participated in the Battle of Plum Point, but did not do any fighting. Participated in the Battle of Memphis. During the battle the *Thompson* was set on fire by shells fired from the Union ironclads and ran aground. As a result of the fire its magazine exploded, and it burned to the waterline.[8]

General Price

(Also known as the *General Sterling Price*.) Previously named the *Laurent Milledon*, and worked as a commercial towboat in the New Orleans area before the war. Named after Confederate General Sterling Price. Commissioned by the Confederacy in early spring 1862. Participated in the Battle of Plum Point and rammed the USS *Cincinnati*. Participated in the Battle of Memphis, but was accidentally rammed and disabled by the CSS *Beauregard*. Sinking in shallow water, the *General Price* was raised by the Federals and placed into their service as the USS *Sterling Price*. In Union service, the *Sterling Price* ran the Vicksburg batteries with Porter and ferried troops across the river. Prior to joining the Red River Expedition, it accidentally rammed and sank the USS *Conestoga*. After the Red River Expedition, it was assigned to patrolling the Mississippi. Decommissioned on July 24, 1865, and sold on October 3, 1865.[9]

General Van Dorn

(Also known as the *General Earl Van Dorn.*) Named after Confederate General Earl Van Dorn. Commissioned by the Confederacy in early spring 1862. Participated in the Battle of Plum Point, firing at the mortar boat and then ramming the *USS Mound City.* Participated in the Battle of Memphis and was the only Confederate ram to escape. While defending the Yazoo River, it was burned, along with the CSS *Livingston, General Clark,* and *Polk,* by the Confederates when the USS *Lancaster* and *Monarch* approached their position.[10]

Little Rebel

Previously named the *R. E. & A. N. Watson* or *R. & J. Watson.* Named the *Little Rebel* due to her small size compared to the other ships in Montgomery's fleet. Commissioned by the Confederacy in early spring 1862 and was the only screw-driven boat in the Confederate fleet. Participated in the Battle of Plum Point by firing her guns. Participated in the Battle of Memphis and was hit by projectiles below the waterline and disabled. Was run aground, captured, and added to the Union fleet as the USS *Little Rebel.* Spent the rest of the war patrolling the Mississippi and ferrying troops. Decommissioned on July 24, 1865, and sold on November 29, 1865. Was renamed the *Spy* and became a merchant ship until 1874.[11]

Louisville

A Pook-designed ironclad. Named after Louisville, Kentucky. Commissioned by the Army on January 16, 1862. Fought at Fort Donelson. Participated in the fight for Island No. 10. Fought at Plum Point and Memphis. Transferred to the Navy in October 1862. Ran past the Vicksburg batteries and participated in the bombardment of Grand Gulf. Was part of the Red River Expedition. Decommissioned on July 21, 1865, and sold on November 29, 1865.[12]

Monarch

Converted from a towboat to an Ellet ram. During the Battle of Memphis, it rammed and disabled the CSS *Sumter*; was actively engaged against some of the other Confederate rams; and participated in the pursuit of the two escaping Confederate vessels. Operated along the

Mississippi, until the Mississippi Marine Brigade was disbanded. Placed in reserve and sunk by ice in December 1864 and was later broken up.[13]

Mound City

A Pook-designed ironclad. Named after Mound City, Illinois. Commissioned by the Army on January 16, 1862. Participated in the capture of Island No. 10. Was rammed and sunk during the Battle of Plum Point. Raised, repaired, and returned to service. While on the White River Expedition, was penetrated by a Confederate projectile that caused the boiler to explode, killing and wounding most of her crew. Was again repaired, and participated in the Vicksburg Campaign and the Red River Expedition. Transferred to the Navy on October 1, 1862. After the war, was decommissioned and then sold on November 9, 1865.[14]

Pittsburg

(Also spelled *Pittsburgh*.) A Pook-designed ironclad. Named after Pittsburgh, Pennsylvania. Commissioned by the Army on January 16, 1862. Seriously damaged at Fort Donelson, was repaired, and participated in the capture of Island No. 10. Was the second ironclad to run past the Confederate batteries at Island Number 10. Fought at Plum Point and Memphis. Transferred to the Navy in October 1862. Was one of the ironclads that ran past the Vicksburg batteries and attacked Grand Gulf. At Grand Gulf, she was heavily damaged. Participated in the Red River Expedition. Decommissioned after the war, and sold on November 29, 1865.[15]

Queen of the West

Converted from a towboat to an Ellet ram. Was Colonel Ellet's flagship. At the Battle of Memphis, rammed the CSS *Colonel Lovell* and was then rammed by the CSS *Sumter*. Disabled, the *Queen of the West* was run aground, then repaired and returned to service. In July 1862 rammed, but did not seriously damage, the CSS *Arkansas* when it was docked at Vicksburg. When on an expedition up the Black River, it was disabled by Confederate artillery fire and captured on February 14, 1863. Renamed the CSS *Queen of the West*, she and the CSS *Webb* forced the ironclad USS *Indianola* to surrender. Attacked by three Union ships on April 14, 1863, on the Atchafalaya River, was hit by artillery fire and set on fire. Drifting down river, it ran aground and exploded.[16]

St. Louis

A Pook-designed ironclad (later named the *Baron De Kalb*). Named after St. Louis, Missouri, and then Revolutionary War General Baron De Kalb. Commissioned by the Army on January 31, 1862. Fought at Fort Henry, Fort Donelson, and Island No. 10. Participated in the Battles of Plum Point and Memphis. Renamed the *Baron De Kalb* in September 1861, and transferred to the US Navy in October 1862. Sunk by a Confederate mine on the Yazoo River on July 13, 1863.[17]

Sumter

(Also known as the *General Sumter.*) Named after the Revolutionary War General Thomas Sumter. Previously named the *Junius Beebe*, had worked as a towboat in the New Orleans area prior to the war. Commissioned by the Confederacy in early spring 1862. Participated in the Battle of Plum Point, ramming the USS *Cincinnati*. At the Battle of Memphis, rammed and seriously damaged the USS *Queen of the West.* Rammed and disabled by the *Monarch*, she tried to escape but ran aground and was captured. Recommissioned as the USS *Sumter*, it patrolled the Mississippi until running aground near Bayou Sara, Louisiana, and was abandoned. After being stripped by both the locals and the Union Navy, was burned by the Confederates.[18]

Appendix B

Biographies

Rear Admiral Charles Henry Davis (1807–1877) was born in Boston, Massachusetts, died in Washington, DC, and is buried in Cambridge Cemetery in Cambridge, Massachusetts.[1] He was appointed a midshipman in 1823. He became well known for his scientific work and served as Superintendent of the Nautical Almanac Office for a number of years. During the war, he helped plan and organize the South Atlantic blockade as well as the expeditions against Hatteras Inlet and Port Royal. At Port Royal, he served as Rear Admiral Samuel DuPont's chief of staff.[2] Flag Officer Andrew Foote personally requested that Davis be his temporary replacement as commander of the Western Flotilla while he recovered from his wound.[3] After destroying the Confederate fleet at Memphis, Davis was replaced by David D. Porter on October 15,

Charles Henry Davis, taken before his promotion to Rear Admiral. From the author's collection.

1862, and reassigned to Washington, DC.[4] In February 1863, he was promoted to rear admiral and became one of the founders of the National Academy of Sciences.[5] He later served as Chief of the Bureau of Navigation; Superintendent of the Naval Observatory; Commander in Chief of the South Atlantic Squadron; Commandant of the Norfolk Navy Yard; and member of the Lighthouse Board. He died while on active duty. TB-12, DD-65, and DD-395 were all named in his honor.[6]

Colonel Charles Ellet Jr. (1810–1862) was born near Philadelphia, Pennsylvania, died while being transported to Cairo, and is buried in the Laurel Hill Cemetery in Philadelphia.[7] He was a famous engineer prior to the war and was best known for designing and building bridges. The iron suspension bridge he designed and constructed across the Ohio River at Wheeling was completed in 1849; at the time, it had the longest single span in the world.[8] Before the bridge was completed, steamboat interests filed suit to stop its construction. The attorney for the plaintiffs was Edwin M. Stanton, future secretary of war, who later authorized Ellet to build his ram fleet. In the end, Ellet succeeded in getting the bridge built after it was declared part of a postal road and thus not subject to court decisions.[9] Ellet also developed plans for bridges across the Mississippi River at St. Louis and the Potomac River at Georgetown, and designed and began building a temporary suspension bridge across the Niagara River below the falls. Beyond bridges, Ellet was known for his work and recommendations in flood control as well as for improving navigation to include canal and railroad construction. Ellet's skills as a civil engineer have been recognized by the American Society of Civil Engineers, and he is one of the 170 entries in its biographical dictionary of American civil engineers born before the Civil War.[10] Beyond his skills as an engineer, Ellet was a prolific writer, but most of his works attacked someone directly or indirectly, alienating potential friends and employers.[11]

Although Ellet was an excellent engineer and writer, he was a difficult manager to work for and an even more difficult manager to supervise. One of his major problems was that he did not tolerate people who disagreed with him because he felt that his ideas were the correct ones. Consequently, he eventually found it difficult to obtain jobs. However, the start of the Civil War provided Ellet with new opportunities, as described in this book. The wound Ellet received at Memphis—which became infected—along with the measles he contracted, forced him to give up his command and travel to Cairo on board the *Switzerland*.

Charles Ellet Jr., taken when he worked for the James River and Kanawha Company around 1846. From the only known daguerreotype of Ellet. Courtesy of the Virginia Historical Society (1926.24).

Just prior to reaching Cairo, Ellet died. One of Ellet's great misfortunes is that his wartime exploits overshadow his more significant engineering skills.

The Navy honored Ellet's actions during the war, along with the actions of four other members of the Ellet family (Brigadier General Alfred W. Ellet, Colonel Charles Rivers Ellet, Lieutenant Colonel John A. Ellet, and Edward C. Ellet) who served during the Civil War, by naming DD-398 for them. DD-398 was a Benham-class destroyer that served in the Navy from 1939–1947.[12]

Commodore Joseph Edward Montgomery (1817–1902). Although a significant amount of biographical information can be found on Rear Admiral Charles Henry Davis and Colonel Charles Ellet Jr., very little information can be found on Commodore Joseph Edward Montgomery. Some authors have stated that Montgomery died by drowning at the Battle of Memphis—or, if he survived, that he disappeared. Neither of these stories is true; he survived the battle, wrote a report, and paid off the surviving members of his fleet. Montgomery has an obituary in the *Confederate Veteran*, but its information about his wartime exploits is questionable at best.[13]

Montgomery was born in Kentucky, died in Chicago, and is buried in New Albany, Indiana. He and two of his brothers were well-known Mississippi River pilots and riverboat captains before the war.[14] Mark Twain (Samuel Clemens) served under Montgomery while learning how to be a pilot on the Mississippi before the war.[15] His obituary in the *Confederate Veteran* states that he was a personal friend of Jefferson Davis and that Judah P. Benjamin had been his attorney. These connections probably helped him get authorization from the Confederate government for his ram fleet. However, his obituary falsely states that, when battling Admiral Farragut on the Mississippi, he personally steered his boat into Farragut's ship, ramming and sinking her. The obituary also states that he built and commanded the steamer CSS *Nashville* at Mobile, and that under his command the *Nashville*, with support from a Confederate fort (Spanish Fort) and Confederate torpedoes, sunk all seven Union ships that attacked him and the fort. None of this is true.

There is evidence that Montgomery was in Montgomery, Alabama, and continued being active in the war effort after the Battle of Memphis. James Delancy, pilot and captain of the *Lovell*, informed Union authorities in February 1864 that Montgomery was living in Montgomery, Alabama, and was in command of the *Nashville*.[16] In addition, a report from Secretary of the Navy Steven Mallory includes a statement about a Montgomery and Anderson constructing a large ironclad, side-wheel steamer at Mobile.[17] Unfortunately, I have not been able to determine if the Montgomery building the steamer was, in fact, Joseph E. Montgomery. Challenging these assertions are a series of messages in the Navy's *Official Records*, dated July 1865, between Joseph E. Montgomery's lawyer, John Colerick, and the Treasury Department and Navy Department trying to clarify his claim to raise twenty-seven civilian steamboats that had been sunk by the Confederate government in the Yazoo River.[18] One of the messages states that Montgomery had been "paroled and afterwards took the amnesty oath at General Dix's office in New York."[19] However, the message does not state when Montgomery took the oath, so determining how long he continued to fight for the Confederacy is impossible. As for his claim—regrettably for Montgomery—it must not have been settled in his favor, for his family history states that he had a claim against the government at the

Commodore Joseph Edward Montgomery, probably taken after the war. From his obituary in the *Confederate Veteran*.

time of his death in 1902, for payment for twenty-five boats and cotton that were confiscated from him during the war.[20]

Although most of Montgomery's activities after the Battle of Memphis are clouded in mystery, he probably knew Davis and Benjamin, but his wartime exploits were embellished when he recounted them to his children and grandchildren. Ultimately, Joseph Montgomery was a resourceful, brave man who gave the Confederacy its greatest naval victory by a Confederate naval squadron, and, if he had been better supported and luckier, could have delayed the capture of Vicksburg until at least 1864, which could have changed the outcome of the war.

Appendix C

Acting Volunteer Lieutenant Commander William R. Hoel

William R. Hoel has the honor of being the first volunteer, and the second individual, promoted to the rank of Acting Volunteer Lieutenant Commander during the Civil War.[1] He served the entire war on the Mississippi and its tributaries, participating in a number of actions. His service presents an example of the difficulties the US Navy faced on the inland rivers integrating knowledgeable riverboat men into the service. Ultimately, it was men like Hoel who enabled the Navy to effectively use its gunboats on the Mississippi and its tributaries.

Hoel was born on March 1824 in Sharon, now Sharonville, Ohio, in Hamilton County, just north of Cincinnati. His father was an experienced Ohio and Mississippi River pilot and, in 1840, when Hoel was 16, his father took him on a trip, beginning his training as a riverboat pilot. When Hoel was 19, and had completed 21 trips between Cincinnati and New Orleans, he was considered a qualified pilot.[2] As a new pilot he was paid $50 per month but, by 1861, he was one of the most experienced pilots on the river and was being paid $350 per month.[3]

In 1852, Congress passed steamboat legislation that, beyond regulating safety on passenger steamboats, included a requirement that pilots be licensed. Hoel was one of the first to receive a license, as he passed the examination ten days after the law took effect.[4] Unfortunately, Hoel's personal life was not as successful as his piloting and military career. His first wife, Mary Riley, died during the birth of their first child in 1853, with the baby only surviving six months. Regrettably, Hoel was not present during the birth of his son and subsequent death of his wife, as he was on the river piloting.[5]

In October 1861, Hoel volunteered to be a pilot for the Union at $175 per month and became one of the pilots on the *Lexington*.[6] Not content with being just a pilot, Hoel sought a more active position and resigned as a pilot on February 1, 1862. Once his resignation was approved, he accepted the position of 1st master on the *Cincinnati* with

Acting Volunteer Lieutenant William R. Hoel. Courtesy of the Naval Historical Foundation, NH 49013.

a reduction in pay to $150 per month.[7] As 1st master, he was second in command on the *Cincinnati*. During the Battle of Fort Henry, five days later, the *Cincinnati*—the flagship of the flotilla—took thirty-one hits, and a number of men became casualties—Hoel being among the wounded.[8] Hoel's wounds were minor, and he returned to duty before the flotilla moved south to attack Island No. 10. When it was decided to have the *Carondelet* run past the batteries at Island No. 10, Hoel volunteered to pilot her.[9] His desire for action and courage was on full display during this engagement.

The *Carondelet* ran past Island No. 10 on a dark and rainy night. Because visibility was very limited, Hoel stood exposed on the forward end of the upper deck, and passed his instructions to the pilots inside the protected pilothouse. He took that position even though it exposed him to greater danger, because from there he could see the river better.[10] His service that night resulted in his being specifically mentioned by Commodore Foote in a dispatch: "I would especially call the attention of the Department to Acting First Master Hoel, of the *Cincinnati*, who so creditably volunteered his services to go in the *Carondelet*, and did go in her, although he was attached to the gunboat *Cincinnati*."[11] As a result, Secretary of the Navy Gideon Welles asked Foote, "Be pleased to inform the Department the full name of Master Hoel, who volunteered on board the *Carondelet* on her recent passage of the rebel batteries at Island No. 10. The Department desires to appoint him an acting lieutenant in the U.S. Navy as a reward for his gallantry."[12] Hoel turned down the offer and, in a letter to Secretary of the Navy Gideon Welles, stated:

> For the complimentary manner in which the Navy Department has seen fit to recognize the performance of a simple act of duty, please accept my thanks—but under the circumstances I do not think I will be doing myself justice in a pecuniary point of view in retaining the Commission which you have been Kind Enough to Confer upon me. I Entered the Gunboat Service on the 19th of last October in the position of Pilot at $175 per month. Wishing a more active position, and believing at the same time I could be of more Service to my Country, I resigned my position as Pilot on the 1st of last February to accept that of 1st Master at $150 per month. In accepting, as I understand it, the position of Acting Volunteer Lieutenant, my pay will again be reduced, to $125 per month, and that as the Commission reads, "on temporary duty" only. [Capitalization and punctuation are as in the original.][13]

However, an agreement was reached because Hoel became an acting volunteer lieutenant at his previous pay of $150 per month, on April 29, 1862.[14]

Fewer than two weeks later, during the Battle of Plum Point, the *Cincinnati* was rammed, and her captain, Roger Stembel, was wounded and disabled. Hoel took command and ordered that the *Cincinnati* be run aground to keep from sinking. Hoel was still in command when the *Cincinnati* was raised and taken upriver to be repaired.[15] As acting commander, Hoel did such a good job that Commodore Charles Davis wrote to Welles, "After he [Stembel] was wounded, the command of the *Cincinnati* devolved upon Acting [Volunteer] Lieutenant William R. Hoel. I can not praise more than they deserve his high valor and ability. He sets the highest example to those below him, and if it were possible to give him a permanent position worthy of his merits, the Navy would be the gainer as well as himself."[16]

After the Battle of Memphis, although Hoel had not been in the battle, Commodore Davis gave Hoel command of the captured *Little Rebel*, the former Confederate flagship.[17] Then, on October 6, 1862, Hoel was given command of the ironclad *Pittsburg*.[18] At this time, he was the only non-regular officer in command of an ironclad as well as the lowest ranking commanding officer in such a position, as all of the other ironclad commanders were at least lieutenant commanders.[19]

Hoel commanded the *Pittsburg* during the flotilla's run past Vicksburg, and all of the fighting that took place during that campaign, to include being on the same mission when the *Cairo* was sunk by a torpedo. He was also in command of the *Pittsburg* during the Red River Campaign.[20] Hoel was frequently requested to do independent missions and, probably due to his expertise of the Mississippi River, was sent to inspect and report on the wreck of the *Indianola*.[21] Hoel stayed commander of the *Pittsburg* until March 1865, when he was ordered to take command of the *Vindicator*, an equally armed, but faster, ram.[22]

It was at the Battle of Grand Gulf, on April 29, 1863, that Hoel achieved his greatest glory. During the battle, the flotilla's flagship, *Benton*, was hit by a large projectile in the pilothouse, wounding the pilot and disabling the wheel. This damage made the *Benton* unmanageable, and she drifted down river with her stern exposed to the Confederate guns.[23] Hoel, seeing what had happened, gallantly positioned the *Pittsburg* between the *Benton* and the Confederate guns. The *Pittsburg* remained in that exposed position until the *Benton* regained control and was able to return to her position in the battle line. Until then, the *Pittsburg* absorbed all of the artillery projectiles meant for the *Benton*. Porter wrote in his report, "The *Pittsburg*, Acting Volunteer Lieutenant Hoel, for a short time bore the brunt of the fire, and lost 8 killed and 16 wounded."[24] Porter further complimented Hoel later in his report:

> It will not, I am sure, be an invidious distinction if I mention the handsome manner in which Acting Volunteer Lieutenant W. R. Hoel handled and fought the *Pittsburg*. I was much indebted to him for so promptly taking the place of the *Benton* when the loss of our wheel made us turn downstream.
>
> All the commanders fought their boats gallantly, and, I think, effectively. The gentleman mentioned had the advan-

> tage of being one of the best pilots on the river, and knew exactly where to place his ship. I only hope that I may always go into a fight with as good officers to back me.[25]

In May 1864, Porter learned that Congress had created the grade of volunteer lieutenant commander. Consequently, he asked that Hoel be promoted to that rank as, "He is one of the best officers of the squadron, and nobly deserves promotion. He has been in nearly all the battles on this river, and conducted himself as a cool and gallant officer." In July 1864, when Porter was asked by Welles to provide a list of acting volunteer lieutenants belonging to the Mississippi Squadron whom he could recommend for promotion to acting lieutenant commander, Porter replied, "Acting Volunteer Lieutenant W. R. Hoel, commanding U.S.S. *Pittsburg*, is the only one that I could recommend at present. He has distinguished himself throughout the war."[26] The government worked slowly, and it was not until November 10, 1864, that Hoel was promoted to acting volunteer lieutenant commander.[27] Hoel was one of the few volunteers to be promoted to this grade, and only one of two volunteers with this rank in the Mississippi Squadron.[28]

After the war, Hoel returned to piloting, earning, in April 1865, $500 for a nineteen-day trip from Cincinnati to New Orleans and then to St. Louis.[29] Hoel married again in 1869 to Elizabeth Hunt, who was eighteen years younger than he was. They had two children, a daughter in 1869, and a son in 1871.[30] Hoel became a well-respected member of his community. The local veterans recognized his service and leadership by naming the Waynesville, Ohio, Grand Army of the Republic (GAR) Post 230 after him.[31] Hoel was also not forgotten by his former commander, as Admiral Charles Davis recommended that he be appointed the master of the lighthouse tender *Lily*. In December 1875, Hoel assumed that position, and served as master of the *Lily* until his sudden and unexpected death.[32]

Hoel was a strong-willed man, and his second marriage did not seem to be a happy one. He was a jealous husband, and there were hints of abuse. His frequent absences due to his duties with his lighthouse boat left his wife alone on their farm with just the children and servants. Elizabeth Hoel seemed to have chronic complaints that required the local physician, Jake Hough, to frequently visit her. Hoel became suspicious, and arranged for a friend to send a telegram to him at his farm requesting that he return to his boat. Hoel left his home, but secretly returned well armed, as Hough was substantially larger than he

Photograph of Acting Volunteer Lieutenant Commander William R. Hoel's jacket. Courtesy of The Sons and Daughters of Pioneer Rivermen and on display in the Ohio River Museum, Marietta, Ohio.

was. When Hoel entered the house, he encountered his maid and asked her to secretly observe with him what was happening between the doctor and Elizabeth Hoel. After a few minutes, Hoel declared that he had seen enough and, with a drawn pistol, entered the room the doctor and Elizabeth were in. There was a struggle, and somehow Hoel was shot through the heart and died. An inquest was held but no charges were ever filed.[33] Hoel was buried in Spring Grove Cemetery in Cincinnati next to his first wife and their son.[34]

The Navy honored Hoel in July 1943 by naming the USS Hoel-DD 533, a Fletcher-class destroyer after him.[35] The USS *Hoel* lived up to Hoel's gallantry when her captain, Commander Leon S. Kinterberger, placed his ship between the escort carriers he was assigned to protect and the Japanese task force trying to destroy the landing forces at Leyte. During the battle, the *Hoel* attacked the Japanese battleship *Kongo* and the heavy cruiser *Haguro*, but, in return, was severely damaged and sunk, with heavy loss of life. Later, the Navy again honored Hoel and the USS *Hoel* by continuing the name through the USS *Hoel*, DDG-13.[36]

Notes

Preface

1. *Admiral David D. Porter, The Naval History of the Civil War* (Secaucus, NJ: Castle, 1984), 173.
2. US War Department, *Official Records of the Union and Confederate Navies in the War of the Rebellion*, series I, vol. 23 (Washington, DC: U.S. Government Printing Office, 1895–1929), xiv. Henceforth cited as *ORN.*
3. Although only the Confederate River Defense Fleet and Ellet's Ram Fleet were referred to as fleets during this time period, I decided to describe all of the units as fleets in this sentence.
4. A search was made for additional information on Reeder, but none was found. However, information was found on individuals named W. Reeder, but no positive link could be made. Reeder's first name was found in Joe Barbiere's *Scraps from the Prison Table at Camp Chase and Johnson's Island* (Doylestown, PA: W.W.H. Davis, 1868). 207.
5. *ORN*, series I, vol. 25, 156; *ORN*, series I, vol. 24, 433.
6. "The Last Roll, Commodore J. E. Montgomery," *Confederate Veteran* (Nashville, TN) 10, no. 9 (September 1902), 416–17; *ORN*, series I, vol. 27, 268–71; David B. Montgomery, *A Genealogical History, The Montgomerys and Their Descendants*, (Owensville, IN: J.P. Cox, 1908), 58–59; J. Thomas Sharf, *History of the Confederate States Navy* (New York: The Fairfax Press, 1977), 257; *ORN*, series I, vol. 26, 266; *ORN*, series I, vol. 26, 267; *ORN*, series I, vol., 269; *Confederate Veteran*(Nashville, TN) 10, no. 9 (September 1902), 416–17.
7. *ORN*, series I, vol. 27, 268–71.
8. Montgomery, *Genealogical History*, 58–59.
9. Sharf, *History of the Confederate*, 257.
10. *ORN*, series I, vol. 26, 266.
11. *ORN*, series I, vol. 26, 267.
12. *ORN*, series I, vol. 26, 269.

13. The 1861 report by Brevet Brigadier-General Joseph Totten, Colonel of Engineers, specifically discussed the number of coal barges on the Ohio River and stated that Pittsburg coal was the best, with Pomeroy coal nearly as good. *The War of the Rebellion: A Compilation of the Official Records of the Union and Confederate Armies* (Washington, DC: U.S. Government Printing Office, 1884), series I, vol. LII, part I, 164. Henceforth cited as *ORA*.
14. Naval History Division, Navy Department, *Civil War Naval Chronology 1861–1865* (Washington, DC: U.S. Department of the Navy, 1971), 111–12. The common belief that the surrender of Vicksburg on July 4, 1863, opened the Mississippi River to shipping is not correct, as Port Hudson was still controlled by the Confederate Army.

Chapter 1. The Importance of the Mississippi River

1. Rear Admiral H. Walke, *Naval Scenes and Reminiscences of the Civil War in the United States, on the Southern and Western Waters* (New York: F.R. Reed & Company, 1887), 17.
2. Sharf, *History of the Confederate*, v.
3. Although the Confederate Congress had passed an act stating that free navigation would be allowed on the Mississippi River, being at war, the Union did not trust this assurance.
4. *ORN*, series I, vol. 23, 443.
5. *ORA*, series I, vol. VII, 798.
6. *ORN*, series I, vol. 22, 376–77. I used the title of Captain for Andrew Foote, as that is how he signed the report and the order.
7. J. C. G. Kennedy, *United States Census Office 8th Census 1860* (Washington, DC: U.S. Government Printing Office, 1864). The four larger cities in the Confederacy were New Orleans, Charleston, Richmond, and Mobile. Louisville and St. Louis were also larger than Memphis, but as Kentucky and Missouri did not secede, I did not count them.
8. A good view of the four railroads coming into Memphis is on Plate CLIV, in Major George B. Davis, Leslie J. Perry, and Joseph W. Kirkley, compiled by Captain Calvin D. Cowles, *The Official Military Atlas of the Civil War* (Gettysburg, PA: The National Historical Society, 1978).

9. Judge J. P. Young, *Standard History of Memphis, Tennessee* (Knoxville, TN: H. W. Crew & Co., 1912), 82–83.
10. Sharf, *History of the Confederate*, 242.
11. *ORA*, series I, vol. X, part I, 776–77.
12. *ORA*, series I, vol. LII, part I, 167. The number of river miles from Cairo to Memphis and from Cairo to New Orleans was determined by the Army Corps of Engineers. The distance to Memphis at the time was actually 250.7 miles, but I decided to round up and make it 251. Later, the Mississippi River Commission calculated Memphis to be 229 miles from Cairo on its maps, 1881–1897. Obviously, the Mississippi had changed channels between the Civil War and the time the commission did its measurements.
13. The 150 miles comes from a map measurement done by the author.
14. Fort Harris/Harrison was constructed about six river miles upriver from Memphis but was never completed. *ORA*, series I, vol. LII, part II, 80–81 and 93; and series I, vol. IV, 408.
15. Edward Dearing Mansfield lived in Morrow, Ohio, a small port on the Little Miami River just north of Cincinnati. Mansfield was offered a commission in the Corps of Engineers upon graduation from the United States Military Academy, but turned it down and did not serve in the Army. Instead, he went to Princeton and became a lawyer. Moving to Ohio, he became a newspaper editor and author, as well as a law and history professor. Biographical information on Mansfield was obtained from Bvt Major General George W. Cullum, *Biographical Register of the Officers and Graduates of the U.S. Military Academy at West Point, N.Y. from its Establishment, in 1802, to 1890 with the Early History of the United States Military Academy*, 3rd ed. vol. I., nos. 1 to 1000 (Boston and New York: Houghton, Mifflin and Company, 1891), 207; the *Twelfth Annual Reunion of the Association of the Graduates of the U.S. Military Academy at West Point, New York, June 9, 1881* (East Saginaw, MI: E.W. Lyon, 1881), 25–31; Elaine McConnell, Rare Book Curator, United States Military Academy, e-mail message to author, August 15, 2012.
16. *ORA*, series I, vol. LII, part I, 157–59.
17. *ORA*, series I, vol. VII, 894.
18. *ORA*, series I, vol. VI, 398.

19. The naval vessels on the western rivers had previously been under the command of Major General George McClellan and then Major General John Frémont, with Commander John Rodgers being the first naval officer to be under their command. *ORN*, series I, vol. 22, 280.
20. *ORA*, series I, vol. X, part II, 130–31. Stanton was not being fully honest, as he was telling the Navy one thing and Ellet something different. This command relationship is more fully explained in Chapter Three.
21. Unfortunately, the Navy's and Army's *Official Records* state that Montgomery's first name is James, a mistake that has been perpetuated by many authors. Montgomery's first name is Joseph. Full discussion of his first name can be found in Appendix B.
22. *ORN*, series I, vol 17., 160–61.

Chapter 2. The Confederate River Defense Fleet

1. Captain James H. Townsend is one of those individuals who makes a difference in history, and then quickly disappears. Unfortunately, I have not been able to determine what happened to him after his boat, the *Price*, reached Memphis. Something happened to Townsend at Memphis, for his boat, the *Price*, is under the command of First Officer J. E. Henthorne during the Battles of Plum Point and Memphis. The only place I found Townsend's first name was in a footnote in Donal J. Stanton, Goodwin F. Berquist, and Paul C. Bowers, eds., *The Civil War Reminiscences of General M. Jeff Thompson* (Dayton, OH: Morningside, 1988), 152. In another case of name confusion, Commodore Montgomery uses the name Thomas E. Henthorne in one of his reports. *ORN*, series I, vol. 23, 56.
2. *ORA*, series I, vol. VII, 798.
3. *ORN*, series II, vol. 1, 695–96.
4. Sharf, *History of the Confederate*, 251.
5. C. W. Read, *Reminiscences of the Confederate States Navy* (Richmond, VA: Southern Historical Society Papers, May 1876, vol. 1, Issue 5), 10.
6. Read, *Reminiscences of the Confederate*, 17. Charles Read, a graduate of the United States Naval Academy, resigned his commis-

sion as a midshipman when his native state, Mississippi, seceded. Assigned to the CSS *McRae*, he eventually became her executive officer. After the loss of the *McRae*, Read rejoined the remnants of the regular Confederate fleet at Fort Pillow under Commander Pinkney. Pinkney, at the urging of General Pierre G. T. Beauregard, had taken the guns off of the *Polk* and *Livingston* and mounted them at Fort Randolph, with sailors manning them. Read was assigned command of two of the heavy naval guns. After the evacuation of Fort Pillow, Commander Robert F. Pinkney quickly left, but Lieutenant Sardine Graham Stone (referred to as Lieutenant S. G. Stone), in disobedience of Pinkney's orders, was able to save two of the guns that were later mounted to defend the Yazoo River. Read then joined the *Arkansas* and was with her until she was destroyed by her crew. He ended the war as a prisoner after he burned his ship, CSS *Webb*, during his failed attempt to break out into the Gulf of Mexico in 1865.

7. Thompson's rank was not a regular Confederate Army rank; rather, he was a Brigadier General in the Missouri State Guard; however, reports and messages referred to him as General Thompson.
8. *ORN*, series I, vol. 23, 54.
9. R. Thomas Campbell, *Confederate Naval Forces on Western Waters* (Jefferson, NC: McFarland & Company, 2005), 15–16.
10. Sharf, *History of the Confederate*, 242.
11. *ORN*, series I, vol. 22, 811.
12. *ORN*, series II, vol. 1, parts 1 to 4, 780.
13. *ORN*, series I, vol. 22, 792–93.
14. *ORN*, series II, vol. 1, parts 1 to 4, 780; Sharf, *History of the Confederate*, 304. The contractor stated in his testimony to the Joint Special Committee of Both Houses of the Confederate Congress to Investigate the Affairs of the Navy Department that the bolts and spikes were seized by Lieutenant Issac Brown of the Confederate Navy. However, Sharf states in his book that bolts and spikes were seized by Confederate officers, but does not mention who they were. Sharf may not have mentioned any names as he did not want to embarrass any former Confederate naval officers.
15. *ORN*, series II, vol. 1, parts 1 to 4, 780.
16. *ORN*, series I, vol. 22, 755–57.

17. *ORA*, series I, vol. X, part II, 380–81.
18. *ORN*, series II, vol. 1, parts 1 to 4, 779–83.
19. George N. Hollins was a former US Navy officer and started the war defending the Potomac River. He was transferred to New Orleans and became commander of the ships afloat and the naval station. After disobeying the orders of the Confederate Secretary of the Navy, Hollins was reassigned to Richmond, Virginia, for courtmartial duty. His rank varies from Captain, to Commodore, to Flag Officer in both the Army's and Navy's *Official Records.* I have decided to use Captain, as that was the most common reference.
20. *ORA*, series I, vol. VI, 610.
21. Information on Hollins's US Navy career was obtained from *Navy History and Heritage Command.* accessed September 2012, http://www.history.navy.mil/
22. *ORA*, series I, vol. VI, 610.
23. *ORA*, series I, vol. VI, 611.
24. *ORA*, series I, vol. VII, 798.
25. *ORN*, series II, vol. 1, parts 1 to 4, 688. Even though Sharf states in his *History of the Confederate States Navy* that it was the Mississippi delegation, Secretary of War Judah Benjamin wrote to General Mansfield Lovell that it was the Missouri delegation.
26. Confederate States of America, The Statutes at Large of the Provisional Government of the Confederate States of America, Chapter XXXIV, January 9, 1862.
27. Confederate States of America, The Statutes at Large of the Provisional Government of the Confederate States of America, Chapter XXXIX, January 14, 1862.
28. *ORN*, series I, vol. 17, 159.
29. *ORN*, series I, vol. 17, 160–61.
30. *ORN*, series I, vol. 17, 161.
31. *ORN*, series II, vol. 1, parts 1 to 4, 688–89.
32. *ORN*, series II, vol. 1, parts 1 to 4, 688–89.
33. Captain Thomas P. Leathers later commanded the *Natchez* in its famous postwar race against the *Robert E. Lee.*
34. Montgomery, *Genealogical History*, 58; "The Last Roll Call" *Confederate Veteran* 10, no. 9 (September 1902): 416.

35. Ibid.
36. Montgomery, *Genealogical History*, 58. Although there were more Confederate boats at New Orleans, they were under different commands, and the regular Confederate Navy on the upper Mississippi had fewer than eight boats. To this author's knowledge, no other Confederate fleet had this number of boats.
37. *ORN*, series I, vol. 17, 160–61 and series II, vol. 1, parts 1 to 4, 663–64.
38. Although General Albert S. Johnston was department commander when the boats were being built, he died prior to the boats leaving New Orleans for Memphis.
39. The actual definition, *FM 101-5-1, Operational Terms and Graphic* (Headquarters, Department of the Army, Washington, DC, 1997), 1–86, is that the units need to be assigned or attached to two different military departments. Because the River Defense Fleet was part of the Confederate War Department, General Beauregard does not meet the exact definition, but he does meet, in my opinion, the spirit of the definition.
40. *ORA*, series I, vol. LII, part I, 37–38.
41. *ORN*, series II, vol. 1, parts 1 to 4, 667.
42. *ORN*, series II, vol. 1, parts 1 to 4, 662.
43. *ORN*, series II, vol. 1, parts 1 to 4, 672.
44. *ORN*, series II, vol. 1, parts 1 to 4, 689.
45. *ORA*, series I, vol. LII, part I, 37–38. Montgomery takes a lot of credit in his report for actions that other people did.
46. *ORA*, series I, vol. LII, part I, 37–38; *ORA*, series I, vol. VI, 513.
47. *ORN*, series II, vol. 1, parts 1 to 4, 691. The distance in river miles from Cairo to Columbus came from *ORA*, series I, vol. LII, part I, 166.
48. *ORN*, series II, vol. 1, parts 1 to 4, 691.
49. *ORA*, series I, vol. LII, part I, 37–38. The *General Sumter* is also spelled *Sumpter* and referred to as the *Sumter* in both the *ORA*s and *ORN*s. I decided to use the full name to help differentiate it from the cruiser CSS *Sumter*. However, when the *General Sumter* was captured at Memphis, the Union Navy changed her name to the USS *Sumter*.
50. Unfortunately, I was not able to find additional information about Montgomery's commanders. There is some confusion with

Henthorne's first name. In his report on the Battles of Plum Point and Memphis, Montgomery wrote J. E. Henthorne, but in all other reports it is written Thomas (T) E. Henthorne. I believe that the J in Montgomery's report is just a typographical error.

51. *ORA*, series I, vol. LII, part I, 38.

52. The log of the *Price* from New Orleans to the Battle of Memphis can be found in Joe Barbiere's *Scraps from the Prison Table at Camp Chase and Johnson's Island* (Doylestown, PA: W.W.H. Davis, 1868), 209–14. Barbiere was a prisoner at Johnson's Island with all of the officers from Montgomery's fleet who had been captured at Memphis, including L. F. Delisdemier, the purser of the *Price*, who wrote the log. Unfortunately, Barbiere does not state how Delisdemier got the log to Johnson's Island.

53. Barbiere, *Scraps*, 210; *ORA*, series I, vol. LII, part I, 38.

54. When I first read the log of the *Price*, I doubted the part about the crew of the *Price* tearing up the railroad even though everything else in the log fit with all of the other reports. My doubts increased as I could not find Eunice on any of the maps in the *Official Atlas* and did not see any railroad lines near the Mississippi between New Orleans and Memphis except the one going into Vicksburg. In addition, I could not imagine that the Confederate authorities would have allowed three miles of precious railroad to be torn up without complaining. These factors, along with no mention of the destruction in the *Official Records*, made me continue to doubt the log. However, a further search of the *Official Records* showed that Eunice, Arkansas, did exist—with the mention that it was not shown on the maps. In addition, reports were found about Union expeditions being sent there to destroy the railroad and its depot. I contacted the Arkansas Railroad Museum in Pine Bluff, Arkansas, hoping that it could provide some additional information, which it did. The railroad at Eunice was the incomplete Mississippi, Ouachita and Red River Railroad. The part of the railroad that was finished could only handle very light traffic, such as track cars. It was a railroad that went nowhere, and the Confederacy did not lose anything when Townsend had his crew tear it up. The log of the *Price* can also be found in Sharf's *The History of the Confederate States Navy,* although he does not cite his source of his information. In reality, Sharf plagiarized from Barbiere, not giving Barbiere credit.

55. *ORA*, series I, vol. LII, part I, 38–39.

56. Barbiere, *Scraps*, 205.
57. The weight of the 8-inch cannon came from Warren Ripley, *Artillery and Ammunition of the Civil War* (New York: Promontory Press, 1970), 368–69.
58. *ORA*, series I, vol. VI, 598.
59. The drafts for only three of the Confederate boats could be found: *General Bragg*, twelve feet; *General Sterling Price*, thirteen feet; and *Little Rebel*, twelve feet, in *ORN*, series II, vol. 1, parts 1 to 4, 91, 92, and 128. The draft for the *Carondelet* was six feet, with the assumption that all of the City Class Ironclads had the same draft; the draft for the *Benton* was five feet, *ORN*, series II, vol. I, parts 1 to 4, 52 and *ORN*, series I, vol. 22, 438. This makes a difference in the drafts at a minimum of six feet between the Confederate and Union boats.
60. Stanton, Berquist, and Bowers, *Civil War Reminiscences*, 155.
61. *ORN*, series I, vol. 23, 57; *ORN*, series II, vol. 1, parts 1 to 4, 91.
62. *ORN*, series II, vol. 1, parts 1 to 4, 91. Paul H. Silverstone, *Civil War Navies 1855–1883* (Annapolis, MD: Naval Institute Press, 2001), 168.
63. *ORN*, series II, vol. 1, parts 1 to 4, 91.
64. Naval Historical Foundation, NH 46642.
65. Silverstone, *Civil War Navies*, 169.
66. *ORN*, series II, vol.1, parts 1 to 4, 216, states that the *General Sumter* was 400 tons, but CSS *General Sumter*, *Navy History and Heritage Command*, accessed September 2012, http://www.history.navy.mil/, states that she was 524 tons.
67. CSS *General Sumter*, *Navy History and Heritage Command*,
68. Tony Gibbons, *Warships and Naval Battles of the Civil War* (New York: Gallery Books, 1989), 98, states that her top speed was twelve knots, which would have made her the fastest boat in the Confederate fleet. I decided to use the order of battle, as provided by *The Civil War Reminiscences of General M. Jeff Thompson*, as he was an eyewitness and stated that the Confederate fleet was arranged according to each boat's speed with the fastest being first (p. 155).
69. *ORN*, series II, vol. 1, parts 1 to 4, 92–93.
70. USS *General Price*, *Navy History and Heritage Command*.
71. Naval Historical Foundation, NH 16863.
72. *ORN*, series II, vol. 1, parts 1 to 4, 253; CSS *General Earl Van Dorn*, *Navy History and Heritage Command*.

73. CSS *General Beauregard, Navy History and Heritage Command.*
74. Ibid.
75. CSS *Colonel Lovell, Navy History and Heritage Command.*
76. *ORA*, series I, vol. VI, 597. To the best of my knowledge, General Mansfield Lovell and Colonel William S. Lovell were not related.
77. *ORA*, series I, vol. VI, 597.
78. Ibid.; Dot Abbott, Special Collections Librarian, United States Naval Academy, e-mail message to author, January 26, 2010.
79. *ORA*, series I, vol. VI, 596–99; Dot Abbott, Special Collections Librarian, United States Naval Academy, e-mail message to author, January 26, 2010.
80. Unfortunately, too many authors misidentify the boat as the *General Lovell* because they assume that it was the boat named after the general rather than the colonel. A ram named the *General Lovell* did exist and was one of the boats converted at New Orleans; however, it was one of the boats kept by General Lovell for the defense of New Orleans and was lost when the city was captured by Farragut.
81. CSS *General M. Jeff Thompson, Navy History and Heritage Command*; Stanton, Berquist, and Bowers, *Civil War Reminiscences*, 156.
82. Stanton, Berquist, and Bowers, *Civil War Reminiscences*, 156; *ORN*, series I, vol. 23, 57.
83. *ORN*, series II, vol. 1, parts 1 to 4, 128.
84. *ORA*, series I, vol. VI, 612–613.
85. *ORA*, series I, vol. VI, 642. *ORA*
86. Sharf, *History of the Confederate*, 286.

Chapter 3. The Union Fleets

1. *ORA*, series III, vol. II, 816.
2. *ORA*, series III, vol. II, 14.
3. A semantic issue is why the smaller of the two organizations was officially called a fleet while the larger one was officially called a flotilla and later a squadron. The answer to that question lies in the different views the Army and Navy had of groups of warships.
4. *ORN*, series I, vol. 22, 307.

5. *ORA*, series I, vol. LII, part I, 164. The previously mentioned Edward Mansfield was probably one of these individuals.
6. *ORA*, series I, vol. LII, part I, 164–65.
7. I have spelled Pittsburgh, Pennsylvania, "Pittsburg," as that was the spelling used to designate the ironclad *Pittsburg*. In the Navy and Army's *Official Records,* both spellings can be found, with Pittsburg being the most common. Wheeling is shown as part of Virginia, which is correct for this time period, as West Virginia had not yet been created.
8. *ORA*, series I, vol. LII, part I, 164–65.
9. *ORA*, series I, vol. LII, part I, 164.
10. *ORA*, series I, vol. LII, part I, 167, although it is omitted in vol. LII; Lenthall's report can be found in ORA, series III, vol. II, 814–15.
11. *ORA*, series I, vol. LII, part I, 167–68.
12. *ORN*, series I, vol. 22, 277–80; *ORN*, series I, vol. 22, 286.
13. *ORN*, series I, vol. 22, 281–82.
14. James Kennedy Moorhead, *Biographical Directory of the United States, Congress*, http://bioguide.congress.gov; *ORA*, series I, vol. LI, part 1, 637 and *ORA*, series II, vol. VI, 107–8.
15. *ORN*, series I, vol. 22, 282.
16. Captain William J. Kountz later captained steamboats in the West Virginia campaign under McClellan. However, when he went west and served under Grant, there were a number of problems, and Grant put him under arrest. *ORA*, series I, vol. VII, 552.
17. *ORN*, series I, vol. 22, 286.
18. *ORN*, series I, vol. 22, 284–85.
19. *ORN*, series I, vol. 22, 285–286.
20. *ORN*, series I, vol. 22, 281.
21. *ORA*, series III, vol. II, 792–93. Fleet was how the Army's Quarter-Master's Officer designated the flotilla.
22. *ORN*, series I, vol. 22, 385 states, "the men are to be paid by the Army, the officers by the Navy." However, the message implied that "officers" meant regular Navy officers. *ORN*, series I, vol. 22, 404, gives a list of officers and their pay on the *Lexington* as of November 11, 1861, but the list only includes the pay for the

nonregular officers and does not list the pay for the one regular Navy officer, Roger Stembel. As further evidence, there is the problem Fleet Paymaster Elisha Dunn had in closing out the pay of the Army's naval officers. *ORN*, series I, vol. 24, 573–74.

23. Schuyler, Hartley & Graham, *Illustrated Catalog of Civil War Military Goods*, (New York: Dover Publications, 1985) 87.
24. *ORN*, series I, vol. 22, 294.
25. *ORN*, series I, vol. 22, 283.
26. *ORN*, series I, vol. 22, 298 has the rate of pay the men were receiving in August 1861.
27. *ORN*, series I, vol. 22, 477.
28. Schuyler, Hartley & Graham, *Illustrated Catalog*, 87.
29. Ibid.
30. *ORN*, series I, vol. 22, 342.
31. *ORN*, series I, vol. 13, 376–77.
32. Information on the ranks obtained by the captains of the ironclads was obtained from *Navy History and Heritage Command*, accessed September 2012, http://www.history.navy.mil/. Information on Phelps's postwar career was obtained from Jay Slagle, *Ironclad Captain, Seth Ledyard Phelps & the U.S. Navy, 1841–1864* (Kent, OH: Kent State University Press, 1996).
33. *ORN*, series I, vol. 22, 391–92.
34. *ORN*, series I, vol. 7, 514.
35. *ORN*, series I, vol. 23, 351.
36. *ORN*, series I, vol. 22, 429.
37. *ORN*, series I, vol. 23, 86.
38. *ORN*, series I, vol. 23, 213–14.
39. *ORN*, series I, vol. 23, 388–89; *ORN*, series I, vol. 23, 348–52.
40. *ORN*, series I, vol. 24, 573–74.
41. *ORN*, series I, vol. 22, 341.
42. *ORN*, series I, vol. 22, 483–84.
43. *ORN*, series I, vol. 22, 657.
44. Albert A. Nofi, *A Civil War Treasury* (Conshohocken, PA: Combined Books, 1992), 383.
45. *ORN*, series I, vol. 22, 478.
46. *ORN*, series I, vol. 22, 493.
47. *ORN*, series I, vol. 23, 64.

48. *ORN*, series I, vol. 23, 343–44.
49. *ORN*, series I, vol. 23, 355.
50. *ORN*, series I, vol. 23, 443.
51. *ORN*, series I, vol. 22, 374.
52. *ORN*, series I, vol. 22, 393.
53. *ORN*, series I, vol. 22, 434, 648.
54. *ORN*, series I, vol. 22, 435.
55. *ORN*, series I, vol. 22, 464–65.
56. *ORN*, series I, vol. 22, 454.
57. *ORN*, series I, vol. 22, 504.
58. *ORN*, series I, vol. 23, 343.
59. *ORN*, series I, vol. 22, 475–76.
60. *ORA*, series I, vol. VII, 534.
61. *ORN*, series I, vol. 22, 632.
62. *ORN*, series I, vol. 24, 233.
63. *ORN*, series I, vol. 24, 232.
64. *ORN*, series I, vol. 22, 736–37; H. Walke, *Naval Scenes and Reminiscences*, 124.
65. *ORN*, series I, vol. 22, 337.
66. *ORN*, series I, vol.18, 499.
67. *ORN*, series I, vol. 23, 355–56.
68. *ORN*, series I, vol. 7, 294.
69. *ORN*, series I, vol. 23, 257.
70. *ORN*, series I, vol. 23, 271–72.
71. *ORN*, series I, vol. 23, 638.
72. *ORN*, series I, vol. 23, 449.
73. *ORN*, series I, vol. 23, 619.
74. *ORN*, series I, vol. 22, 603.
75. *Shipmates*, National Park Service, Vicksburg National Military Park.
76. *ORN*, series I, vol. 24, 656.
77. *ORN*, series I, vol. 26, 291.
78. *ORN*, series I, vol. 22, 534–535.
79. *ORN*, series I, vol. 22, 535.
80. *ORN*, series I, vol. 22, 315.
81. *ORN*, series I, vol. 22, 550.

82. John D. Milligan, *From the Fresh-Water Navy: 1861–64, The Letters of Acting Master's Mate Henry R. Browne and Acting Ensign Symmes E. Browne*, (Annapolis, MD: United States Naval Institute, 1970), 29–31.
83. *ORN*, series I, vol. 23, 504.
84. Walke, *Naval Scenes and Reminiscences*, 25.
85. Thomas O. Selfridge, *What Finer Tradition: The Memoirs of Thomas O. Selfridge, Jr.* (Columbia, SC: University of South Carolina Press, 1987), 73. Selfridge was incorrect about most of his crew being former riverboat men. Information on the crew can be found at the Cairo Museum in the Vicksburg National Military Park.
86. *ORN*, series III, vol. II, 334.
87. William R. Hoel Papers, Collection of the Public Library of Cincinnati and Hamilton County.
88. Ibid.
89. Ibid.
90. Ibid.
91. Ibid.
92. *ORN*, series I, vol. 22, 298; Schuyler, Hartley & Graham, *Illustrated Catalog*, 87.
93. *ORN*, series I, vol. 22, 298.
94. *ORN*, series I, vol. 22, 350.
95. *ORN*, series I, vol. 24, 676–77.
96. *ORN*, series I, vol. 25, 217.
97. *ORN*, series I, vol. 25, 557. The *Moose* was one of the gunboats that stopped Brigadier-General John Hunt Morgan's cavalry from crossing the Ohio River at Buffington Island and escaping from Union pursuit in July 1863.
98. James M. Merrill, "Cairo, Illinois: Strategic Civil War River Port," *Journal of the Illinois State Historical Society* (Winter 1983): 252.
99. Schuyler, Hartley & Graham, *Illustrated Catalog*, 87.
100. *ORN*, series I, vol. 27, 32–33.
101. *ORN*, series I, vol. 27, 31–33.
102. Walke, *Naval Scenes and Reminiscences*, 22.
103. *ORN*, series I, vol. 22, 657.

104. Milligan, *From the Fresh-Water Navy*, 36.
105. *ORN*, series I, vol. 26, 53.
106. *ORN*, series I, vol. 22, 283.
107. *Civil War Naval Chronology, 1861–1865* (Washington, DC: U.S. Government Printing Office, 1971), 1–14, 1–22.
108. The definition of a combined command can be found in *Field Manual 101–5–1, Operational Terms and Graphics* (Headquarters Department of the Army, 1997), 1–158.
109. *ORN*, series I, vol. 22, 366.
110. Should someone reject this reasoning, as the timberclads were still part of the Army, he must remember that the boats were commanded by regular Navy officers and, thus, the command structure meets the spirit of the definition. The full definition was met when Andrew Foote was appointed a flag-officer on November 13, 1861, as his orders read, "You are hereby appointed flag-officer in command of the U.S. naval forces employed on the Mississippi River and its tributaries." *ORN*, series I, vol. 22, 429. On that date, Major-General David Hunter was the temporary commander of the Western Department, having relieved Major General John Frémont on November 2. Hunter remained temporary commander until relieved by Major-General Henry Halleck on November 19. E. B. Long, *The Civil War Day by Day*, (Garden City, NY: Doubleday & Company, 1971), 134 and 141. Because Foote was commander of US Naval forces and reported to the commander of the Western Department, that would make Hunter, by definition, a combined commander.
111. *ORA,* series III, vol. II, 814–815.
112. *ORN*, series I, vol. 25, 756.
113. Navy History and Heritage Command, accessed September 2012 http://www.history.navy.mil/photos/sh-usn/usnsh-c/cincnti.htm.
114. The contract can be found in the *ORA*, series III, vol. II, 816–34.
115. *ORA*, series III, vol. II, 820.
116. The tonnage, speed, and draft on the City Class Ironclads came from the description of the *Carondelet* in the *ORN*, series II, vol. 1, 52. As the City Class Ironclads were constructed based on the same specifications, the abilities of one can be assumed to be the same for all.

117. Many people studying the Civil War use today's impression of the Mississippi River and its tributaries and cannot understand why these boats had to have a shallow draft. Today, the Corps of Engineers regulates the depth of the Mississippi and its tributaries through a series of dams; however, during the Civil War these dams did not exist, and the depth of the rivers varied tremendously.
118. Edwin C. Bearss, *Hardluck Ironclad* (Baton Rouge, LA: Louisiana State University Press, 1980), 189.
119. *ORN*, series I, vol. 22, 493.
120. *ORN*, series I, vol. 22, 378.
121. *ORN*, series I, vol. 22, 459.
122. *ORN*, series I, vol. 22, 456. Later in the war, Winslow was captain of the USS *Kearsarge*, and was in command of her when she sunk the CSS *Alabama*.
123. *ORN*, series I, vol. 22, 448.
124. *ORN*, series I, vol. 22, 297.
125. *ORN*, series I, vol. 22, 495.
126. *ORN*, series I, vol. 23, 324.
127. Milligan, *From the Fresh-Water Navy*, 65–66.
128. *ORN*, series I, vol. 22, 777.
129. *ORN*, series I, vol. 22, 314. The salvage boat No. 7 was also known as wrecking boat No. 7 and submarine boat No. 7.
130. *ORN*, series I, vol. 22, 438.
131. *ORN*, series I, vol. 22, 505.
132. *ORN*, series I, vol. 22, 503. William Faulkner, Acting Engineer in Chief, made an examination of the *Benton*'s machinery and boiler and gave a very negative report on the equipment. His report was included in Pennock's and Stembel's report to Foote. *ORN*, series I, vol. 22, 506.
133. *ORN*, series I, vol. 22, 520.
134. *ORN*, series I, vol. 22, 523.
135. *ORN*, series I, vol. 22, 659.
136. *ORN*, series I, vol. 22, 660.
137. Paul H. Silverstone, *Civil War Navies, 1855–1883* (Annapolis, MD: Naval Institute Press, 2001), 114
138. Ibid.

139. Ibid., 116.

140. *ORA*, series III, vol. II, 792.

141. *ORN*, series I, vol. 22, 560. Interestingly, General Tilghman was allowed to write his report as a prisoner in Alton, Illinois, although it had not reached Richmond by the time he was exchanged.

142. *ORN*, series II, vol. 1, 52.

143. *ORN*, series I, vol. 22, 583.

144. Charles H. Davis, *Life of Charles Henry Davis Real Admiral* (Cambridge, MA: Houghton, Mifflin and Company, 1899), 272.

145. *ORA*, series I, vol. XXIV, part III, 152.

146. *ORN*, series I, vol. 22, 688–89. The paddle wheels were located in the middle of the boat, and there was very little clearance between the front of the paddle wheel and the boat. As a consequence, when the boat was backed up, the water being thrust forward by the paddle wheel would have hit the boat and been forced back into the water being thrust forward by the paddle wheel. This dynamic would have had a tremendous lessening impact upon the force that could be generated.

147. Walke, *Naval Scenes and Reminiscences*, 95.

148. *ORN*, series I, vol. 22, 705.

149. Bearss, *Hardluck Ironclad*, 189.

150. James B. Eads, "Recollection of Foote and the Gun-Boats," in *Battles and Leaders of the Civil War*, vol. I ed. Robert U. Johnson and Clarence C. Buel, (Secaucus, NJ: Castle, 1982) 339–40.

151. *ORN*, series II, vol. 1, 148.

152. Donald L. Canney, *The Old Steam Navy*, vol. II (Annapolis, MD: Naval Institute Press, 1993), 54.

153. Ibid.

154. William R. Hoel, Papers in the Collection of the Public Library of Cincinnati and Hamilton County.

155. *ORN*, series I, vol. 22, 665.

156. The only exception is the USS *Cairo*. It was sunk by a Confederate torpedo (mine) in the Yazoo River, was recovered in the 1960s, and is currently on display at the Vicksburg National Military Park.

157. "Charles Ellet, Jr.," *A Biographical Dictionary of American Civil Engineers*, (ASCE Historical Publication No. 2, 1972), 40–41.

158. Chester G. Hearn, *Ellet's Brigade* (Baton Rouge, LA: Louisiana State University Press, 2000), 3.
159. Lewis, *Charles Ellet,* 183.
160. *ORN*, series I, vol. 22, 288.
161. Lewis, *Charles Ellet*, 183–84.
162. Hearn, *Ellet's Brigade*, 3–4.
163. Lewis, *Charles Ellet,* 186.
164. *ORA*, series I, vol. XI, part III, 25–26 and 42–43.
165. *ORA*, series I, vol. XI, part III, 46. The rams were not able to attack the *Virginia* farther up river than Fort Monroe due to the channel becoming narrow and crooked.
166. *ORA*, series I, vol. VIII, 642–643. One of the other sources of information may have been Charles Ellet, as he had met with Stanton on March 14. *ORN*, series I, vol. 22, 665.
167. *ORA*, series I, vol. VIII, 643.
168. *ORA*, series I, vol. X, part II, 68–69.
169. *ORA*, series III, vol. I, 950–51.
170. *ORA*, series III, vol. I, 952–53.
171. *ORA*, series I, vol. X, part II, 76.
172. *ORA*, series III, vol. II, 1–2.
173. *ORA*, series III, vol. II, 12.
174. *ORA*, series I, vol. X, part II, 69.
175. *ORN*, series I, vol. 23, 29.
176. *ORA*, series III, vol. II, 794.
177. *ORN*, series I, vol. 23, 73.
178. *ORN*, series I, vol. 23, 74–75.
179. *ORN*, series I, vol. 23, 65.
180. *ORN*, series I, vol. 23, 43.
181. *ORN*, series I, vol. 23, 73.
182. *ORN*, series I, vol. 23, 741.
183. *ORN*, series I, vol. 23, 80.
184. *ORN*, series I, vol. 23, 39–40.
185. "From the Mississippi Flotilla," *New York Daily Tribune*, June 11, 1862.
186. *ORN*, series I, vol. 22, 683.
187. *ORN*, series I, vol. 22, 684.

188. *ORN*, series I, vol. 23, 87; Norman E. Clarke, Sr., ed., *Warfare along the Mississippi: The letters of Lieutenant Colonel George E. Currie* (Ann Arbor, MI: Edwards Brothers, 1961), 47. Currie stated that each boat had fifteen sharpshooters, but Lieutenant Warren on the *Monarch* stated in his description of the Battle of Memphis that the *Monarch* had eleven sharpshooters (Warren D. Crandall, *History of the Ram Fleet*, St. Louis: Buschart Brothers, 1907, 80).
189. *ORA*, series III, vol. II, 25.
190. *ORN*, series I, vol. 23, 65.
191. *ORN*, series I, vol. 23, 79.
192. *ORN*, series II, vol. 1, parts 1 to 4, 169.
193. *ORN*, series I, vol. 23, 79.
194. *ORN*, series I, vol. 23, 79.
195. *ORN*, series I, vol. 22, 682. Although the rate of flow of the Mississippi varies, a good estimate would be four or five miles per hour based on information shown on one of the maps in Henry Walke's autobiography, *Naval Scenes and Reminiscences*, 252. Thus, the unaided speed of the rams was at least thirteen miles per hour, or about eleven knots.
196. Norman E. Clarke Jr., *Warfare Along the Mississippi*, 47. Crandall, *History of the Ram Fleet*, (Mount Pleasant, MI: Central Michigan University, 1961), 80. Information on the loopholes came from a report in the *Chicago Tribune*, June 10, 1862.
197. *Dictionary of American Naval Fighting Ships*, vol. I (Washington, DC: U.S. Government Printing Office, 1959), 412; *ORA*, series III, vol. II, 834–35; *ORN*, series I, vol. 19, XVI.
198. *Dictionary of American Naval*, 412; *ORA*, series III, vol. II, 834–35; *ORN*, series I, vol. 19, XVI.
199. *ORN*, series I, vol. 1, 244.
200 *ORA*, series III, vol. II, 834–35.
201. *ORN*, series I, vol. 24, 151.
202. *ORN*, series I, vol. 18, 752.
203. *ORA*, series III, vol. II, 834.
204. There were both sailing ships and steam ships in the Navy's Mortar Flotilla. Only the sailing ships were used as mortar boats or bomb vessels, whereas the steam ships were armed with cannon and used to tow the mortar ships into position. A good

description of the Mortar Flotilla can be found in the *ORN*, series I, vol. 18, 25–26. Only descriptions of the steamers can be found in the *ORN*.

205. Names can become confusing, as there was an Army quartermaster with the name of Major R. Allen in St. Louis who was responsible for paying for the construction of the mortar boats.

206. *ORN*, series I, vol. 22, 314.

207. *ORN*, series I, vol. 22, 489.

208. *Instruction for Heavy Artillery* (Washington, DC: U.S. Government Printing Office, 1862), 40.

209. *ORN*, series I, vol. 22, 621.

210. *Instruction for Heavy Artillery*, 35.

211. *ORN*, series I, vol. 23, 279.

212. *ORN*, series I, vol. 23, 622.

213. *ORN*, series I, vol. 22, 314.

214. *ORN*, series I, vol. 22, 492.

215. *ORN*, series I, vol. 22, 462–63.

216. *ORN*, series I, vol. 22, 526.

217. *ORN*, series I, vol. 22, 483–84; *ORN*, series I, vol. 22, 521.

218. *ORN*, series I, vol. 23, 280.

219. *ORN*, series I, vol. 22, 373.

220. *ORN*, series I, vol. 22, 492.

221. *ORN*, series I, vol. 22, 483; *ORN*, series I, vol. 22, 492. Captain Robert Constable later became a Lieutenant Colonel in the 75th Ohio Volunteer Infantry.

222. *ORN*, series I, vol. 22, 636; *ORN*, series I, vol. 22, 636; *ORN*, series I, vol. 23, 16.

223. *ORN*, series I, vol. 22, 373–74; *ORN*, series I, vol. 22, 369.

224. *ORN*, series I, vol. 22, 471–72.

225. *ORN*, series I, vol. 22, 511–12.

226. *ORN*, series I, vol. 22, 516.

227. *ORN*, series I, vol. 22, 694–95.

228. *ORN*, series I, vol. 23, 278–81.

229. *ORN*, series I, vol. 23, 280.

230. *ORN*, series I, vol. 23, 290.

231. *ORN*, series I, vol. 23, 422.

Chapter 4. The Situation

1. *ORN*, series I, vol. 23, 71.
2. *ORA*, series II, vol. I, part 1, 691.
3. Campbell, *Confederate Naval Forces*, 15–16.
4. Naval History Division, Navy Department, *Civil War Naval Chronology*, 1–14, 1–22.
5. Silverstone, *Civil War Navies*, 114.
6. *ORA*, series I, vol. VII, 578.
7. *ORN*, series I, vol. 22, 537–39.
8. *ORA*, series I, vol. VII, 124–25.
9. *ORA*, series I, vol. VII, 131.
10. *ORN*, series I, vol. 22, 538; *ORN*, series I, vol. 22, 545.
11. *ORN*, series I, vol. 22, 540.
12. Walke, *Naval Scenes and Reminiscences*, 65. Walke mentions one Sailor, Jasper P. Breas, who died that night.
13. Ibid., 66.
14. Ibid.
15. *ORN*, series I, vol. 22, 544.
16. *ORN*, series I, vol. 22, 539.
17. *ORN*, series I, vol. 22, 560.
18. *ORN*, series I, vol. 22, 553.
19. *ORN*, series I, vol. 22, 548.
20. *ORN*, series I, vol. 22, 585–87 and 592.
21. *ORN*, series I, vol. 22, 586.
22. *ORN*, series I, vol. 22, 626.
23. Milligan, *From the Fresh-Water Navy*, 27.
24. Walke, *Naval Scenes and Reminiscences*, 87.
25. *ORN*, series I, vol. 22, 597.
26. *ORN*, series I, vol. 22, 315.
27. Island No 10 was given that name as it was the 10th island down river from Cairo.
28. *ORN*, series I, vol. 22, 657.
29. Milligan, *From the Fresh-Water Navy*, 36.
30. *ORN*, series I, vol. 22, 693.
31. *ORN*, series I, vol. 22, 693–94.

32. *ORN*, series I, vol. 22, 732. The canal was dug by Colonel Josiah Bissell's engineer regiment; it took them nineteen days to dig the canal.
33. ORN, series I, vol. 22, 738 & 749–50; *ORN*, series I, vol. 22, 701.
34. *ORN*, series I, vol. 22, 701.
35. *ORN*, series I, vol. 22, 732.
36. *ORN*, series I, vol. 22, 697, 703–4.
37. *ORN*, series I, vol. 22, 705–6.
38. Walke, *Naval Scenes and Reminiscences*, 117–19.
39. *ORN*, series I, vol. 22, 706–8.
40. *ORN*, series I, vol. 22, 709 and 711.
41. *ORN*, series I, vol. 22, 721. When Island No. 10 was captured, seventy heavy cannon were part of the equipment seized along with sixteen heavy cannon from the floating battery.
42. Walke, *Naval Scenes and Reminiscences*, 129.
43. Ibid., 124.
44. Ibid.
45. Walke, *Naval Scenes and Reminiscences*, 125; *ORN*, series I, vol. 22, 704.
46. *ORN*, series I, vol. 22, 839.
47. *ORN*, series I, vol. 22, 733.
48. *ORN*, series I, vol. 22, 712–13.
49. *ORN*, series I, vol. 22, 714.
50. *ORA*, series I, vol. VIII, 655–57.
51. *ORN*, series I, vol. 22, 714–15.
52. *ORN*, series I, vol. 22, 700.
53. *ORN*, series II, vol. 1, parts 1 to 4, 464; ORA, series I, vol. LII, part 1, 166.
54. Read, *Reminiscences of the Confederate; ORN*, series I, vol. 22, 497–98.
55. *ORN*, series I, vol. 22, 315 and 531.
56. *ORN*, series I, vol. 22, 531. On January 19, 1862, there was no artillery defending Cairo, *ORA*, series I, vol. VII, 544. On February 21, 1862, there were twelve field guns at Bird's Point, sixteen field guns at Fort Holt, and six guns at Cairo, *ORA*,

series I, vol. VII, 649. My assumption is that at the beginning of February, when the Union flotilla was attacking Forts Henry and Donelson, the majority of these guns had not yet been emplaced and that Cairo was weakly defended by the Army.

57. *ORN*, series I, vol. 22, 532.
58. *ORA*, series I, vol. VII, 893–94.
59. *ORN*, series I, vol. 22, 824. The regular Confederate naval force that was sent from New Orleans is referred to as both a squadron and a fleet. Because its commander, George N. Hollins, is referred to as captain and flag-officer in the *ORN*s, I have decided to use the same term the regular Union Navy would have used for such an organization under a flag-officer, Hollins's highest rank—a squadron.
60. *ORN*, series I, vol. 22, 842. Read, *Reminiscences of the Confederate.* Read names the two gunboats that Hollins brought with him and states that one was the *Joy*, but there was no Confederate boat with that name in any of the sources I used. However, there is mention of a Confederate gunboat with the name of *Ivy*, and I believe that Read forgot the real name of the second gunboat. In addition, James Morris Morgan in his autobiography, *Recollections of a Rebel Reefer* (New York: Houghton Mifflin Company, 1917), calls the boat the *Ivy.*
61. *ORA*, series I, vol. VII, 437–38.
62. *ORN*, series I, vol. 22, 738, 749–50. Read, *Reminiscences of the Confederate.*
63. *ORN*, series I, vol. 22, 738.
64. *ORN*, series I, vol. 22, 713–14; Alfred T. Mahan, *The Navy in the Civil War, The Gulf and Inland Waters* (New York: Charles Scribner's Sons, 1883), 41.
65. *ORN*, series I, vol. 22, 842. Read, *Reminiscences of the Confederate.*
66. Read, *Reminiscences of the Confederate.*
67. *ORN*, series I, vol. 22, 839.
68. *ORN*, series I, vol. 22, 840.
69. The CSS *Ivy* is one of the boats whose history is hard to determine. Charles Read states in his reminiscences that Hollins went to New Orleans in the *Joy,* but the *Joy* was not part of Hollins's fleet; however, James Morgan, in his reminiscences, states that

Hollins took the *Ivy* to New Orleans. In addition, an article in the *New York Times*, dated April 26, 1862, states that Commodore Hollins had gone to New Orleans in the *Ivy*. The *Ivy* is mentioned in the Navy's *Official Records* as being at New Orleans when it was attacked. It must have escaped, for the Statistical Data for Confederate Ships in the Navy's *Official Records* states that she was burned by the Confederates on the Yazoo River in 1863 to avoid capture. Based on this information, I made the assumption that the *Ivy* took Hollins to New Orleans and not the *Joy*, as stated by Read.

70. *ORN*, series I, vol. 23, 4–5. Read, *Reminiscences of the Confederate.*
71. *ORN*, series I, vol. 23, 4–5.
72. *ORA*, series I, vol. LII, part I, 38.
73. Stanton, Berquist, and Bowers, *Civil War Reminiscences,* 152.
74. *ORN*, series I, vol. 23, 54.
75. Stanton, Berquist, and Bowers, *Civil War Reminiscences*, 153–54. Read, *Reminiscences of the Confederate.*
76. Stanton, Berquist, and Bowers, *Civil War Reminiscences*, 152–55.
77. Ibid., 155.
78. *ORN*, series I, vol. 23, 54, 697–98; Read, *Reminiscences of the Confederate.*
79. *ORN*, series II, vol. I, 259 and 263. The *Maurepas* was later sunk to obstruct the White River and the *Pontchartrain* burned to avoid capture. The *Livingston* and *Polk* were burned per the orders of Commander Pinkney. Pinkney was court-martialed for this action, but it must not have hurt his career because he later commanded ships in North Carolina. *ORN*, series II, vol. 2, 242.
80. Read, *Reminiscences of the Confederate.*
81. Ibid.
82. Ibid.
83. Ibid. *ORN*, series I, vol. 23, 204. Two rifled guns were taken from Fort Randolph to St. Charles, and I have made the assumption that they were the two cannon saved by Lieutenant Stone. Lieutenant Sardine Graham. Stone was better known as S. G. Stone. Lieutenant Stone later served onboard the CSS *Florida*.
84. Read, *Reminiscences of the Confederate.*

85. *ORN*, series I, vol. 22, 316; *ORN*, series I, vol. 23, 4–5.
86. *ORN*, series I, vol. 23, 8. Foote was worried that the ironclad *Louisiana* being built in New Orleans would be sent upriver; his fear was real, as this was one of the options the Confederates were considering.
87. *ORN*, series I, vol. 23, 7.
88. *ORN*, series I, vol. 23, 8–11.
89. *ORN*, series I, vol. 23, 76.
90. *ORN*, series I, vol. 23, 63–64.
91. *ORN*, series I, vol. 23, 11–12.
92. *ORN*, series I, vol. 22, 466; Walke, *Naval Scenes and Reminiscences*, 249.
93. Barbiere, *Scraps*, 212.
94. Walke, *Naval Scenes and Reminiscences*, 249.
95. *SORA*, part III, vol. 1, 554.
96. *ORN*, series I, vol. 22, 703.
97. *ORN*, series I, vol. 23, 63.
98. *ORN*, series I, vol. 23, 109.
99. Stanton, Berquist, and Bowers, *Civil War Reminiscences*, 155.
100. Ibid.

Chapter 5. The Battle of Plum Point

1. *ORN*, series I, vol. 23, 54.
2. Davis, *Life of Charles Henry*, 223.
3. The Battle of Plum Point was the first naval squadron action of the Civil War, even though it occurred after the battles at Hampton Roads and New Orleans. At Hampton Roads, while the Confederacy had a naval squadron involved in the battles, they only fought individual Union ships and not a Union squadron. At New Orleans the same is true, as the Confederates boats fought as individuals and were under different commands. Statements that this was the first naval squadron action of the Civil War can be found in Davis, *Life of Charles Henry*, 228; Walke, *Naval Scenes and Reminiscences*, 249; Admiral David D. Porter, *The Naval History of the Civil War* (Secaucus, NJ: Castle, 1984), 166. The thirty-minute length of the battle is from Stanton, Berquist, and Bowers, *Civil War Reminiscences*, 158, and

Montgomery's report in ORA, series I, vol. LII, part I, 39, in which he states that the "boats were exposed for thirty minutes to a most terrific fire." In his official report, Captain Davis stated that the action lasted "the better part of an hour" (*ORN*, series I, vol. 23, p. 14). Second Master Thomas Gregory stated in his official report that the battle lasted about forty minutes. However, the log of the mortar division states that the battle lasted about an hour. The log of the *Benton* states that the Union boats continued to fire until all of the Confederate boats returned behind the point, which could account for the one-hour time frame.

4. Mark Twain, *Life on the Mississippi* (New York: Harper and Brothers, 1917), 231.
5. *ORN*, series I, vol. 23, 56.
6. G.P.U., "Com. Foote's Progress," *Chicago Tribune*, April 17, 1862.
7. Walke, *Naval Scenes and Reminiscences*, 246.
8. Information on the time of sunrise is from the National Oceanic & Atmospheric Administration website, which shows that sunrise on May 10 in Memphis is at 5:01 standard time.
9. Information on the weather and level of the river is from Walke, *Naval Scenes and Reminiscences,* 250. A Union newspaper reporter onboard the St. Louis stated in a dispatch published in the *Chicago Tribune* on April 14, 1862, that the river had overflowed its banks, and that the surrounding shores were thickly overgrown with timber and brush.
10. Walke, *Naval Scenes and Reminiscences,* 252.
11. *ORN*, series I, vol. 23, 18–20; Walke, *Naval Scenes and Reminiscences,* 252; Eliot Callender, "What a Boy Saw on the Mississippi," *Speeches of a Veteran* (Chicago, IL: The Blue Sky Press, 1901).
12. Second Master Thomas Gregory stated in his official report (*ORN*, series I, vol. 23, pp. 15–16) that he started firing at 6:00 a.m. as per Captain Henry E. Maynadier's, Commander of the Mortar Boats, orders. Captain Henry Walke wrote in his postwar memoirs that the mortar boat opened fire at 5:00 a.m. As Gregory was in charge of the mortar boat and considering that it would have been dark at 5:00 a.m. during that time of the year—which would have made it difficult to tow the mortar boat into position—I decided to use Gregory's time for when his mortar commenced firing.

13. Walke, *Naval Scenes and Reminiscences,* 250–251.
14. The best Union official description of the battle—although he dramatically overestimates the damage to the Confederate fleet—is Lieutenant S. Ledyard Phelps's, commander of the *Benton.* His report can be found at *ORN*, series I, vol. 23, 18–19. There is also an excellent description of the battle along with some detailed maps and a detailed discussion of various contemporary controversies about the battle in Walke, *Naval Scenes and Reminiscences,* 249–268.
15. Stanton, Berquist, and Bowers, *Civil War Reminiscences,* 155.
16. *ORN*, series I, vol. 23, 54.
17. Although Montgomery does not give the exact order of the Confederate boats in his report, Thompson gives it in his reminiscences, and a man who was onboard the *Bragg* wrote a letter to the Houston Telegraph that was published on June 2, 1862, giving the same order of battle as in Thompson's reminiscences. However, one of the soldiers on board the *General Bragg* gave a slightly different order of battle in a report to the *Memphis Avalanche* newspaper. I decided not to use his order of battle, as he probably could not differentiate among all of the boats and because he stated that the *General Bragg* was the flagship, which it was not.
18. The best official Confederate descriptions of the battle are Montgomery's and Thompson's official reports. Their reports can be found at *ORN*, series I, vol. 23, 54–57.
19. *ORN*, series I, vol. 23, 15. Gregory stated that he was only able to fire five shells before he saw the Confederate gunboats. The sustained rate of fire for his 13–inch mortar was about five minutes per projectile, and if he started firing at 6:00 a.m., he would have seen the Confederate boats about 6:25 a.m. Walke stated in his report that the battle began about 6:30 a.m. The log of the mortar division agrees with Gregory; however, Davis stated in his report that the battle began a little after 7:00 a.m. The log of the *Benton* does not agree with Davis, and states that the engagement started at 7:25 a.m., which is a surprise as Davis was on the *Benton.* Symmes Browne, in a letter to his family, stated that it was at 7:00 a.m. when the drums beat to quarters on the *Mound City.* He also states that the *Cincinnati* had been sent down to guard the mortar boat thirty minutes prior to that. In agreement

with Browne, the *Memphis Avalanche* newspaper reported that the battle began at about 7:00 a.m. So, there is a range of times for the start of the battle. Based on the time the Confederate fleet left its mooring site and Gregory's statements, I decided to go with 6:30 a.m.

20. Callender, "What a Boy Saw."
21. Ibid.
22. Stanton, Berquist, and Bowers, *Civil War Reminiscences,* 156.
23. Walke, *Naval Scenes and Reminiscences*, 251.
24. Ibid., 264.
25. Ibid., 251.
26. During this time period, the normal order of battle for a fleet was for the flagship to be in the lead. The fact that Davis allowed Walke's boat to precede his shows how serious Davis thought the situation was.
27. Walke, *Naval Scenes and Reminiscences*, 249. Walke's statements in his reminiscences can be verified by how long it took each ironclad to get into action. The ones that did not have their steam up were the slowest.
28. Walke, *Naval Scenes and Reminiscences*, 252–253.
29. Slagle, *Ironclad Captain,* 219.
30. Much of the information on the actions onboard the *Cincinnati* was taken from *SORA*, part III, vol. I, 554–56.
31. The only reference I found about the *Bragg* going upriver and then turning back to ram the *Cincinnati* was in A. T. Mahan's *The Gulf and Inland Waters* (New York: Charles Scribner's Sons, 1883), 43. Although Mahan was not an eyewitness, I felt that he was reliable enough to justify using his information. In addition, if the *Cincinnati* were going downriver, the *Bragg* would have had to ram her from upriver to have hit her on the starboard quarter. Thus, beyond Mahan, logic would dictate that the *Bragg* was upriver from the *Cincinnati* when she rammed her.
32. Stanton, Berquist, and Bowers, *Civil War Reminiscences,* 155.
33. *SORA*, part III, vol. I, 555; Callender, "What a Boy Saw."
34. Walke, *Naval Scenes and Reminiscences*, 253. One result of the collision was that it appeared to some of men on the approaching Union ironclads that the *Cincinnati* was steaming upriver to escape from the enemy.

35. *ORN*, series I, vol. 23, 55.
36. The only reference I found that specifically stated when the man on the *Bragg* was killed was in log of the *Price* in Barbiere's *Scraps*, 212.
37. *ORN*, series I, vol. 23, 55–56.
38. Callender, "What a Boy Saw."
39. Information on the damage suffered by the *Cincinnati* came from reports written by Fleet Captain Alexander Pennock, who was in charge of the Navy Depot at Cairo where the *Cincinnati* was repaired. His reports can be found in *ORN*, series I, vol. 23, 20–21, and 102.
40. Callender, "What a Boy Saw."
41. Ibid. It is hard to say if those were the exact words, or if the phrase was created by Callender to make his speeches more interesting. However, considering the personalities of Stemble and Hoel, it would have been very like either one of them to make such a response.
42. "[S]kulking crew" is how Stemble described the Confederate sailors in a letter to Eads. *SORA*, part III, vol. I, 555.
43. *ORN*, series I, vol. 23, 17; *ORN*, series I, vol. 23, 24–25. Although I was unable to find any direct reference that Hoel gave the order to run the *Cincinnati* aground, the timing of Stembel's wounding and subsequent partial paralyzation makes it unlikely that he was able to issue such an order. Consequently, I gave Hoel credit for ordering that the *Cincinnati* be run aground.
44. Callender, "What a Boy Saw."
45. *ORN*, series I, vol. 23, 15–16. Gregory stated, "I at once trained my mortar upon them, loaded for that short range, and fired, bursting my shell directly over them." Because mortars are not designed for direct fire, I made the assumption that Gregory fired his mortar almost vertically, which would have been possible as he stated that they were three-fourths of a mile away.
46. *ORN*, series I, vol. 23, 65.
47. *ORN*, series I, vol. 23, 15–16.
48. Walke, *Naval Scenes and Reminiscences*, 253, 256–257.
49. *ORN*, series I, vol. 23, 56.
50. *ORN*, series I, vol. 23, 55.

51. *ORN*, series I, vol. 23, 19.
52. Walke, *Naval Scenes and Reminiscences*, 255.
53. Ibid.
54. *ORN*, series I, vol. 23, 56.
55. Walke, *Naval Scenes and Reminiscences*, 256.
56. *ORN*, series I, vol. 23, 13.
57. *ORN*, series I, vol. 23, 14 and 18–19.
58. Davis, *Life of Charles Henry*, 233.
59. *ORN*, series I, vol. 23, 19. Interestingly, Phelps's official correspondence about the battle was sent to Foote rather than to Davis, which must irritated Davis, but it is understandable, as Foote had just left the flotilla and was expected to return.
60. *ORN*, series I, vol. 23, 24.
61. *ORN*, series I, vol. 23, 14.
62. Walke is particularly bitter in his autobiography. To demonstrate how important it was to everyone that his boat was heavily involved in the fighting, George Yost states in his diary that the *Mound City* was "closely followed by the *Cairo*," and that the *Cairo* poured "shot & shell into the rebel boat." George R. Yost, Diary, Manuscripts, Illinois State Historical Library, Springfield, Il.
63. *SORA*, part III, vol. I, 556.
64. *ORN*, series I, vol. 23, 17.
65. *ORN*, series I, vol. 23, 54–57.
66. Porter, *Naval History*, 166. Although Porter does not get the details of the battle correct, his observations on the limitations of the Union boats are perceptive—but he should know, as he eventually commanded them.
67. *ORN*, series I, vol. 23, 26, 115.
68. Stanton, Berquist, and Bowers, *Civil War Reminiscences*, 158.
69. *ORN*, series I, vol. 23, 56.
70. *ORN*, series I, vol. 23, 14 and 16–17.
71. Stanton, Berquist, and Bowers, *Civil War Reminiscences*, 157.
72. Milligan, *From the Fresh-Water Navy*, 79–80.
73. *ORN*, series I, vol. 23, 14–15.
74. Porter, *Naval History*, 167.
75. *ORN*, series I, vol. 23, 15.

76. Callender, "What a Boy Saw."
77. *Memphis Avalanche*, May 12, 1862, 3–1.
78. *Memphis Avalanche*, May 14, 1862, 1–1.

Chapter 6. The Fall of Fort Pillow

1. *ORA*, series I, vol. X, part I, 898–99.
2. *ORA*, series I, vol. X, part I, 902.
3. Barbiere, *Scraps*, 213.
4. Ibid.
5. *ORN*, series I, vol. 23, 20, 106–7. Fleet Captain Alexander Pennock also took credit for sending the *Champion* downriver, but as the Army Quartermaster Department was responsible for paying all of the expenses except the pay of the naval officers, I decided that Quartermaster Wise was the individual who actually made the decision.
6. *ORN*, series I, vol. 23, 20, 106–7.
7. *ORN*, series I, vol. 23, 13.
8. *ORN*, series I, vol. 23, 19.
9. Milligan, *From the Fresh-Water Navy*, 74. Reports in the *ORN*s give the reader the impression that the *Mound City* was repaired at Cairo. However, letters from the Browne brothers—who were on the *Mound City*—in *From the Fresh-Water Navy*, state that the boat was repaired at Mound City. The misunderstanding occurs as the commander of the naval facilities was located in Cairo, and all of his reports on the damage to the *Mound City* and its repairs were written in Cairo.
10. *ORN*, series I, vol. 23, 92–93.
11. Milligan, *From the Fresh-Water* , 78; *ORN*, series I, vol. 23, 28.
12. *ORN*, series I, vol. 23, 21.
13. Davis, *Life of Charles Henry*, 228.
14. *ORN*, series I, vol. 23, 23–24.
15. *ORN*, series I, vol. 23, 102.
16. *ORN*, series I, vol. 23, 115.
17. *ORN*, series I, vol. 23, 13.
18. *ORN*, series I, vol. 23, 88–89.
19. *ORN*, series I, vol. 23, 89.
20. *ORN*, series I, vol. 23, 17.

21. *ORN*, series I, vol. 23, 93.
22. *ORN*, series I, vol. 23, 95.
23. *ORN*, series I, vol. 23, 18.
24. *ORN*, series I, vol. 23, 108–9.
25. *ORN*, series I, vol. 23, 29.
26. *ORN*, series I, vol. 23, 53, 105.
27. *ORN*, series I, vol. 23, 105.
28. *ORN*, series I, vol. 23, 108.
29. *ORN*, series I, vol. 23, 24–25. Hoel later commanded the *Pittsburg*.
30. *ORN*, series I, vol. 23, 22. Gregory started the war as a carpenter onboard the *Cincinnati* and, as such, was an officer. After the Battle of Memphis, he became commander the *Little Rebel*. Later, he commanded the *Springfield*, *St. Clair*, and *Juliet*. His boats were involved in a number of actions, and he stayed on active duty until the end of the war.
31. *ORA*, series I, vol. X, part I, 897. *ORN*, series I, vol. 23, 30–31.
32. *ORA*, series I, vol. X, part I, 898. *ORN*, series I, vol. 23, 30–31.
33. *ORA*, series I, vol. X, part I, 897–98; *ORN*, series I, vol. 23, 30–31.
34. *ORN*, series I, vol. 23, 24.
35. *ORN*, series I, vol. 23, 109.
36. Davis, *Life of Charles Henry*, 232. I researched who or what Kilhard was, but was unsuccessful in finding anything about him. Kilhard appears to be a saying that has lost its meaning.
37. *ORN*, series I, vol. 23, 29.
38. Davis, *Life of Charles Henry*, 233.
39. *ORN*, series I, vol. 23, 32–33.
40. *ORN*, series I, vol. 23, 33.
41. *ORN*, series I, vol. 23, 34.
42. *ORN*, series I, vol. 23, 38.
43. *ORN*, series I, vol. 23, 39.
44. *ORN*, series I, vol. 23, 41.
45. *ORN*, series I, vol. 23, 41.
46. *ORN*, series I, vol. 23, 42.
47. *ORN*, series I, vol. 23, 43.
48. *ORN*, series I, vol. 23, 43.

49. *ORN*, series I, vol. 23, 48.
50. *ORA*, series I, vol. X, 901.
51. *ORN*, series I, vol. 23, 45–46.

Chapter 7. The Battle of Memphis

1. *ORN*, series I, vol. 23, 140.
2. Davis, *Life of Charles Henry*, 242.
3. *ORA*, series I, vol. IV, 408.
4. *ORA*, series I, vol. LII, part II, 93–94.
5. *ORA*, series I, vol. IV, 408.
6. *ORA*, series I, vol. LII, part II, 80–81; 93–94; *ORA*, series I, vol. IV, 408.
7. *ORA*, series I, vol. LII, part I, 39. It is my assumption that these four 8-inch guns were mounted on the largest boats, as they would have been the best ones to handle the extra stress and due to their placement in the battle line at Memphis.
8. *ORN*, series I, vol. 23, 699–700; *ORA*, series I, vol. X, part II, 589
9. *ORA*, series I, vol. X, part II, 589; *ORN*, series I, vol. 23, 699–700.
10. *ORA*, series I, vol. X, part II, 578.
11. *ORA*, series I, vol. X, part II, 578–79.
12. *ORA*, series I, vol. X, part II, 588–89.
13. *ORA*, series I, vol. X, part I, pp. 912–13.
14. Barbiere, *Scraps*, 213–214.
15. Navigating the Mississippi was hazardous even for experienced river pilots, as at Fort Randolph the *Van Dorn* ran aground, and her crew had to go ashore and cut wood to make spars to push her off the sandbar. Barbiere, *Scraps*, 214.
16. *ORA*, series I, vol. X, part I, 912–13. Island No. 40 was a relatively large and important island just upriver from Memphis. It was important enough that in July 1863, Admiral Porter had the USS *Hastings* based there. *ONR*, series I, vol. 25, 218–219.
17. Barbiere, *Scraps*, 214.
18. Ibid.
19. *ORA*, series I, vol. LII, part I, 39. Captain J. Henry Hart [*sic*] (His name was James H. Hurt. Another example of a misspelled

name.) stated in *History of the Confederate* (p. 259) that it was not until the fleet was in a battle line on the morning of t 6t June that he was told that they were going to fight.

20. *ORA*, series I, vol. X, part I, 912–13; *ORA*, series I, vol. LII, part I, 37–40. Montgomery stated in his report that he purchased the coal but that General Lovell refused to pay for it, which is contradictory. What probably happened was that Montgomery contracted for the coal but Lovell refused to honor the contract.
21. Walke, *Naval Scenes and Reminiscences*, 292.
22. *ORA*, series I, vol. LII, part I, 39.
23. Barbiere, *Scraps*, 214.
24. *ORN*, series I, vol. 23, 133.
25. *ORN*, series I, vol. 23, 119.
26. Walke, *Naval Scenes and Reminiscences*, 275. Anyone who has been in a military convoy that is trying to safely negotiate treacherous terrain can appreciate how a column of boats/vehicles can easily spread out such that the lead boat/vehicle ends up being far ahead of the rest of the convoy.
27. Walke, *Naval Scenes and Reminiscences*, 275.
28. *ORN*, series I, vol. 23, 119.
29. The weather on the morning of June 6 is based on a statement in Charles Coffin's *The Boys of '61* (Boston: Estes and Lauriat, 1881), 102. Coffin was a reporter, and on board the *Jessie Benton* during the battle.
30. The order of the ironclads is based on Walke's reminiscences with one variation. Charles Coffin, a reporter on board the tug *Jessie Benton*, stated in his reminiscences, *Drum-Beat of the Nation* (New York: Harper & Brothers, 1888, 229), that the order of the boats was, starting at the Tennessee side, the *Benton*, *Carondelet*, *Louisville*, *St. Louis*, and *Cairo*. I have decided to use most of the information provided by Walke, as he was captain of the *Carondelet* and, as a professional naval officer who had been with the fleet for quite a while, could distinguish the boats based on the colored bands on their smoke stacks better than the reporters. I also believe that Davis would have kept his flagship toward the middle of the line to maintain better control. Another problem with Coffin's story is that it changes. In the *Drum-Beat of the Nation*, published in 1887, he boards the *Jessie Benton* from the *Benton*, whereas in *The Boys of '61*, published in 1881, he boards

the *Jessie Benton* from the *J. H. Dickey*, one of the supply boats. As the reporters were quartered aboard the supply boats, he probably boarded the *Jessie Benton* from the *J. H. Dickey*. However, I changed Walke's placement of the *St. Louis* and *Cairo*, as eyewitnesses agreed that the Union boat closest to the Arkansas shore fired first, and George Roberts Yost, who was on the *Cairo*, stated that it was the first boat to fire. Another reporter, from the Missouri *Democrat*, was onboard the *St. Louis*, and his report in Walke's reminiscences (p. 293) states that the *St. Louis* was to the starboard, right, of the *Benton*.

31. Coffin, *Drum-Beat of the Nation*, 229. Coffin, *Boys of '61*, 103–4
32. *ORN*, series I, vol. 23, 139–40.
33. Sharf, *History of the Confederate*, 259.
34. The initial disposition of the Confederate fleet is based on Montgomery's report in *ORA*, series I, vol. LII, part I, 39–40 and the eyewitness account of W. H. Reeder, 1st Assistant Engineer on the *Little Rebel* in the *Houston Telegraph*, June 20, 1862.
35. *ORN*, series I, vol. 23, 136. The reporter for the *Chicago Tribune* estimated that there were 15,000 people watching the battle,. Alexander Simplot's diary noted that there were 40,000 people watching the battle. Alexander Simplot, Papers and drawings 1866–1911, Papers in the Wisconsin Historical Society, Madison, WI. Young, *Standard History of Memphis*, 344, states that almost the entire population of the city watched the battle.
36. Joseph C. Kennedy, *Population of the United States in 1860; Compiled from the Original Returns of the Eighth Census* (Washington, DC: U.S. Government Printing Office, 1864), 467. Even though the 1860 census had Memphis at a population of 22,623, the population of the city may have increased by 1862 due to the war. The First Battle of Bull Run/Manassas was observed by a number of civilians who drove their carriages from Washington to view the battle. Due to the distance of the battle from Washington, not many people would have made the journey especially, as they would not have known when, or if, the battle would take place. Therefore, it is very unlikely that more than a couple of thousand civilians saw the First Battle of Bull Run/Manassas, far fewer than the 15,000 who would have viewed the Battle of Memphis.
37. Information on the speed of the current and the location of the channel comes from a map in Walke's, *Naval Scenes and Reminiscences*, 279.

38. Coffin, *Boys of '61*, 104.
39. *Chicago Tribune*, June 10, 1862; *New York Tribune*, June 11, 1862.
40. *ORA*, series I, vol. LII, part I, 39.
41. Coffin, *Boys of '61*, 105.
42. A reporter from the Missouri *Democrat*, who was onboard the St. Louis stated that "The position of this boat, by rank of the commander, is the rear, her captain being the youngest commanding officer in the fleet." Walke, *Naval Scenes and Reminiscences*, 293.
43. When the *Cairo* sunk in December 1862, she had a 32-pounder smooth bore gun and a 30-pounder rifled Parrott gun in her stern. I have made the assumption that she and all of the other boats in the fleet were similarly armed at this time.
44. Coffin, *Boys of '61*, 105.
45. Walke stated in *Naval Scenes and Reminiscences*, 290, that the shot that hit the *Carondelet* on the bow broke her anchor and anchor stock, in addition to slightly wounding three to four men, which was only minor damage. This information can also be found in Walke's official report, *ORN*, series I, vol. 23, 123.
46. "From the Mississippi Flotilla," *New York Tribune*, June 11, 1862.
47. Walke, *Naval Scenes and Reminiscences*, 276.
48. Barbiere, *Scraps*, 205.
49. Walke, *Naval Scenes and Reminiscences,* 288. The Mississippi was dangerous even near a major port like Memphis, as the *Carondelet* temporarily went aground as she chased the *Van Dorn* (*ORN*, series I, vol. 23, 123.). In addition, the *Bragg* ran aground while trying to escape at Memphis.
50. Walke, *Naval Scenes and Reminiscences*, 288.
51. *ORN*, series I, vol. 23, 125.
52. *ORN*, series I, vol. 23, 133.
53. *ORN*, series I, vol. 23, 129.
54. Coffin, *Boys of '61*, 106; *ORN*, series I, vol. 23, 122.
55. Lieutenant Colonel Alfred Ellet stated after the war that the smoke was so thick that the only part of the *Queen of the West* he could see was the top of her smoke stacks. Alfred W. Ellet, *Ellet and His Steam-Rams at Memphis*, *Battles and Leaders of the Civil War*, vol. I (Secaucus, NJ: Castle:,1982), 456.

56. *ORN*, series I, vol. 23, 133.

57. As with any battle, newspaper reports often do not agree with the reports written by the commanders. The *Memphis Avalanche* reported the captain of the *Lovell* as W. H. Cabel and that he died when he was shot in the forehead. The *Avalanche* also reported the *Van Dorn* as the flagship. Although the *Avalanche* does give an accurate description of most of the battle, these two items are incorrect. In his report, Montgomery states that Delaney was the captain of the *Lovell*, Cabel was the pilot, and that Cabel was killed as the *Lovell* was sinking. In addition, Montgomery states that the *Little Rebel* was his flagship. I have decided to use the information in Montgomery's report rather then the report in the *Avalanche*.

58. Union reports imply that the captain of the *Lovell* lost his nerve and swerved to avoid the collision; however, Montgomery's report states that one of the engines of the *Lovell* went out of order. As the captain of the *Lovell*, Captain James C. Delancy was an experienced river boat pilot and captain—he would have been well aware of the time, speed, and distance factor of a steamboat moving down the river. I find it hard to believe that he would have deliberately turned broadside to the rapidly moving *Queen of the West*. Consequently, I decided to use the information in Montgomery's report.

59. *ORN*, series I, vol. 23, 133.

60. *SORA*, part III, vol. 3, 320–21.

61. *ORN*, series I, vol. 23, 133.

62. In one of his reports, Ellet uses the term larboard to indicate the port side of the boat. Larboard is a much older term for the left side of a boat and, although the Navy no longer used the term, the riverboat men on the Mississippi did.

63. *ORN*, series I, vol. 23, 134.

64. *ORA*, series I, vol. LII, part I, 40; Lewis, *Charles Ellet*, 204. A search was made to determine the first name of Quartermaster J. Sullivan, to no avail.

65. Montgomery's report after the Battle of Plum Point gives Henthorne's first name as Thomas (*ORN*, series I, vol. 23, 56), but in the same report in *ORA*, series I, vol. X, 889, shows it as J. E. Henthorne. My belief is that because a T can easily be confused with a J, the name shown in the Navy's records is correct.

Interestingly, the same report in different official records has such subtle differences.

66. *ORA*, series I, vol. LII, part I, 40; Crandall, *History of the Ram,* 82. Crandall's book has a report of the battle by Lieutenant William Warren, who was on board the *Monarch*. Warren states that the *Monarch* was rammed by the *Beauregard*, then missed by the *Bragg* and *Price*, then rammed the *Price*, pushed the *Little Rebel* onto the shore, secured the *Little Rebel*, assisted the crew of the *Beauregard*, and finally pursued the *Van Dorn*. Although parts of Warren's narrative support statements from other sources, other parts do not. Consequently, I have been selective in deciding which parts of Warren's narrative to include.
67. *ORA*, series I, vol. LII, part I, 40.
68. *ORN*, series I, vol. 23, 134.
69. *ORN*, series I, vol. 23, 125.
70. Lewis, *Charles Ellet,* 204.
71. *ORN*, series I, vol. 23, 135.
72. *ORN*, series I, vol. 23, 136.
73. *ORA*, series I, vol. LII, part I, 40.
74. *ORN*, series I, vol. 23, 120.
75. *ORN*, series I, vol. 23, 120; *ORA*, series I, vol. LII, part I, 40; Walke, *Naval Scenes and Reminiscences*, 281.
76. *ORN*, series I, vol. 23, 137.
77. *ORN*, series I, vol. 23, 120; Davis, *Life of Charles Henry,* 242.
78. *ORA*, series I, vol. LII, part I, 40; *ORN*, series I, vol. 23, 120, 136.
79. "The Grand Naval Engagement," *Chicago Tribune*, June 10, 1862; *ORN*, series I, vol. 23, 141.
80. *ORA*, series I, vol. LII, part I, 40.
81. Walke, *Naval Scenes and Reminiscences*, 291, 295–296; George R. Yost Diary, Manuscripts, Illinois State Historical Library, Springfield, Illinois.
82. *ORN*, series I, vol. 23, 125.

Chapter 8. The Aftermath

1. Davis, *Life of Charles Henry,* 242.

2. *Journal of the Congress of the Confederate States of American, 1861–1865*, (Washington, DC: U.S. Government Printing Office, 1904), 58th Congress 2d Session.
3. *Harper's Weekly* from June 28, 1862 has a good drawing by Alexander Simplot—who was at the battle—of the *Lioness* approaching Memphis.
4. *ORN*, series I, vol. 23, 126–27.
5. *ORN*, series I, vol. 23, 127; Young, *Standard History of Memphis*, 347–51.
6. Clarke, *Warfare Along the Mississippi*, 51.
7. One interesting aspect is that in the Confederate version of events, they were subject to frequent and undeserved mistreatment at the hands of Union officials and that the vast majority of civilians were always loyal to the Confederacy. However, in Union versions, mistreatment of civilians seldom happened, and when it did, it was justified. In addition, a large number of civilians were very pro-Union. The interpretation of events is always subject to the bias of the reporter.
8. *ORN*, series I, vol. 23, 121.
9. *ORN*, series I, vol. 23, 122.
10. *ORN*, series I, vol. 23, 121.
11. *ORN*, series I, vol. 23, 119.
12. *ORN*, series I, vol. 23, 119.
13. Walke, *Naval Scenes and Reminiscences*, 291.
14. *ORN*, series I, vol. 23, 121 and 35–136.
15. *ORN*, series I, vol. 23, 209.
16. *ORN*, series I, vol. 23, 211.
17. *ORN*, series I, vol. 23, 218–219.
18. SORA, part III, vol. 3, 320–21.
19. Barbiere, *Scraps*, 206–207 and 336–92.
20. *ORA*, series I, vol. LII, part I, 40; *ORN*, series I, vol. 23, 123.
21. *ORN*, series I, vol. 23, 140. *Memphis Avalanche*, June 9, 1862, 1:2. Civil War Prisoner of War Records, 1861–1865 for James C. Delancy, accessed October 10, 2013, http://www.ancestry library.com.
22. *ORA*, series I, vol. LII, 40.

23. *ORN*, series I, vol. 18, 649.
24. *ORN*, series I, vol. 23, 120.
25. Warren Crandall, the Assistant Adjutant General of the Marine Brigade, wrote in his book *History of the Ram Fleet and the Mississippi Marine Brigade* (St. Louis, MO: Society of Survivors, 1907) that prize money was distributed only after the Ram Fleet became part of the Navy, 241–242.
26. *ORN*, series I, vol. 23, 120.
27. *ORN*, series I, vol. 23, 233–234 and 243; *ORA*, series I, vol. LII, part I, 40. Even though Montgomery states in his report that the *Van Dorn* was burned on June 25, I decided to use the date in the log from the *Lancaster*, which states that the *Van Dorn* was burned on June 26. C. W. Read has a very low opinion of Pinkney and of his actions in burning the boats on the Yazoo River; see Read, *Reminiscences of the Confederate.*
28. *ORN*, series I, vol. 23, 149.
29. *ORN*, series I, vol. 23, 136.
30. *ORN*, series I, vol. 23, 141.
31. *ORN*, series I, vol. 23, 144.
32. *ORN*, series I, vol. 23, 208–209.
33. *ORN*, series I, vol. 23, 143–44.
34. *ORN*, series I, vol. 23, 147.
35. *ORN*, series I, vol. 23, 149.
36. *ORN*, series I, vol. 23, 143.
37. *ORA*, series I, vol. XIII, 426.
38. *ORN*, series I, vol. 23, 163.
39. *ORN*, series I, vol. 23, 171.
40. *ORN*, series I, vol. 23, 209.
41. *ORN*, series I, vol. 23, 172–74.
42. *ORN*, series I, vol. 23, 218.
43. *ORN*, series I, vol. 23, 389.
44. *ORN*, series I, vol. 23, 388.
45. *ORN*, series I, vol. 23, 427.
46. *ORN*, series I, vol. 23, 429.
47. *ORN*, series I, vol. 23, 430.
48. *ORN*, series I, vol. 23, 428.

49. *ORN*, series I, vol. 23, 465.
50. *ORN*, series I, vol. 23, 468.
51. *ORN*, series I, vol. 23, 469.
52. *ORN*, series I, vol. 24, 448.
53. Davis, *Life of Charles Henry*, 242.
54. *ORN*, series I, vol. 18, 561.

Chapter 9. Rams versus Guns

1. *ORN*, series I, vol. 22, 672.
2. *ORN*, series II, vol. 1, p. 785.
3. John L. Porter, *The Plan and Construction of the "Merrimac," Battles and Leaders of the Civil War*, vol. I (Secaucus, NJ: Castle, 1982), 717.
4. Sharf, *History of the Confederate*, 155.
5. *ORN*, series II, vol. 1, 787.
6. *ORN*, series II, vol. 1, 787.
7. John Coddington, "*Farragut at Mobile Bay,*" Battles and Leaders of the Civil War, vol. IV, ed. Robert U. Johnson and Clarence C. Buel (Secaucus, NJ: Castle, 1982), 395. Coddington was a Union Army Signal Officer who was assigned to the Hartford for the Battle of Mobile Bay for the purpose of communicating between the ships and between the fleet and the Army.
8. Coddington, "*Farragut at Mobile Bay,*" 395.
9. Ibid., 396–97.
10. James D. Johnston, "*The Ram 'Tennessee' at Mobile Bay,*" Battles and Leaders of the Civil War, vol. IV, ed. Robert U. Johnson and Clarence C. Buel (Secaucus, NJ: Castle, 1982), 404–5.
11. Ibid., 404.
12. *ORN*, series I, vol. 23, 15; *ORN*, series I, vol. 23, 123. The log of the *Carondelet* from the Battle of Memphis states that she fired sixty-six projectiles, but I decided to use the number that Commander Walke, the captain of the *Carondelet*, states in his official report. My assumption was that he would have had time to confirm how many projectiles were fired by the time he wrote the report, in contrast to the log, which would have been written immediately following the action.
13. *ORN*, series I, vol. 23, 120.

14. *ORN*, series I, vol. 19, 45–46 & 48–49.
15. *ORN*, series I, vol. 19, 45–50.
16. *ORN*, series I, vol. 24, 174.
17. *ORN*, series I, vol. 25, 757.
18. Information on the construction of the Cincinnati monitor was provided by Bill Roberts, Civil War Ironclads (Baltimore, MD: The Johns Hopkins University Press, 2002); *ORN*, series I, vol. 24, 374.
19. *ORN*, series I, vol. 24, 374.
20. *ORN*, series I, vol. 24, 377.
21. *ORN*, series I, vol. 24, 375–76.
22. *ORN*, series I, vol. 24, 378.
23. *ORN*, series I, vol. 24, 379.
24. The distance from the mouth of the Red River to Grand Gulf is 115 river miles based on information in *ORA*, series I, vol. LII, 167. Brown was some distance upriver from the mouth of the Red River when he decided to continue steaming upriver the afternoon of February 22nd. He reached Grand Gulf the morning of February 24th, taking about thirty-six hours. After calculating time and distance, I determined that the *Indianola* was making much less than three miles per hour, or a little over two knots.
25. *ORN*, series I, vol. 24, 380.
26. *ORN*, series I, vol. 24, 403.
27. To emphasize how slow the *Indianola* was, Major Joseph Brent, commander of the Confederate boats pursuing it, stated that it had a forty-eight–hour head start on the four Confederate boats at Acklin's Landing. *ORN*, series I, vol. 24, 402. Acklin's Landing is just up and across the Mississippi River from the mouth of the Red River and is named for Acklin's Plantation.
28. Information on the capture of the *Indianola* was taken from *ORN*, series I, vol. 24, 374–412.
29. The Confederacy was not able to take advantage of the captured *Indianola* because they destroyed her when they thought a Union ironclad had been sent to attack the salvage operation. In reality, the Union ironclad was a dummy ironclad built for the express purpose of getting the Confederates to destroy the *Indianola*.
30. Ericcson to Fox, October 5, 1862, Private, Box 3, Ltrs Rcvd 1862 A–K, information provided by William Roberts.

31. Information on the Battle of Lissa came from E. B. Potter and Chester W. Nimitz, *Sea Power* (Englewood, NJ: Prentice Hall, 1960), 328–31 and Oscar Parkes, *British Battleships* (Hamden, CN: Archon Books, 1972), 175–76.
32. Parkes, *British Battleships*, 27.
33. Information on Convoy SC104 was taken from Correlli Barnett, *Engage the Enemy More Closely* (New York: W.W. Norton & Company, 1991), 483–89.

Conclusion: The Impact of the Battle of Memphis

1. *ORN*, series I, vol. 23,110.
2. *ORA*, series I, vol. LII, part I, 39.
3. Ulysses S. Grant, *Personal Memoirs of U S. Grant*, vol. I (New York: Charles L. Webster & Company, 1885), 574.
4. Davis, *Life of Charles Henry*, 242–243.
5. Although the Confederates would still achieve naval victories on the Mississippi and its tributaries, there was never any future threat to Union naval control of the upper Mississippi. Even the CSS *Arkansas* was not much of a threat, as it could barely steam upriver. Any attempt by the *Arkansas* to steam up river to raid the northern cities would have been, at best, a very long process, and would have required her to stop and regularly refuel. Such a slow trip would have made the *Arkansas* vulnerable to any Union boat that may be chasing her as well as given Union authorities time to prepare for her upriver.

Appendix A. History of the Boats

1. *Dictionary of American Naval Fighting Ships*, vol. I (Washington DC: U.S. Government Printing Office, 1959), 119; Silverstone, *Civil War Navies*, 116.
2. *Dictionary of American Naval*, vol. II, 9; Bearss, *Hardluck Ironclad; Silverstone, Civil War Navies*,, 114–15.
3. *Dictionary of American Naval*, vol. II, 40; Walke, *Naval Scenes and Reminiscences*, 114–15.
4. *Dictionary of American Naval*, vol. II, 119; Silverstone, *Civil War Navies*, 114–15.

5. *Dictionary of American Naval*, vol. II, 510; *ORA*, series I, vol. VI, 597
6. *Dictionary of American Naval*, vol. II, 522.
7. *Dictionary of American Naval*, vol. II, 522–23 and vol. III, 37–38; *ORN*, series II, vol. 1, parts 1 to 4, 91; Silverstone, *Civil War Navies*, 168.
8. *Dictionary of American Naval*, vol. II, 524; *ORN*, series I, vol. 23, 57.
9. *Dictionary of American Naval*, vol. II, 525 and vol. III, 59–60.
10. *Dictionary of American Naval*, vol. II, 523–24; *ORN*, series II, vol. 1, parts 1 to 4, 253.
11. *Dictionary of American Naval*, vol. II, 543–44 and vol. IV, 125.
12. *Dictionary of American Naval*, vol. IV, 148–49; Silverstone, *Civil War*, 114–15
13. *Dictionary of American Naval*, vol. IV, 414; Silverstone, *Civil War Navies*, 120.
14. *Dictionary of American Naval*, vol. IV, 443–44; Silverstone, *Civil War Navies*, 114–15.
15. *Dictionary of American Naval*, vol. V, 321–22; Silverstone, *Civil War Navies*, 114–15.
16. *Dictionary of American Naval*, vol. II, 559 and vol. V, 412.
17. *Dictionary of American Naval*, vol. I, 98; Silverstone, *Civil War Navies*, 114–15.
18. *Dictionary of American Naval*, vol. II, 525–26 and vol. V, 672.

Appendix B. Biographies

1. Davis, *Life of Charles Henry*, 4 & 333–34.
2. Ibid. Naval History & Heritage website, accessed December 2013, http://www.history.navy.mil.
3. *ORN*, series I, vol. 23, 63.
4. *ORN*, series I, vol. 23, 388 & 395.
5. Davis, *Life of Charles Henry*, 286 & 285–86.
6. Naval History & Heritage website.
7. Lewis, *Charles Ellet*, 5 and 207.
8. *Biographical Dictionary of American*, 39.
9. Lewis, *Charles Ellet*, 121–28.

10. *Biographical Dictionary of American*, 38–40.
11. A list of Ellet's publications can be found in *A Biographical Dictionary of American Civil Engineers*, 40.
12. Naval History & Heritage website
13. "The Last Roll, Commodore J. E. Montgomery," *Confederate Veteran* 10, no. 9 (September 1902), 416–17.
14. Montgomery, *Genealogical History*, 58–59.
15. Twain, *Life on the Mississippi*, 216.
16. *SORA*, part III, vol. 3, 320–21.
17. *ORN*, series II, vol. 2, 753.
18. *ORN*, series I, vol. 27, 268–271.
19. *ORN*, series I, vol. 27, 269.
20. Montgomery, *Genealogical History*, 59–60.

Appendix C. Acting Volunteer Lieutenant Commander William R. Hoel

1. A search of the Navy's *Official Records* for acting volunteer lieutenant commander was made and those names were then crosschecked with *Officers of the Continental and U.S. Navy and Marine Corps 1775–1900* in *Navy History and Heritage Command*, accessed September 2012, http://www.history.navy.mil/. Only two men were shown to have been promoted to acting volunteer lieutenant commander prior to Hoel; however, one entry is incorrect, as it shows that the individual, Thomas A. Harris, was promoted directly from acting master to acting volunteer lieutenant commander on April 17, 1863, which would not have been possible as Congress did not authorize the rank until 1864. In addition, the Navy's *Official Records* show that Harris was an acting volunteer lieutenant as late as April 1865 (*ORN*, series I, vol. 27, 138), and do not show him to be an acting volunteer lieutenant commander until July 1865 (*ORN*, series I, vol. 27, 285). The first individual to be promoted to acting volunteer lieutenant commander was Joseph D. Danels. The *Officers of the Continental and U.S. Navy and Marine Corps 1775–1900* shows that he was promoted to acting lieutenant commander on May 18, 1864, and the Navy's *Official Records* indicates that he was an acting volunteer lieutenant commander in January 1865 during the attack on Fort Fisher. The *Officers of the Continental and U.S.*

Navy and Marine Corps 1775–1900 also shows that Danels was a lieutenant in the regular US Navy prior to the war, resigned his commission in April 1861, and became an acting master in September 1862. After Danels was promoted to acting volunteer lieutenant commander, he was given a backdated promotion to lieutenant commander, effective July 16, 1862. Thus, he was not a "true" volunteer, but rather a former regular US Navy officer who came back to active duty and was, eventually, given a regular commission.

2. Joseph W. Rutter, "Capt. William Rion Hoel: The Life of a 19th Century Riverman," part I, *S&D Reflector* (June 1996): 8.
3. Rutter, "Capt. William Rion Hoel," 8. William R. Hoel, Papers in the Collection of the Public Library of Cincinnati and Hamilton County. Henceforth cited as Hoel Papers.
4. Rutter, "Capt. William Rion Hoel," 10.
5. Ibid.
6. Hoel Papers; Rutter, "Capt. William Rion Hoel,"13.
7. Hoel Papers.
8. *ORN*, series I, vol. 22, 539 & 544.
9. *ORN*, series I, vol. 22, 712–13.
10. Rutter, "Capt. William Rion Hoel," 15.
11. *ORN*, series I, vol. 22, 712–13.
12. *ORN*, series I, vol. 22, 729.
13. Hoel Papers.
14. Hoel Papers.
15. *ORN*, series I, vol. 23, 23–24.
16. *ORN*, series I, vol. 23, 17.
17. *ORN*, series I, vol. 23, 136.
18. *ORN*, series I, vol. 23, 391.
19. Acting Rear-Admiral David D. Porter's memorandum on the operations of the Mississippi Squadron from October 1862 to May 1863 lists, in various places, the commanders of each boat. Hoel was the only nonregular in command of an ironclad. All of the other commanders were regular Navy officers with a rank of lieutenant commander or higher. *ORN*, series I, vol. 23, 395–416. In June 1863, Porter sent a message to Secretary of the Navy Gideon Welles listing all of the vessels in the Mississippi Squadron, their stations, and commanders. *ORN*, series I, vol. 25, 145–

47. Hoel was the only nonregular Navy officer in command of an ironclad and was the lowest ranking individual in such a position.

20. *ORN*, series I, vol. 24, 560; *ORN*, series I, vol. 23, 550–51; *ORN*, series I, vol. 26, 24–25.
21. *ORN*, series I, vol. 24, 543.
22. *ORN*, series I, vol. 27, 82.
23. *ORN*, series I, vol. 24, 611.
24. *ORN*, series I, vol. 24, 611. Porter overstated the *Pittsburg*'s losses, as Hoel reported that he had six men killed and thirteen wounded during the battle, *ORN*, series I, vol. 24, 616.
25. *ORN*, series I, vol. 24, 612.
26. *ORN*, series I, vol. 26, 316.
27. Hoel Papers. *Navy History and Heritage Command*, accessed September 2012, http://www.history.navy.mil/.
28. A search of the Navy's *Official Records* and a comparison of the names to the *Officers of the Continental and U.S. Navy and Marine Corps 1775–1900* in *Navy History and Heritage Command* was made. The searched showed the whereas some individuals in the Mississippi Squadron are shown as acting volunteer lieutenant commanders, they were in reality acting volunteer lieutenants, but commanders of boats. Thus, their signature on reports could be written as acting volunteer lieutenant-commander. The other individual who was an acting volunteer lieutenant commander in the Mississippi Squadron was Thomas A. Harris, who spent most of the war with the Atlantic Blockading Squadron.
29. Rutter, "Capt. William Rion Hoel,"11.
30. Ibid., 13.
31. Library of Congress, *The Grand Army of the Republic and Kindred Societies, accessed January 2013,* http://www.loc.gov.
32. Rutter, "Capt. William Rion Hoel,"13.
33. All of the information in this paragraph was taken from Rutter, "Capt. William Rion Hoel," 22–24, and various papers in the William R. Hoel file in the Mary L. Cook Public Library, Waynesville, OH.
34. Spring Grove Cemetery records. William Hoel is buried in Section 35, Lot 184.
35. *Navy History and Heritage Command.*
36. Ibid.

Bibliography

Primary Sources

Barbiere, Joe. *Scraps from the Prison Table, at Camp Chase and Johnson's Island.* Doylestown, PA: W. W. H. Davis, 1868.

Callender, Eliot. *Speeches of a Veteran.* Chicago: The Blue Sky Press, 1901.

Clarke, Norman E. Jr. ed. *Warfare Along the Mississippi, The Letters of Lieutenant Colonel George E. Currie.* Mount Pleasant, MI: Central Michigan University, 1961.

Coffin, Charles Carleton. *The Boys of '61.* Boston: Estes and Lauriat, 1881.

———. *Drum-Beat of the Nation.* New York: Harper & Brothers, 1888.

———. *My Days and Nights on the Battle-Field.* Boston: Ticknor and Fields, 1864.

Cullum, George W., Bvt, Major General. *Biographical Register of the Officers and Graduates of the U.S. Military Academy at West Point, N.Y. from its Establishment, in 1802, to 1890 with the Early History of the United States Military Academy.* 3rd ed. Vol. I., Nos. 1 to 1000. Boston and New York: Houghton, Mifflin and Company, 1891.

Davis, Major George B., Leslie J. Perry, and Joseph W. Kirkley. Compiled by Captain Calvin D. Cowles. *The Official Military Atlas of the Civil War.* Gettysburg, PA: The National Historical Society, 1978.

Ellet, Charles, Jr. *The Army of the Potomac and its Mismanagement; Respectfully Addressed to Congress.* New York: Ross & Tousey, 1862.

Grant, Ulysses S. *Personal Memoirs of U. S. Grant.* 2 vols. New York: Charles L. Webster & Company, 1885.

Hewett, Janet B., ed., *Supplement to the Official Records of the Union and Confederate Armies.* Wilmington, NC: Broadfoot Publishing Company, 1999.

Hoel, William R. Papers in the Collection of the Public Library of Cincinnati and Hamilton County.

Hoel, William R. File in the Mary L. Cook Public Library, Waynesville, OH.

House of Representatives. *Armed Flotilla on the Western Waters, Communication from the Secretary of War, on the Subject of the Armed Flotilla on the Western Rivers. 37th Cong., 2d sess, Ex. Doc. No. 5.*

Instruction for Heavy Artillery. Prepared by a Board of Officers for the use of the Army of the United States. Washington, DC: U.S. Government Printing Office, 1862.

Johnson, Robert U., and Clarence C. Buel, eds. Battles and Leaders of the Civil War. Vols. I and IV. Secaucus, NJ: Castle, 1982.

Journal of the Congress of the Confederate States of America, 1861–1865. Washington, DC: U.S. Government Printing Office, 1904.

Kennedy, J. C. G., *United States Census Office 8th Census 1860.* Washington, DC: U.S. Government Printing Office, 1864.

Matthews, James M., ed. *Confederate States of America, The Statutes at Large.* Richmond, VA: R. M. Smith, 1864.

Milligan, John D., ed. *From the Fresh-Water Navy: 1861–64, The Letters of Acting Master's Mate Henry R. Browne and Acting Ensign Symmes E. Browne.* Annapolis, MD: United States Naval Institute, 1970.

Mississippi River Commission. *Maps of the lower Mississippi from the mouth of the Ohio River to the head of the passes, in thirty-two sheets, 1881–1897. Gardner Family Map Room, Thompson Library, The Ohio State University.*

Morgan, James Morris. Recollections of a Rebel Reefer. New York: Houghton Mifflin Company, 1917.

Official Records of the Union and Confederate Navies in the War of the Rebellion. Washington, DC: U.S. Government Printing Office, 1884.

Potter, David D., Admiral. *The Naval History of the Civil War.* Secaucus, NJ: Castle, 1984.

Selfridge, Thomas O., Jr. *What Finer Tradition.* Columbia, SC: University of South Carolina Press, 1987.

Shipmates. National Park Service, Vicksburg National Military Park.

Simplot, Alexander. Papers and drawings, 1866-1911. Papers in the Wisconsin Historical Society, Madison, WI.

Stanton, Donal J., Goodwin F. Berquist, and Paul C. Bowers, eds. *The Civil War Reminiscences of General M. Jeff Thompson.* Dayton, OH: Morningside House, 1988.

The War of the Rebellion: A Compilation of the Official Records of the Union and Confederate Armies. Washington, DC: U.S. Government Printing Office.

Twain, Mark. *Life on the Mississippi.* New York: Harper and Brothers, 1917.

Twelfth Annual Reunion of the Association of the Graduates of the U.S. Military Academy at West Point, New York, June 9, 1881. East Saginaw, MI: E.W. Lyon, 1881.

Walke, H. *Naval Scenes and Reminiscences.* New York: F. R. Reed & Company, 1877.

Yost, George R. Diary, Manuscripts. Illinois State Historical Library, Springfield, Il.

Period Newspapers and Periodicals

Baltimore Sun, The, June 9, 1862; June 10, 1862

Chicago Tribune, April 17, 1862; June 7, 1862; June 10, 1862

Gift, George. "The Story of the Arkansas." *Southern Historical Society Papers* 12., Issue 3, March 1884, 48-55.

Harper's Weekly, May 10, 1862; May 31, 1862; June 28, 1862; July 5, 1862

Houston Telegraph, June 2, 1862

Littell's Living Age, August 2, 1862

Macon Weekly Telegraph, June 12, 1862; June 18, 1862

Memphis Appeal, June 6, 1861; June 9, 1862

Memphis Avalanche, April 19, 1861; May 13, 1862; May 14, 1862; June 9, 1862; June 13, 1862

New York Herald, *The, May 11, 1862; May 12, 1862; June 9, 1862*

New York Times, *The, February 13, 1855; April 26, 1862; April 27, 1862; June 12, 1862*

New York Tribune, *The, June 7, 1862; June 11, 1862; June 12, 1862*

Philadelphia Inquirer, *The,* May 30, 1862

Read, Captain C. W. "Reminiscences of the Confederate States Navy." *Southern Historical Society Papers*, Vol 1, Issue 5, May 1876., 1–33.

San Francisco Bulletin, July 21, 1862.

"The Last Roll, Commodore J. E. Montgomery." *Confederate Veteran* 10 (9), (September 1902)., 416–17.

Tri-Weekly Telegraph, June 20, 1862

Maine Farmer, *The,* June 12, 1862.

New York Evangelist, The, June 19, 1862.
Wisconsin State Register, The, June 14, 1862.

Secondary Sources

A Biographical Dictionary of American Civil Engineers. ASCE Historical Publication No. 2, 1972. American Society of Civil Engineers, 345 East 47th Street, New York 10017.

Barnett, Correlli. *Engage the Enemy More Closely*. New York: W. W. Norton & Company, 1991.

Bearss, Edwin C. *Hardluck Ironclad*. Baton Rouge, LA: Louisiana State University Press, 1980.

Bogan, Dallas. *The History of Warren County, Ohio*. Chicago, IL: W. H. Beers & Co., 1982.

Campbell, R. Thomas. *Confederate Naval Forces on Western Waters*. Jefferson, NC: McFarland & Company, 2005.

Canney, Donald L. *The Old Steam Navy, Volume II, The Ironclads, 1842–1885*. Annapolis, MD: Naval Institute Press, 1993.

Civil War Naval Chronology, 1861–1865. Washington, DC: U.S. Government Printing Office, 1971.

Clark, Ira G. *Then Came The Railroads*. Norman, OK: University of Oklahoma Press, 1958.

Coombe, Jack D. *Thunder Along the Mississippi*. New York: Sarpedon, 1996.

Crandall, Warren Daniel. *History of the Ram Fleet and the Mississippi Marine Brigade*. St. Louis, MO: Buschart Brothers, 1907.

Davis, Charles H. *Life of Charles Henry Davis*. New York: Houghton, Mifflin and Company, 1899.

Dictionary of American Naval Fighting Ships. VIII vols. Washington, DC: U.S. Government Printing Office, 1959.

Dorsey, Florence. *The Story of James B. Eads, Road to the Sea and the Mississippi River*. New York: Rinehart & Company, 1947.

Ferreiro, Larrie D. "The Social History of the Bulbous Bow." *Technology and Culture* 52, no. 2 (2011): 335–59.

Field Manual 101-5-1. *Operational Terms and Graphics, Headquarters Department of the Army*, 1997.

Gibbons, Tony. *Warships and Naval Battles of the Civil War*. New York: Gallery Books, 1989.

Gibson, Charles Dana with E. Kay Gibson. *The Army's Navy Series, Dictionary of Transports and Combatant Vessels Steam and Sail*

Employed by the Union Army, 1861–1868. Camden, ME: Ensign Press, 1995.

Gibson, Charles Dana with E. Kay Gibson. *The Army's Navy Series, Volume II, Assault and Logistics, Union Army Coastal and River Operations 1861–1866*. Camden, ME: Ensign Press, 1995.

Gosnell, H. Allen. *Guns on the Western Waters*. Baton Rouge, LA: Louisiana State University Press, 1949.

Greene, F. V. *Campaigns of the Civil War, The Mississippi*. New York: Charles Scribner's Sons, 1882.

Hearn, Chester G. *Ellet's Brigade*. Baton Rouge, LA: Louisiana State University Press, 2000.

Holley, Alexander L. *A Treatise on Ordnance and Armor*. Vol. I & II. New York: D. Van Nostrand, 1865.

Hoppin, James Mason. *Life of Andrew Hull Foote*. New York: Harper & Brothers, 1874.

Joiner, Gary D. *Mr. Lincoln's Brown Water Navy*. New York: Rowman & Littlefield Publishers, 2007.

Konstam, Angus. *Mississippi River Gunboats of the American Civil War 1861–65*. Oxford, England: Osprey Publishing, 2002.

Lewis, Gene D. *Charles Ellet, Jr.* Urbana, IL: University of Illinois Press, 1968.

Long, E. B., and Barbara Long. *The Civil War Day By Day: An Almanac 1861–1865*. Garden City, NY: Doubleday & Company, 1971.

Mahan, A. T. *The Navy in the Civil War, The Gulf and Inland Waters*. New York: Charles Scribner's Sons, 1883.

McPherson, James M. *War on the Waters*. Chapel Hill, NC: The University of North Carolina Press, 2012.

Milligan, John D. *Gunboats Down the Mississippi*. Annapolis, MD: United States Naval Institute, 1965.

Montgomery, David B. *A Genealogical History, The Montgomerys and Their Descendants*. Owensville, IN: J.P. Cox, 1908.

Naval History Division, Navy Department. *Civil War Naval Chronology 1861–1865*. Washington, DC: U.S. Department of the Navy, 1971.

Nofi, Albert A. *A Civil War Treasury*. Conshohocken, PA: Combined Books, 1992.

Parkes, Oscar. *British Battleships*. Hamden, CN: Archon Books, 1972.

Patterson, Benton Rain. *The Mississippi River Campaign, 1861–1863*. Jefferson, NC: McFarland & Company, 2010.

Potter, E. B., and Chester W. Nimitz, eds, *Sea Power*, Englewood Cliffs, NJ: Prentice Hall, 1960.

Ripley, Warren. *Artillery and Ammunition of the Civil War.* New York: Promontory Press, 1970.

Rutter, Joseph W. "Capt. William Rion Hoel: The Life of a 19th Century Riverman." *S&D Reflector*, Marietta, OH, June 1996, September 1996, December 1996, March 1997.

Schuyler, Hartley and Graham. *Illustrated Catalog of Civil War Military Goods.* New York: Dover Publications, 1985.

Sharf, J. Thomas. *History of the Confederate States Navy.* New York: Crown Publishers, 1977.

Sellers, William. *Memoir of James Buchanan Eads, 1820–1887.* Read before the National Academy, April, 1888.

Silverstone, Paul H. *Civil War Navies, 1855–1883.* Annapolis, MD: Naval Institute Press, 2001.

Slagle, Jay. *Ironclad Captain, Seth Ledyard Phelps & the U.S. Navy, 1841–1864.* Kent, OH: Kent State University Press, 1996.

Smith, Myron J., Jr. *The USS Carondelet.* Jefferson, NC: McFarland & Company, 2010.

The American Society of Mechanical Engineers, *U.S.S. Cairo Engine & Boilers, A National Historic Mechanical Engineering Landmark*, Vicksburg, MS, June 15, 1990.

Still, William N., Jr., ed. *The Confederate Navy.* Annapolis, MD: Naval Institute Press, 1997.

Tucker, Spencer C. *Andrew Foote.* Annapolis, MD: Naval Institute Press, 2000.

Young, Judge J. P. ed. *Standard History of Memphis Tennessee.* Knoxville, TN: H. W. Crew & Co., 1912.

Newspapers and Periodicals

Adamiak, Stanley J. "A Naval Depot and Dockyard on the Western Waters; The Rise and Fall of the Memphis Naval Yard, 1884–1854." *International Journal of Naval History,* April 2002:.Volume 1, Issue 1, April 2002, http://www.ijnhonline.org/, accessed September 2012.

Burpo, Robert S., Jr. "Notes on the first fleet engagement in the Civil War." *American Neptune* 19 (1959): 265–73.

Gaden, Elmer L., Jr. "Eads and the Navy of the Mississippi." *Invention & Technology* Spring 1994. 24–31.

Merrill, James M. "Cairo, Illinois: Strategic Civil War River Port." *Journal of the Illinois State Historical Society* 76, no. 4 (Winter 1983): 242–56.

Websites

"Civil War Prisoner of War Records, 1861–1865 for James C. Delancy." Ancestry.com. Accessed October 2013. http://ancestrylibrary.com.

Biographical Directory of the United States Congress. Accessed September 2012. http://bioguide.congress.gov.

Library of Congress. Accessed January 2013. http://www.loc.gov.

Navy History and Heritage Command. Accessed September 2012. http://www.history.navy.mil/.

Unpublished Sources

Abbott, Dorothea V. Special Collections Librarian. United States Naval Academy, Annapolis, MD. Information about the naval career of William S. Lovell. E-Mail Message 26 January 2010; letter dated 26 January 2010.

Gaines, Elizabeth. Secretary Cotton Belt Rail Historical Society, Inc. Information about the railroad depot at Eunice, Arkansas; letter dated 19 February 2010.

McConnell, Elaine B. Rare Book Curator. United States Military Academy. Information on Edward D. Mansfield; e-mail dated 15 August 2012.

Reynolds, Bill. The Sons and Daughters of Pioneer Rivermen. Ohio River Museum, Marietta, Ohio. Photograph of Willaim Hoel's Civil War coat.

Roberts, William. Information on the construction of monitors; e-mails dated 4 May 2011 and 13 June 2011.

Index

Page numbers in **boldface** refer to illustrations and photographs.